W9-BTN-011

Building Engaged Schools

Gary Gordon

with Steve Crabtree

GALLUP PRESS
New York

GALLUP PRESS
1251 Avenue of the Americas
23rd Floor
New York, NY 10020

ISBN: 1-59562-010-9
First Printing: 2006
10 9 8 7 6 5 4 3 2 1

CONTENTS

INTRODUCTION

"It is not necessary to change. Survival is not mandatory."
— *W. Edwards Deming*

The expectations that America's public schools face appear daunting and, to some, increasingly demoralizing. New challenges to the way we approach public education are emerging from the social, political, and economic changes taking place inside and outside the United States.

Can our school systems, which have been very resistant to change, meet these challenges? Not by doing more of what they're doing today. Outdated assumptions and a lack of consensus about the fundamental goals of America's schools have cast the future of public education as we know it in doubt. Thus, we hear a lot of talk about the need to reform the schools. The trouble is, many of the plans for doing so are subject to the same faulty assumptions that have prevented schools from keeping up with the times in the first place.

The current efforts to remake our public schools began with a land-mark 1983 report, *A Nation at Risk*. The document was the result of an 18-month study by the National Commission on Excellence in Education, which had been created by the secretary of education to make recommendations for improving U.S. schools. "If an unfriendly foreign power had attempted to impose on America the mediocre educational performance that exists today, we might well have viewed it as an act of war," the report declared. "As it stands, we have allowed this to happen to ourselves. . . . We have, in effect, been committing an act of unthinking, unilateral educational disarmament."[1]

A Nation at Risk drew widespread attention, launched a national dialogue about education reform, and led to the statewide standards and accountability testing programs that are prevalent today. Almost a quarter-century later, we have even more compelling evidence that our educational system is outdated. And the report's warning that "our once unchallenged preeminence in commerce, industry, science, and technological innovation is being overtaken by competitors throughout the world"[2] is at least as relevant now as it was then.

In his 2005 book *The World Is Flat*, Thomas Friedman argues that the capacity to distribute information and services globally has created a new reality. For the first time in history, jobs that demand intellectual capital aren't tied to geography. Jobs that can be considered commodities will go where the labor is cheapest. But when it comes to providing cheap labor, America can't compete with mammoth emerging economies like India and China. Instead, as economists, business leaders, and journalists have noted, if we're to maintain our dominant world position, it has to be through innovation. It has to come from the steady flow of fresh ideas that result in new goods and services.

In this new world, it's even more critical to ensure that *all* students receive a high-quality education. Friedman quotes Cisco Systems CEO John Chambers as saying, "The jobs are going to go where the best-educated workforce is with the most competitive infrastructure and environment for creativity and supportive government. It is inevitable. And by definition those people will have the best standard of living. This may not be the countries who led the Industrial Revolution."[3] In other words, the United States' economic preeminence isn't a given in the 21st century. It will depend in large part on the capacity of our schools to make greater use of the energy and natural talents of more students than ever before.

That seems like a very tall order — particularly in relation to the rest of the developed world. Consider the following unflattering statistics:

- In the 2003 Trends in International Mathematics and Science Study (TIMSS), students in 11 countries outperformed American fourth graders in math, and those in nine countries posted higher average math scores than American eighth graders.[4]

- Similarly, 2003 results from the Program for International Student Assessment (PISA) indicated that students from 20 out of 28 industrialized nations scored at higher levels in math than American students.[5] This test included a special section on problem solving — a cross-subject assessment of students' ability to make strategic, innovative decisions to achieve a goal. Here, U.S. students scored below those from 25 other countries.[6]

- In the International Literacy Survey, the United States ranked below 18 other industrialized countries in average literacy proficiency among adults under age 35.[7]

- Among 30 highly developed countries, the United States ranks first in high school completion rates among adults 45 and older — but places 10th for adults 25 to 34 years old. The U.S. graduation rate isn't declining, but graduation rates in other countries are rising faster.[8]

Certainly, many Americans have the sense that too often, public schools aren't getting the job done. In response to a May 2005 Gallup Poll, just 37% said they had "a great deal" or "quite a lot" of confidence in the public schools — a trend that has remained flat since the early 1990s.[9] In April 2005, the Educational Testing Service asked Americans the following question: "If 25 years from now high schools haven't changed, what effect will this have on America's ability to compete?" Just 22% said it would have a positive effect or wouldn't make a difference. Just over *three-fourths* (76%) said it would have a negative effect. Forty-three percent felt the effect would be *very* negative.[10]

NEW DEMANDS

The day-to-day routines in most schools haven't changed much in decades. In fact, the basic curriculum required of today's students has remained substantially the same for almost a century. And contemporary classroom techniques still focus on the lectures, worksheets, drills, and tests familiar to the grandparents of today's students.[11] But the expectations faced by today's schools have been transformed in several important respects.

First, until the states adopted uniform standards and accountability testing, public schools saw themselves as accountable for executing a *process* — providing instruction in facts and skills. It was enough for schools to claim, "We taught it." Today, schools are accountable for *outcomes* in the form of student progress. The question has become, "Did students *learn* it?"

4

Second, as the very title of the No Child Left Behind law makes clear, public schools are now expected to provide *all* students — regardless of background, socioeconomic status, or disability — with a level of education once reserved for a small percentage of Americans who were college bound.

Even as America's schools face increased pressure to demonstrate outcomes, they must accommodate a more diverse group of students than ever before. In 2000, only about 6 in 10 elementary and high school students were white non-Hispanics. The remaining 40% reflected a rainbow of ethnicities and cultures. More than 100 languages are spoken in the Fairfax County Public Schools outside of Washington, D.C. Students attending Grant High School in the Los Angeles Unified School District come from 61 different countries and speak 41 different languages.[12] And all schools must now accommodate the needs of special education students who wouldn't have attended public schools 25 years ago. But schools are still typically structured to treat students as more alike than different.

Adding to the complexity of the situation is the increasingly diverse set of choices facing education consumers (i.e., parents of school-aged kids). Private and parochial schools have always been around, but they have traditionally catered to limited segments of the population. These days, district- or state-wide open-enrollment programs, charter schools, new resources for home schooling, and the ability (under No Child Left Behind) to transfer their children out of low-performing schools give parents more options. Technology-based "distance education" approaches may further crowd the field of alternatives in the not-too-distant future. But entrenched assumptions have made it difficult for public schools to deviate from the status quo.

Rising international pressure, expanded state and federal expectations, and new forms of competition are combining to force America's public schools to demonstrate their value to society and to individual students. Failing to do so increasingly means losing students to competitors who are better geared to deliver that value.

THE LOGJAM

Why, with such pressing new demands, has there been so little change in the average American classroom over the past 20 years? After all, in the same period of time, thousands of U.S. businesses have reinvented their entire manufacturing, marketing, and distribution strategies in response to new technological and geopolitical conditions. Obviously, public schools haven't been under the same competitive pressures that most for-profit companies are under — nor should they be. Even so, if they're to continue to meet society's needs over the long haul, they have to be capable of evolving in response to profound social changes. Despite all the talk about upgrading public schools for the 21st century, most of the resulting strategies are based on an ongoing cycle of curricular revisions and new testing plans. The engagement levels of students, the interaction between students and teachers, and the importance of teachers and principals to student performance have been largely ignored.

The inertia is due at least in part to a logjam between two opposing perspectives on how best to ensure students get what they need from their education to succeed in life. Both perspectives are represented by powerful forces with strong — but incomplete — visions for helping students get more from the schools. In his 1993 book *Multiple Intelligences: The Theory in Practice*, education theorist Howard Gardner framed the competing camps as "educational researchers and policy experts" vs. "government, business and community 'opinion leaders.'"[13]

As Gardner's description implies, the first perspective comes largely from within the education establishment itself. This view maintains that effective schooling must be flexible wherever possible in order to accommodate the infinite complexity of the developing brain. It has been articulated most often by scholars, including many veteran teachers, whose primary concern is that America's schools focus on meeting the learning needs of individual students. As educators themselves, this group would seem to have credibility. But their recommendations for reform don't lend themselves to easy, consistent measurement and are therefore seen by many as unreliable.

The second perspective, Gardner notes, is advocated by concerned citizens outside the education establishment. This view holds that a more consistent set of academic requirements is essential to school improvement, as are more reliable forms of measurement and accountability. This view is verbalized primarily by business and political leaders — but it also resonates with the general public, the majority of whom see the need for a higher standard of success in American education. This group is justifiably worried about evidence that too many students aren't coming away from their school years with the knowledge and skills they need to succeed.

Both perspectives have merit — and flaws. But the more important point is that they consistently undermine one another rather than seeking commonalities. Gardner noted there had been little substantive dialogue between the two sides. "Unless the reasons for the lack of communication can be identified and dealt with satisfactorily," he wrote, "it is unlikely that the critical problems of precollegiate education can be dealt with effectively."[14]

Today, the two camps are more entrenched than ever, exemplified by the Bush administration's No Child Left Behind (NCLB) initiative

— passed into law in 2002 — and growing opposition to NCLB in its current form that includes major education advocates like the National Education Association. And the friction is rising, having taken on distinct political overtones.

Students are stuck in the middle of all this, and they can't afford to be there for long. It's time to take a step back, reconsider our goals and assumptions regarding America's schools, and then move forward with greater unity. That means finding common ground — the basis for a new, third path.

Can it be done? Certainly. The two perspectives aren't mutually exclusive. From both an educator's perspective and a "bottom line" perspective, the most promising guiding principle is the need to maximize the human potential within America's schools by raising engagement levels among students and teachers.

What does that mean? I believe we've been too oriented toward top-down direction, enforcement systems, and technical changes to instruction. Our fascination with correcting the system as a whole has distracted us from the more important process of considering, on a school-by-school basis, how to get the most out of the people who work there. A high-quality education isn't something that can be mandated by law. It's something that has to come about "on the ground" — in the school itself, in the effectiveness of its teachers, and in the frequency of "aha" moments among its students.

In more than 20 years as a teacher, principal, and district administrator, I came to understand that the school improvement efforts that succeeded did so first and foremost because they were able to capture the devotion and enthusiasm of highly talented people. That led me to believe that we should be thinking less in terms of developing systems to hand down to schools, and more in terms of finding new and better

ways to enlist talented teachers and principals — and helping them cultivate the potential within each student day by day.

That conviction became even stronger when I joined The Gallup
Organization. Guided by Chairman Don Clifton until his death in 2003,
Gallup's education and management experts have spent nearly 40 years
studying teachers, 25 years studying principals, and 35 years investigating the common aspects of healthy workplaces. That research, along
with many other important studies like the ones cited in this book,
makes a compelling case that when it comes to education reform, we've
put processes ahead of people for far too long.

The message of this book is, whatever your perspective on improving America's schools, educational excellence relies more on the talent
and the engagement levels of the people within an individual school
than on any other factor. Identifying and leveraging the underutilized talent of students, teachers, support staff, and principals should be the first
consideration in improving outcomes for students.

The first step is to challenge some of the assumptions that hold back
our students and schools. Chapter 1 previews six of those assumptions,
and the remaining chapters deal with those assumptions and alternatives that can lead to student success.

PART ONE

The Predicament of Public Schools

CHAPTER ONE

OLD ASSUMPTIONS, NEW PERSPECTIVES

*"Get the assumptions wrong and everything that follows
from them is wrong." — Peter Drucker*

We can begin to move schools forward by reexamining some of the assumptions that — because they are outdated or only partially correct — may be holding us back. We constantly rely on assumptions to provide shorthand ways to make decisions by recalling previous situations in response to current circumstances. Obviously, the more that current conditions are like those of the past, the more accurate our assumptions and appropriate the decisions that spring from them.

But inertia can be a powerful force, leading individuals and organizations to cling to old assumptions even though circumstances underlying them have changed. The results can be disastrous. Let me offer a couple of historical examples from the world of industry that illustrate the way assumptions drive behaviors.

GOLDEN AGE TO END OF THE LINE

The golden age of railroads began in the spring of 1869 with the completion of the transcontinental railroad. In the period between the Civil War and World War I, America's population tripled — but the rail systems expanded by nearly seven times. By the beginning of World War I, railroads dominated transportation in America.[1]

But that dominance wasn't sustainable against competition from the fledgling automobile and airline industries. In 1940, airlines carried only about 3% of the passenger traffic between cities. But by 1987, the situation was reversed — only 2% of passengers traveled by rail.[2] Today, besides commuter traffic along the East coast, inter-city passenger trains are quaint reminders of another era.

While a number of reasons contributed to the railroads' fall, reasons cited by contemporary historians point to the lens through which railroad executives viewed the rest of the world. Partly because of their monopoly status, they developed paternalistic attitudes and mistrusted feedback from their customers. They responded to intense government regulation by hunkering down in a "siege mentality," assuming they could ride out their troubles by doing more of what they had always done.[3] But in light of new technologies that could move passengers more quickly and conveniently, maintaining the status quo was no longer a viable option.

Railroad industry leaders remained focused on a limited mission — shipping freight — rather than enthusiastically embracing the more expansive prospect of providing passenger transport. A more forward-thinking perspective would have led rail executives to invest in more localized rail lines transporting commuters from the rapidly expanding suburbs into the inner cities. Or it might have led them to purchase emerging bus and airline companies, capitalizing on their brand names and building interconnected transportation networks. But the entrenched railroad culture obscured social change, generated complacency — and led to the decline of a once-dominant industry.

IBM AND THE PC

A more recent example comes from the computer industry. In the relatively short span between 1974 and 1985, the personal computer evolved from a toy for electronics whiz kids to a mainstream tool in offices across the United States. Though IBM was already a technological behemoth by the mid-1970s, it lost the chance to make personal computing a part of everyday life to a little-known company named Apple Computer.

IBM's initial forays into PCs ended in frustration, and then-chairman Frank Cary decided that the company itself was part of the problem. In 1980, Cary authorized a group to design a personal computer outside of IBM's normal corporate structure. Given unprecedented latitude, a small, renegade group built the new IBM personal computer with components purchased from existing sources and sold through retail sources. Within a calendar year, the group delivered a personal computer with more power than the Apple — but only by breaking many of IBM's corporate rules and operating as outsiders with a mission separate from that of the rest of the company.[4]

IBM's PC was a hit. By 1983, it accounted for 75% of the total personal computers bought by businesses. The combined revenues for IBM PCs and related products reached $4 billion in 1984.[5] But that remarkable level of success was short-lived. IBM was unable to keep up with intense competition, and its share of the business market for PCs dropped to 40%. In 1992, IBM declared the largest profit loss seen to that date by a U.S. company.[6] In 2004, IBM accounted for just 5.2% of worldwide PC sales, and controlling interest in IBM's PC division was sold to China's largest manufacturer of computers.[7]

15

What went wrong? Again, observers point to faulty assumptions by IBM's leaders to explain much of the IBM PC's fall from dominance. IBM's near-monopoly of the mainframe and PC computer business in the early 1980s made the lucrative status quo seem sustainable and unquestionable. The PC craze notwithstanding, IBM executives assumed that their primary mission was still to sell mainframe computers to businesses. As profitable as it was, the PC was never seriously presented as a complementary part of IBM's range of computer offerings.[8]

IBM's centralized management was slow to appreciate the opportunities inherent in the advent of personal computing. Indeed, the success of the PC became possible only when Cary created an independent group outside the company's sluggish bureaucracy.

It's not hard to see how continually reassessing their assumptions could have improved these outcomes for passenger railroads and the IBM PC. The same can be said of countless other historical endeavors. As America's schools face rising pressure to meet new demands, they need to be fully mindful of that simple idea: The assumptions that hold sway within an organization — regarding such fundamentals as the nature of its mission or its need for adaptability — tend to drive its success or failure.

ASSUMPTIONS AND AMERICA'S SCHOOLS

We're now seeing another time of rapid social and technological change. Schools have had trouble keeping up, so much so that they haven't had enough breathing room to thoughtfully examine the critical assumptions under which they operate. Educator and child psychologist Paul Brandwein described this "dogpaddling" tendency as far back as 1981. Brandwein predicted that as American society entered the post-industrial age, education would undergo a major change. But he also noted that it would probably lag behind social change. "Schools have not been given a time of peace to undertake the intelligent, progressive development a major social institution must have," Brandwein wrote. "The schools have been too busy serving the nation's growth to tend to their own. Reforms and policies directed at advancing schooling have been, of necessity, short term, if not ad hoc."[9]

Now full swing into the Information Age, we're experiencing the growing pains Brandwein predicted even more acutely. And the knee-jerk reaction still consists of stopgap solutions — increased testing, school vouchers — that do little to help schools adapt to changing social conditions.

THE SIX ASSUMPTIONS

Six outdated assumptions represent significant barriers to improving schools' outcomes — and to reconciling the differences between the two major perspectives on education reform. None of them is exclusive to either side, though some are more characteristic of one side than the other. Confronting these assumptions in America's public schools won't be easy. State and federal governments propagate and support some of them. Others are simply ingrained in the way most public schools operate. But even entrenched assumptions can — and *will* — eventually be discarded if successfully challenged.

The assumptions were selected because they involve critical aspects of education quality, and because there is compelling evidence that they should be reexamined. Are there other important assumptions underlying the education process? Of course, a myriad of them. But the purpose here is to identify a manageable few for which replacement with *alternative* viewpoints carries the most potential for improving the experiences of students and educators.

Each of the assumptions is embedded within current approaches to school improvement. In some cases, the assumptions simply take schools in the wrong direction. In others, they constitute half-truths that yield some student gains, but in the long run, those gains will be costly and uneven. All impede the changes needed to prepare America's schools for a globally competitive future.

ASSUMPTION 1. *Higher expectations and accountability testing are the keys to ensuring that students are learning what they need to be successful in life.*

Today, this assumption translates to the idea that raising standards for proficiency — and holding schools accountable for ensuring that students reach those standards — will improve the quality of education. This belief originated within individual states following the release of *A Nation at Risk*, then became a nationwide strategy in 2002 as the basis of President Bush's No Child Left Behind law. Focusing on standards and accountability testing may produce short-term gains, but it also threatens to undermine any and all ideas about how to more fundamentally update — and upgrade — American education.

ASSUMPTION 2. *Focusing on and improving areas of weakness for students and teachers is the key to making them more successful.*

In other words, put your efforts into fixing your weaknesses, because when it comes to your strengths, you've already got the bases covered. The basis of this assumption is hardly exclusive to America's schools. We are a remedial society that focuses tremendous energy and resources on fixing weaknesses. At every turn, we comment on people's areas of weakness and design developmental activities around them. In some cases, we even assign people to tasks or jobs that emphasize their areas of weakness in the belief that doing so will force them to improve. Indeed, focusing on weaknesses may help raise performance in a given area from poor to adequate. But we need to recognize that weakness fixing is an entirely different process from that of fostering *outstanding* performance in an area of strength.

ASSUMPTION 3. *Selecting and developing teachers and principals on the basis of their knowledge and skills is the most reliable way to promote student success.*

This assumption suggests that learning requisite knowledge and skills makes a teacher or principal successful. It's certainly true that I can't teach something I don't know. But simply knowing a lot about a subject doesn't mean I can effectively engage young people in learning about it. The assumption identifies a *necessary* standard for teachers — but not a *sufficient* one. That's the catch. Knowledge of the subject and an understanding of useful teaching methods should be minimal qualifications to stand in front of students in America's public schools. But as we'll see, there's a critical element missing from the usual criteria for "highly qualified."

ASSUMPTION 4. *There exists a perfect curriculum that can help solve student achievement problems in a way that works for all students and teachers.*

For nearly 50 years, America's public schools have focused heavily on finding the "perfect" curriculum or instructional approach. The assumption is that if the right content is delivered with the right methodology, students will learn at high levels every time. The unstated implication here is that classrooms should be made "teacher-proof." In other words, we need to minimize teacher foibles to ensure that we reach all students in the same way with the same information.

Despite huge financial investments in "prepackaged" learning approaches and a white-water rapids of change for teachers in many school districts, the perfect curriculum or instructional approach eludes schools. In the process, many schools have seen disruptive cyclical change with little substantive improvement. And many teachers have been left with the impression that their jobs are seen as little more than assembly-line work.

ASSUMPTION 5. *Differences in workplace culture are largely irrelevant to schools, because a teacher's working environment doesn't make much difference in the classroom.*

This assumption about workplace cultures applies to businesses and schools alike. Until recently, organizations focused little attention on the emotional climate of a workplace as a factor in performance. We may have noticed differences at an intuitive or gut level — perhaps commenting from time to time on a store with a special "feel" or a school with a "charged" environment. But for the most part, employees' workplace perceptions didn't seem to have much to do with the organization's most significant outcomes.

Today, we know beyond doubt that this assumption is simply not true. We can identify the kinds of workplaces that keep employees motivated and happy, and we know how to establish work environments that support high levels of performance. Moreover, we understand that employees' perceptions are no less important in schools than in other types of workplaces — indeed, they may be more important.

ASSUMPTION 6. *Though greater involvement in America's schools is needed, schools can do little to improve parents' commitment to their children's education.*

If the current approaches to interacting with parents and other community members continue, this assumption will be self-sustaining. Currently, parent-teacher communications typically involve far more telling than listening. Schools can do a better job of establishing positive, two-way dialogues that involve parents in helping their children succeed, make schools a hub of contact and energy within their neighborhoods, and gain community support for increasing student achievement. But educators must first recognize that this assumption is a faulty one.

REORIENTING FOR THE FUTURE

These six assumptions lead America's public schools in the wrong direction. Collectively, they reinforce the status quo among those in America's schools — and those who make policy for them — even as the world changes dramatically around them.

The good news is that we don't have to start from scratch. The push for accountability testing has moved education forward in a number of ways. Schools are now held accountable for ensuring that students learn, rather than for simply carrying out the processes *intended* to help them learn. There is a new focus on building rigor, accountability, and a high degree of professionalism into the country's education system. Perhaps most importantly, reforms like NCLB have unequivocally rejected the implicit assumption that there are some students or some types of students who simply "can't learn."

These are the parts of the standards movement that many teachers like. One veteran high school chemistry teacher we interviewed said, "I feel very positive about the fact that the emphasis is more on academics now. The only thing we rallied around was sports in the past; now, we rally around curriculum."

The discord begins when it comes to how those broad goals should be carried out. The same teacher went on to say, "If you go from the basement to the first floor, that's an improvement. But if you're already on the third floor and you're striving to go to the penthouse, and [focusing on accountability tests] brings you down to the first floor, it's not nice."

Has the traditional goal of helping students be the best they can be been subsumed by the goal of bringing all students to a minimum threshold of knowledge? Many agree that it has. As we'll see, a large percentage of Americans don't feel that local schools are consistently maximizing students' potential. In this regard, the "education researcher" perspective has the preponderance of scientific evidence — and a great deal of public sentiment — on its side.

But it's becoming easier to reconcile the two perspectives. In the business world, there is growing recognition that focusing on the unique needs and development of individuals is both possible and profitable. More and more companies are coming to realize that their biggest opportunity for improvement lies not in new technologies, which their competitors tend to quickly adopt as well, but in drastically underutilized reservoirs of human talent. Organizations concerned with "hard" productivity outcomes are becoming aware of the need to approach those goals by tapping the strengths and emotions of individual employees and customers. The implication for the education standoff may be that new lines of thought emerge that blend education experts' concern about the unique developmental needs of individual students with the outcome-oriented perspective of business and political leaders.

This book is partly an attempt to demonstrate how those lines of thought might develop. The assumptions challenged here can be replaced with alternatives that accommodate the concerns of everyone seeking to move schools forward.

The suggestions for change in this book will no doubt spark some debate. The six assumptions are deeply embedded in the day-to-day practices of schools and in what our society believes about schools. That debate can be cause for optimism, because America's public schools will not provide students with the education they deserve — and the more proficient workforce the country needs — except through a close examination of those practices and beliefs.

CHAPTER TWO

THE REFORM STANDOFF

*"No Child Left Behind treats students as skill-acquiring cogs in
an economic wheel, and the results have been disappointing."*
— *David Brooks,* The New York Times

Let's look at the first of the six faulty assumptions, listed on page 18 —
that public schools can meet all the needs of America's students if we
simply ratchet up our expectations and test more frequently. In other
words, the problem isn't that our approach to educating has become
outdated — it's that we're not using that approach as rigorously as we
should. That idea has been the starting point for most of the high-profile
reform initiatives over the past two decades.

But debate about this assumption goes back much further. In fact,
prevailing ideas about the goals of American education have tended
to swing on a pendulum between student-centeredness and subject-
centeredness since Horace Mann argued in the 1830s that U.S. schools
should educate more than just the elite classes. Soon thereafter,

reformers noted that American education would have to become more adaptive to meet these increased demands.

In the late 19th and early 20th centuries, John Dewey and other prominent members of the progressive education movement argued that the fundamental driver of that adaptation should be the needs of individual students. In 1928, for example, Harold Rugg and Ann Shumaker published their highly influential book *The Child-Centered School*, which put creative self-expression at the heart of what they called the "new education."[1] The movement collapsed in the mid-20th century, but the progressives and the schools they started left a lasting imprint on America's educational landscape.

THE CALL FOR STANDARDS AND ACCOUNTABILITY TESTING

In 1983, the pendulum swung decidedly in the opposite direction. That was the year *A Nation at Risk* denounced what it termed a "rising tide of mediocrity" in America's schools. Chronicling a decline in the quality of performance by high school students across a broad group of measures, the report concluded that most American students failed to take rigorous coursework. It described high school curricula as "homogenized, diluted, and diffused to the point that they no longer have a central purpose." Student choice in a "curricular smorgasbord" led to lack of focus and low achievement.[2] The Excellence Commission proposed an unprecedented set of uniform course requirements for high school graduates — the "New Basics," suitable for all students, not just the college-bound.[3]

The response from states, colleges, and local school districts was predictable: It was time to buckle down. Schools must be made tougher to guarantee a standard of excellence.[4] State universities in 27 states evaluated or changed their requirements for admission in the first half of the 1980s.[5] Local school districts and state legislatures increased the number of academic courses required for graduation.

But that was only the beginning. The report ensured that the agenda for improving America's schools would remain largely focused on standards and requirements through the end of the 20th century. Most state legislatures adopted the "New Basics" and set new benchmarks for what students should know or do in subjects at each grade level. Annual testing in some grades became the norm in most states. By 2000, 44 states had approved standards in English, math, social studies, and science.[6]

Fast-forward to 2002. No Child Left Behind gave the states' standards and accountability testing the stamp of legitimacy as the nation's primary engine of school improvement — and went two steps further. First, as a prerequisite for receiving federal funds, NCLB required that students must be making progress toward the standards set by each state. To track this requirement, as of the 2005-2006 school year, schools must test all third though eighth graders annually. Second, NCLB established sanctions for schools in which students in racial, ethnic, income, and special education subgroups fail to meet adequate yearly progress goals toward the standard for acceptable performance set by each state.

NCLB's requirements constitute unprecedented federal involvement in American education. Still, the law was politically popular because it addressed concerns widely held at the turn of the millennium. Political and business leaders worried about international comparisons to American students, while most Americans were troubled by the persistent achievement gaps between economic, racial, and ethnic groups. A few federal policymakers were frustrated by how slow some states had been to set standards and institute testing.[7] And some state leaders had expressed dismay about the variability in performance among their school districts — at least some of which they felt was due to inconsistent expectations.

Local leaders, meanwhile, often found it difficult to convince principals to make the changes necessary to reorient all their efforts around student learning. And many principals were unable to enforce teaching to standards once classroom doors closed. Some local school leaders welcomed new state and federal requirements, because they recognized that reform wouldn't have been possible at the local level due to inertia. Finally, many felt that the common statewide standards mandated by NCLB would put everyone on the same page.

OVEREMPHASIZING STANDARDS, PART 1: SOLUTIONS FROM 30,000 FEET

There is, however, a flip side to the advantages of greater centralization. Decisions about educational content are being made further and further from the "action" in the classroom. The underlying assertion is that centralized bodies — most often governors and state legislatures consulting with pedagogical experts and teacher representatives — are better suited than individual school districts to set the minimum standard for learning that students at various levels in that district should have.

For teachers, an overemphasis on top-down standards has the capacity to affect how they see themselves and their profession. It implies that many of the day-to-day decisions involving what goes on in the classroom shouldn't be left to teachers, or even to individual schools. That perceived lack of confidence in their judgment takes a toll on teachers' own enthusiasm levels. Gallup's focus groups and interviews with educators confirmed the idea that in too many cases, over-regulation leads talented young teachers to become disillusioned and lose their enthusiasm for the profession.

Retention, not recruitment, is currently the biggest factor in the nation's teacher shortage. In 2002, a special analysis of data from the National Center for Education Statistics found that almost half of America's new teachers leave the profession within their first five years of teaching.[8] New teachers expect long hours and relatively low salaries. But talented young teachers full of mission may have a much harder time coming to grips with the implicit message that they can't be trusted with the outcomes they're yearning to achieve.

Booker T. Washington once said, "Few things help an individual more than to place responsibility upon him, and to let him know that you trust him."[9] Trust and responsibility are empowering — and motivating. Across industries, Gallup has consistently found that one of the strongest predictors of an employee's overall engagement level is whether or not he or she agrees that "At work, my opinions seem to count." That's hardly the message most teachers receive every day.

The result is that many teachers feel like they're in a Catch-22 situation when it comes to top-down education reform. If they vocally oppose it, they appear to be speaking out against raising the bar for education quality — perhaps, it might be assumed, because it would make their jobs more difficult. On the other hand, if they support it, they feel that their own talent and instincts are devalued, and they worry about how the new requirements will affect their ability to engage students.

Effective Innovation Starts Locally

The biggest problem with reform efforts that come from the top down is that often, teachers don't buy into them. A number of the teachers we talked to indicated that they often just try to ride out reform programs, hoping the most obtrusive will prove untenable and eventually go away.

True innovation is much more likely to take root when it starts at the local level — with input and buy-in from all the parties affected — and is highly tailored to local conditions. In his 2002 book *Against School Reform (and in Praise of Great Teaching)*, Peter Temes writes, "Reform that works over time works at . . . the level of one class, one student, one moment at a time. The more removed they are from these small facts, the less likely that reform efforts will succeed."[10]

That principle applies to all organizations. Gallup's management research has revealed that in the attempts of most large companies to maximize the use of their "people" assets (employees and customers), single silver-bullet solutions for an entire workforce don't work. There are two main reasons for this:

1. No "one-size-fits-all" prescription can account for all the specific talents and circumstances that occur within a large organization. A variety of problem-solving strategies can be equally valid. It's most important for teams to be given the freedom to invent their own solutions. "Teams that build a workflow and have control over it are capable of far better performance than teams that don't," says senior Gallup researcher Glenn Phelps. "The challenge is in adopting a management philosophy that emphasizes supporting individuals and teams over processes."

2. Because they weren't asked for their input, employees will automatically feel threatened by the new plan, or at least be highly skeptical of it. After all, it's being implemented by the powers that be to "fix" them. Good employees will at least pay it lip service, but they may end up looking for ways to "satisfice" — that is, to meet the new requirements with as little effort as possible and no connection to the spirit of the reform.[11]

Management expert Margaret Wheatley wrote in 1997: "Most change efforts fail when leaders take an innovation that has worked well in one area of the organization and attempt to roll it out to the entire organization.

This desire to replicate success actually destroys local initiative. It denies the creativity of everyone except a small group."[12]

Real changes are more likely to happen in schools than in districts, in districts than in states, and in states than across the nation as a whole. This may seem somewhat paradoxical given the decades-long search for a uniform "quick fix." Nevertheless, the fastest, most reliable way to improve education is simply to foster the conditions that lead educators to come up with creative approaches to school-level — and even student-level — challenges, one situation at a time.

Outcomes and Process

One way to address this problem of centralized decision making is to be sure we are defining general educational *outcomes*, rather than the specific *steps* used to arrive at them. This approach requires a delicate compromise between the needs for consistency and freedom in education.

Advocates of legislated standards argue that's already happening. Standards are intended as outcomes, they contend, and teachers are not told specifically how to help students achieve them. But teachers often complain that statewide standards can be so detailed that they end up dictating the learning process. They prescribe not only what is to be taught, but *how* it is to be taught. And the accompanying accountability tests divert talented teachers from the broader outcomes that are the real measures of effective education.

One of Gallup's key management discoveries is that great managers avoid the temptation to try to control the steps people use to accomplish goals. There are a couple of reasons for this. The first is that there are typically many different ways to address any task, and often, trying to enforce a single approach as "the best" reduces the efficiency of the organization when it comes to capitalizing on human talent. Second, trusting people with freedom in the way they do their jobs sends a powerful message of respect to those individuals.

Substituting specific and often questionable accountability goals for broad outcomes can be very frustrating to teachers. Obviously, standards are essential to school performance. But those standards must be implemented in terms of outcomes that are broad enough to leave the process of reaching the standards in the hands of talented teachers.

OVEREMPHASIZING STANDARDS, PART 2: OPPORTUNITY COST

We started by challenging the assumption that higher standards and accountability testing are primarily what's needed to ensure that all students learn effectively. The spirit behind the assumption has merit; schools need to expect more of their students. Moreover, many people inside and outside education have rightly argued that such measures bring a sense of business efficiency to schools, and that without them, we don't know that students are learning.[13]

The argument for raising standards goes like this: If we replace low requirements with high expectations, then student performance will increase dramatically. Put simply, schools have failed to expect enough of students — and you get what you expect. Certainly it's true that "stretch goals" can lead many students to higher achievement. The problem with this reasoning is that it assumes any student who does poorly in a given class is simply underperforming.

But applying the same classroom methods more rigorously is unlikely to suddenly kindle the interest and elevate the performance of a faltering student. It's doubtful, for example, that a student who does poorly in Algebra I will be more successful by being required to take Algebra II, unless a significantly different approach is taken. And in many cases, the resulting frustration saps the motivation of the very students the standards are intended to assist.

Schools that refuse to think of their student body as a monolithic group need strategies that help all students learn. Ratcheting up uniform standards may work for students who are able to learn effectively the way we currently teach — most likely those in affluent areas with highly involved parents. But even in schools where most students have these advantages, current educational practices fail to actively involve all too many students whose minds are tailored to learn differently, or who see the subject matter as irrelevant to their lives.

Schools can try to drag underperforming students kicking and screaming to predetermined thresholds of knowledge by mandating that they reach them before moving on. But if the goal is to motivate students to achieve, it's not enough to just apply the same methods more rigorously to kids who weren't responding to those methods in the first place. In the process, schools divert resources and attention away from kids who *were* succeeding — and the result is that *no* student benefits.

Over the long run, just raising standards and administering more tests won't do enough to combat the lack of engagement that is all too common in America's classrooms. In fact, trying to squeeze more output from a process that is itself increasingly outdated may do more harm than good.

Aggregated Measurement

Relying on accountability tests to raise education quality has its own set of problems. The intended result of annual accountability testing is that schools will make it their top priority to help all students reach proficiency in basic skills. Indeed, schools can't manage something they don't measure. That's one of the strengths of the current reform climate;

precise and reliable measures of educational effectiveness have been sorely needed. But the current testing approach fails to meet some important tests of its own.

As required by NCLB, testing in grades 3 through 8 and some testing at the high school level primarily serves to judge the performance of *schools*, rather than students. Usually administered in the spring, state tests evaluate the academic status of an entire school body, as well as at-risk subgroups, at a particular point in time. They are typically written directly from the state's prescribed standards and are criterion-referenced, meaning they are designed to measure achievement of uniform predetermined goals.

As currently mandated, accountability testing can misrepresent the performance of students and schools. Consider these scenarios:

1. An individual student may make substantial growth gains as indicated by the year-end test but still not reach the expected proficiency level. In this case, the student may be held back a grade, smothering her motivation to build on that growth. Or a minority subgroup may be showing gains, but not enough to meet the threshold for adequate yearly progress. In that case, the school may be labeled as "in need of improvement" and face sanctions ranging from student transfers out of the school to complete takeover by the state. In both cases, any momentum that has been established grinds to a halt.

2. On the other hand, an individual student or a targeted subgroup of students may show very little growth in performance, or even a decline. But because they have achieved proficiency, their scores are perceived as acceptable under the law — and the idea that measurement will drive improvement fails.[14]

Part of the problem in these cases is that the system typically gauges progress by simply comparing the scores of today's students with those of last year's students in the same grade. In doing so, it fails to acknowledge growth achieved during the school year on a student-by-student basis. Clearly, the foremost goal of reporting test scores isn't to improve students' learning experiences on an individual basis, but to target low-performing schools or entire student segments for overhaul.

But learning doesn't happen in the aggregate. After all, school improvement is comprised of the continual progress of each student. The degree of student growth is a more important measure of proficiency. Currently, some students clear the proficiency bar without being challenged, while others find it so frustratingly high that they give up. In either case, motivation and development of the students' potential suffer. More sophisticated measures of educational effectiveness would account for — and help elevate — the quality of individual student-teacher interactions. They would be better indicators of the engagement levels of individual students.

Because these tests happen toward the end of the school year, they don't assist teachers in shaping instruction for individual students during the course of that year. One effect the scores *do* tend to have is that they contribute to a remedial mindset at the start of the following school year by telling teachers which standards a student failed to meet during the previous year. By concentrating on the few students meeting minimal standards, the goal may be achieved for the school.

A single year-end test, as currently required, simply does not provide a full picture of the students' achievement. Steve Dunbar heads a company that makes a widely used achievement test battery — the Iowa Test of Basic Skills. He views accountability testing this way: "A test is just a snapshot of where that particular kid is on a particular day."[15] Author and educator John Goodlad describes tests as measuring "the mechanics of learning."[16] They certainly don't measure many of the attributes needed to thrive in an ever-changing global economy: learning independently, communication skills, and the ability to work with others.

Consider also that there are more students at the extremes when it comes to ability than ever before. Teachers are being forced to "teach to the middle" at a time when the range of ability in their classroom is far broader than it was a few decades ago. When speaking to teachers about differentiated education, William Bender, author of *Differentiating Math Instruction*, notes that sixth grade classrooms of the past typically contained students with fourth-grade to eighth-grade reading levels. Today, because schools now include more children with special needs — and because the digital divide has given some kids access to educational resources at home that others don't have — it's not unusual for a sixth grade classroom to contain non-readers and college-level readers.[17]

Given that more and more students do not fall into "average" ability levels, measures of individual progress are more appropriate assessments than absolute thresholds of knowledge. Our notion of accountability seems too narrow if the goal is to maximize student potential: Hard academic outcomes are important, but it may be equally important to track students' learning momentum and degree of emotional engagement with school.

"Is It on the Test?"

Even if these measurement issues are resolved, we're still left with serious concerns about the emphasis placed on statewide assessments. They're often referred to as "high-stakes tests" because poor performance can have severe consequences not just for schools, but for individual students. Moving from one grade level to the next may depend on a passing score. On the surface, that seems reasonable — after all, shouldn't all students learn to a standard level before moving on?

The problem, as opponents of standardized tests often point out, is that the measurement tools are stressed so heavily that they tend to assume greater importance than the learning they're intended to measure. Scott Thompson, executive director of the Panasonic Foundation, said in 2001, "At whatever point a high-stakes, standardized test is imposed as the sole basis for determining student success, that test will replace whatever content and performance standards were previously in place."[18] We've reached this point when students routinely ask, "Is it on the test?" after an assignment is given. Teachers are forced to replace activities that previously sparked engaging classroom discussions with more tedious test preparation.

The reality of high-stakes testing is that the existing "factory" system requires every student at a particular grade level to be at a similar point on the assembly line at any given time. Teachers feel pressured to cover the material required by the accountability tests and move on, even if many of the students don't fully understand the content, or others with a stronger affinity for the topic are so bored by the prescribed presentation that they mentally check out. "Teaching to the test" is similar to relying too heavily on textbooks; both homogenize the classroom experience, forcing students and teachers into limited, uninspired approaches to learning.

"Not only do [standardized] tests not measure basics," said noted educational reformer and activist Deborah Meier in a 2004 *Washington Post* interview, "they also distract us from teaching the kind of stuff that might engage kids' minds and hearts, stuff that would force them to engage in the real discipline of intellectual life — weighing evidence, seeing other ways of looking at the same data or situation, comparing and contrasting, seeking patterns, conjecturing, even arguing."[19]

The "Growth" Approach

We already have examples of more sophisticated tests that aim to more meaningfully capture the academic progress of individual students in a given area. The Tennessee Comprehensive Assessment Program (TCAP) uses year-end test data to measure achievement in a given subject area during the school year. In this way, individual student growth can be calculated in each of the subjects tested for every student, every year.[20] Value-added examples such as Tennessee's are not without their problems, but measures of growth for individuals and groups recognize accomplishments by students and teachers that are ignored by current accountability testing.

There's reason to hope that the U.S. Department of Education is open to such new forms of testing. For the first time, in 2005, it allowed 10 states to experiment with "growth models" that track the progress of individual students. Participating schools will have to establish more sophisticated tracking procedures like the TCAP method, hopefully starting a nationwide trend toward measurement systems that are more student-focused.[21]

But overall, the nation's schools are still far from an effective assessment system. To serve students, the system must: 1) serve the primary purpose of tapping students' potential, 2) incorporate measures of student engagement and learning momentum, and 3) include multiple measures for students and schools.

AN ALTERNATIVE PERSPECTIVE

NCLB and other reform initiatives of the past two decades have met with protest from veteran educators and education scholars. At best, they say, attempting to raise standards without addressing the underlying problems that plague schools is a short-term strategy. At worst, it can further raise the barriers to student engagement. Author and high school principal George Wood neatly summarized this perspective in 1992: "The legislated-excellence movement is, as is to be expected, silent about changing the context of classroom instruction. In fact, preoccupied with content, the advocates of excellence will only further flatten classroom life with their demand for more coverage."[22]

Some experts, recognizing the mismatch between current reforms and changing social conditions, have urged opinion leaders to reconsider the kinds of students we need schools to produce. Howard Gardner, renowned for his work on multiple intelligences, wrote in 1999's *The Disciplined Mind* that education is at a crossroads. A "fact-based" approach to teaching is becoming increasingly outdated as technology makes information easier and easier to access, Gardner argues. People who are adept at different approaches to understanding and interpreting complex topics and situations will thrive in the 21st century.[23] In other words, schools should develop students' creative talents and teach them to use information to solve problems and gain deeper understandings, rather than to recall facts.

The biggest problem with this perspective is that it doesn't easily lend itself to measurement. It doesn't result in independently generated data that are easily comparable across students, school districts, states, and even countries, as standardized test scores are. Therefore, it's often perceived as unmethodical, non-scientific — and highly suspect.

Furthermore, as Gardner noted in describing the current standoff, this perspective remains couched in terms of "complex theories," as opposed to the "quick fix" implied by testing-based reform. It seems far more nebulous to those outside education. Educators like Carol Ann Tomlinson have worked to provide specific guidelines for student-centered classrooms, but lack of hard evidence that their recommendations consistently produce better student outcomes remains a persistent problem for this group.

And so the standoff continues, to the dismay of those who desperately want to find common ground. Education activist Parker Palmer described that frustration in his 1997 book *The Courage to Teach*. "As the debate swings between the teacher-centered model, with its concern for rigor, and the student-centered model, with its concern for active learning, some of us are torn between the poles," Palmer wrote. "We find insights and excesses in both approaches, and neither seems adequate to the task. The problem, of course, is that we are caught in yet another either/or. Whiplashed, with no way to hold the tension, we fail to find a synthesis that might embrace the best of both."[24] Palmer's point about the need for consensus is critical. All parties who have significant influence on what goes on in America's classrooms need to be working in concert, now more than ever.

NEW GROUNDS FOR AGREEMENT

Fortunately, there are signs that the common ground between the two perspectives is expanding. New voices, notably those of influential opinion leaders from outside of education, have begun contending that improving our schools means more than just raising standards. None of these voices has been more prominent than that of Bill Gates. At the 2005 National Education Summit on High Schools, the Microsoft chairman spoke provocatively about the need for fundamental change:

> Training the workforce of tomorrow with the high schools of today is like trying to teach kids about today's computers on a 50-year-old mainframe. It's the wrong tool for the times. Our high schools were designed 50 years ago to meet the needs of another age. Until we design them to meet the needs of the 21st century, we will

keep limiting — even ruining — the lives of millions of Americans every year.[25]

Gates' basic concern is that most schools preclude students from aspiring to excellence. In an effort to promote an alternate model, the Bill and Melinda Gates Foundation supports the development of small, theme-based high schools where students have a greater opportunity to focus on an area of intense interest to them.

Business leaders like Gates have become increasingly appreciative of the difference that harnessing employees' talents and keeping them emotionally connected to their work can make in the success of their enterprises. Demand is rising for workplace measurement and development services. Employee engagement has become a popular topic at business conferences. At the 2005 conference of the International Association of Business Communicators, for example, participants discussed research quantifying the linkages between emotional constructs like engagement and "hard" business outcomes such as productivity and retention.

In this light, opinion leaders are becoming more likely to support the idea that schools must work harder to address students' distinctive interests, to help them locate career paths that tap into natural wellsprings of enthusiasm and motivation. And there is growing recognition that, in order to do that, schools must work harder to find teachers who powerfully and insightfully relate to students.

In his speech on education, Gates reaffirmed that rigor — the need to ensure that all students are given a challenging curriculum that prepares them for college or work — is one of the building blocks of successful schools. But then he added two more "Rs":

- The second "R" is relevance — making sure students have courses and projects that clearly relate to their lives and goals.

- The third "R" is relationships — making sure students have a number of adults who know them, look out for them, and push them to achieve.[26]

School changes must go beyond standards and accountability testing to changing what happens in schools on a daily basis. Relevance and relationships are two good places to start because they are important elements in reorienting the education process around the strengths of students and teachers.

PART TWO

Mapping Common Ground

A COMMON HURDLE:
THE WEAKNESS TRAP

Few stories better illustrate the importance of focusing on students' innate talents and strengths than George Reavis' 1939 children's fable *The Animal School*. His tale (which was published in 1999 by Crystal Springs Books) is highly relevant to the argument made in this book. Here is an adaptation of the story:

> *Imagine there is a tree next to a pond in a meadow. There, a group of young animals is gathered, including a duck, a fish, an eagle, an owl, a squirrel, and a rabbit. They decide they want to have a school so they can be smart, just like people.*
>
> *So the grown-up animals come up with a curriculum they believe will make a well-rounded animal: courses in running, swimming, tree climbing, jumping, and flying.*
>
> *On the first day of school, little br'er rabbit combed his ears, and he went hopping off to his running class.*
>
> *There he was a star. He ran to the top of the hill and back as fast as he could go, and, oh, did it feel good. He said to himself, "I can't believe it. At school, I get to do what I do best."*

After class, the instructor said, "Rabbit, you really have talent for running. You have great muscles in your rear legs. With some training, you will get more out of every hop."

The rabbit said, "I love school. I get to do what I like to do and get to learn to do it better."

The next class was swimming. When the rabbit smelled the water, he said, "Wait, wait! Rabbits don't swim." The instructor said, "Well, you may not like it now, but five years from now you'll know it was a good thing for you." The rabbit remained skeptical and quite apprehensive about the first time he would be asked to get in the water.

In tree-climbing class, a tree trunk was set at a 30-degree angle so all the animals had a chance to succeed. The little rabbit tried so hard to climb that he hurt his leg.

In jumping class, the rabbit got along just fine; in flying class, he had a problem. So the teacher gave him a psychological test and discovered that he belonged in remedial flying. In that class, the rabbit had to practice jumping off a cliff. His teacher told him if he'd just work hard enough, he could succeed.

A few weeks later, the rabbit went to swimming class, and the instructor said, "Today we jump in the pond."

"Wait, wait!" the young rabbit said. "I talked to my parents about swimming. They didn't learn to swim. We don't like to get wet. I'd like to drop this course."

The instructor said, "You can't drop it. This class is part of the core curriculum and required for all animals. At this point, you have a choice: Either you jump in or you flunk."

The rabbit jumped in. He panicked! He went down once. He went down twice. Bubbles came up. The instructor saw that he was drowning and pulled him out. The other animals had never seen anything quite as funny as this wet rabbit who looked more like a rat without a tail, and so they chirped, and jumped, and barked, and laughed at the rabbit. The rabbit was more humiliated than he had ever been in his life. He wanted desperately to get out of class that day. He was glad when it was over.

He thought that he would head home, that his parents would understand and help him. When he arrived, he said to his parents, "I don't like school. I don't want to go to school."

"If the rabbits are going to get ahead, you have to get a diploma," replied his parents.

They argued, and finally the parents made the rabbit go to bed. In the morning, the rabbit headed off to school with a slow hop. Then he remembered that the principal had said that any time he had a problem to remember that the counselor's door is always open.

When he arrived at school, he hopped up in the chair by the counselor and said, "I don't like school."

And the counselor said, "Mmmm, tell me about it."

And the rabbit did.

The counselor said, "Rabbit, I hear you. I hear you saying you don't like school because you don't like swimming. I think I have diagnosed that correctly. Rabbit, I'll tell you what we'll do. You're doing exceptionally well in running. You don't need to work on running. What you need to work on is swimming. I'll arrange it so you don't have to go to running anymore, and you can have two periods of swimming."

When the rabbit heard that, he just threw up!

As the rabbit hopped out of the counselor's office, he looked up and saw his friend, the wise old owl. Br'er rabbit said, "I don't like school! I hardly ever get to do what I'm good at." Wise old owl cocked his head and said, "Br'er rabbit, life doesn't have to be that way."[1]

REMEDIATION NATION?

The *Animal School* fable illustrates that we are all born with certain talents — aptitudes and abilities — that are unique to us. We also have weaknesses — or lesser talents — that we struggle with at times and that seem as unnatural to us as our talents seem natural. The likelihood that the rabbit will excel in running appears high with practice and the right training, and the likelihood that he will achieve at a high level in swimming seems very low. Unlike the animals in this fable, however, humans' areas of talent — and those of lesser talent — aren't always obvious.

Let's first look at the definition of talent Gallup researchers have used through decades of study, because it may not be precisely the definition you're used to. When asked about talent, most people think of entertainment or sports celebrities, famous writers, or other luminaries. In the context of schools, you might associate talent with a particular student's aptitude for math, science, writing, music, art, languages, or athletics.

But thinking about talent only in terms of specific subjects or skills is very limiting. So we use a more inclusive definition: *A talent is any recurring pattern of thought, feeling, or behavior that can be productively applied.*[2] That includes any personal attribute that boosts the effectiveness with which we are able to complete any task in any field. Always striving to be the best is a talent; so is sticking to a goal despite distractions. A tendency to bring out the best in others classifies as a talent, as does a powerful affinity for learning.

Talent is the raw material from which to build *strengths*. Strengths are defined as talent combined with knowledge and skills and productively applied to produce *consistent, near-perfect performance of an activity.*[3] Talent, knowledge, and skills are essential building blocks of strengths; rarely do we see near-perfect performance of an activity

46

without all three. Though highly gifted people may be seen as a "natural" for a task (think Tiger Woods), in reality, a certain degree of knowledge and skill must be present to channel that talent productively. In the same way, knowledge and skill alone rarely explain the near-perfect performance of an activity. There is almost always an element of natural talent.

Few schools are adept at identifying and nurturing students' talents. Instead, the emphasis more typically gravitates to their weaker areas. The counselor's proposed solution for little br'er rabbit underscores the second assumption that we must confront: *Focusing on and improving areas of weakness for students and teachers is the key to making them more successful.*

During one of Gallup's focus groups, a mother's description of a discussion between herself and her son's teacher echoed the little rabbit's predicament. "I asked the teacher at the end of the year what they were going to do about John's math class," she said. "John already knew the content in the *next* year's math class. The teacher said she didn't know. Then she added, 'Maybe John could work on his writing.' That's a perfect alternative, I thought to myself: Be bored for a year in the class he loves or take two hours of a subject he hates!"

Does John need to learn how to write? Of course he does. His teachers should continue to work with John on his writing, albeit with an understanding that he may need to be taught differently from those who love to write. His school is unquestionably responsible for helping John develop his writing skills to an acceptable level. But its greater responsibility is to see that John's math talents are nurtured. As an adult, John's success will most likely spring from his inherent affinity for math rather than his less instinctive writing skills.

Neither perspective on education reform is immune to the weakness assumption — in fact, it's pervasive throughout our society. Gallup tested its prevalence in a 2001 poll, asking 1,016 American adults: *Which would help you be more successful in your life — knowing what your weaknesses are and attempting to improve your weaknesses, or knowing what your strengths are and attempting to build on your strengths?* A slight majority of respondents, 52%, chose working on weaknesses as the best way to help themselves become more successful in life. Forty-five percent opted for identifying and building on their strengths.[4]

Given the emphasis on remediation in many organizations, it's surprising not that the percentage choosing weaknesses was so high, but that it was so *low*. In many cases, our knee-jerk tendency is to notice the weaknesses first in ourselves and others. Viewing human nature through a lens of negativity is an easy habit to fall into because weaknesses *stand out*. It's easy to take positive qualities for granted because they don't create problems. By contrast, weaknesses present concrete challenges in areas of life that *don't* tend to go as smoothly — thus it seems more potentially beneficial to dwell on them. But does doing so lead to success in the long run?

Honing in on weaknesses creates a mindset that is preoccupied with fault, deficits, and failures in organizations and people. As a result, physicians rarely conduct wellness studies (though insurance companies often do). Psychologists study unsuccessful marriages more frequently than successful relationships. Management teams in all types of organizations spend time and resources fixing "weak links" and investing heavily in remediation, rather than figuring out how to get more out of what people do well.

But is this tendency also a problem in schools, which are tasked with helping build a bright future for the next generation? Too often, it is. In fact, in many cases, negativity is ingrained into a school's culture.

Denise, a parent in the Midwest, told me this story about the first parent-teacher conferences at her son's middle school:

"As a sixth grader, this is Trevor's first year in middle school, so I was very excited to go to parent-teacher conferences and meet his teachers, but the evening was a roller coaster ride. The first teacher I sat down with was his social studies teacher. She started out with 'Trevor is a great kid, but . . .' Whenever I hear the 'but,' I cringe. She went on to tell me that basically he was failing the class. The teacher said that she didn't know if it was a comprehension problem or a reading problem. Then she said maybe we should have him tested because he might have a learning disability.

"At this point, I was holding back tears. I asked if she had talked with any of Trevor's other teachers; she hadn't. When I asked what I could do at home to help him, she just shook her head, like, 'Hmmm, you know, I don't know.'

"From there, I went to the math teacher. She actually said that he was doing well. Upon checking the grade book, the math teacher said that Trevor was one point from a B+, and he was good to have in class.

"The third conference was with Trevor's science teacher. Again, he was not doing well. Like the social studies teacher, she was very negative in her delivery and not very helpful in suggestions for what I could do to help.

"The language arts teacher was next, and she made my evening. She said Trevor was doing a great job in class, and she almost has to constantly reassure him that he's doing a great job. She said that Trevor doesn't believe he's doing as well as he is.

"It made me wonder if he's not hearing much positive reinforcement from the other two teachers in the classes he's not doing well in. When I walked away from those two teachers, I felt negativity just from the way they approached me and talked to me at the conference. I just thought, 'Is that how you talk with your students? Is that how you teach?' Because I wouldn't perform very well for a teacher like that."

Were the drastic differences in Denise's meetings with these four teachers due entirely to Trevor's greater affinity for math and language arts than for science and social studies? That's probably part of the story; Denise admits that she didn't have a knack for science in school. But his teachers' negativity probably made things worse for Trevor, compounding his struggles by assuming the worst about him.

That kind of negative spiral made me think of another conversation I had, this one with Ted, a longtime teacher who had been nominated by one of my colleagues as the best he'd ever known. Ted told me that early in his career, he made a decision not to look at other teachers' evaluations of his incoming students prior to the school year. "When I started teaching, I read a young man's folder that was just riddled with all the things he couldn't do, and I was just dreading starting that school year with this kid," Ted recalled. "But I realized he had many, many strengths — and we clicked, and hopefully he had one of his best school years. That taught me a lesson: not to have these preconceived notions of students before the year starts."

LESSONS FROM POSITIVE PSYCHOLOGY

The story of the relatively young Positive Psychology movement provides a compelling example of the drift toward deficit-thinking on a large scale. For most of its history, the discipline of psychology served three purposes: 1) identifying and treating mental disorders, 2) making the lives of ordinary people more fulfilling, and 3) understanding and developing exceptional talent. However, by the end of the 20th century, psychologists had become so preoccupied with mental *illnesses* that the discipline's accompanying focus on mental *healthfulness* had been virtually eclipsed. As Martin Seligman recounted in his 2002 book *Authentic Happiness*, there were a number of reasons for this. Prominent among them was the fact that with the creation of the National Institute of Mental Health and the passage of the Mental Health Act in 1946, the federal government upped the ante on finding effective treatments for mental disorders with unprecedented levels of funding.[5] "Psychology journals have published 45,000 articles in the last 30 years on depression, but only 400 on joy," said a *New York Times* article on Seligman in 1998. "Joy is not covered by insurance, nor does it lead to tenure."[6]

Since the mid-1990s, Seligman and a rapidly growing cadre of psychologists worldwide have been working to restore the discipline's two neglected missions: helping psychologically healthy people find fulfillment and learning about high talent. This group has already made important breakthroughs within the discipline by reigniting interest in emotions that lead to resilience — like hope, subjective well-being, confidence, and joy.

Regardless of how you think about education, that's a critical lesson to keep in mind. In fact, it conveys an important common challenge for both major perspectives on education reform: Preoccupation with weaknesses means that the strengths of individuals may be neglected. Carol Ann Tomlinson, whose 1999 book *The Differentiated Classroom* made individualized instruction seem within the reach of all teachers, suggests how reframing common didactic questions creates a whole different outlook:

Not, What deficits? But, What strengths? Not, How do we remediate? (or even How do we enrich the standard curriculum?) but, How do we maximize access to the richest possible curriculum and instruction? Not, How do we motivate? but, What would it take to tap the motivation already within this learner? Not, Which kind of setting? But, What circumstances maximize the student's full possibilities?[7]

This problem of perspective filters down to every single administrator, principal, teacher, and student. It's inherent both in the status quo in U.S. schools and in proposed education reforms. We need to understand that weakness orientation and constantly guard against it if we're going to promote development by helping students leverage their greatest talents.

MOTIVATIONS FOR WEAKNESS FIXING

Preoccupation with weaknesses may be common to many of life's endeavors — but it seems particularly likely to hold sway in schools. Why should this be? After all, schools are filled with children who carry boundless energy and untold potential — shouldn't the process of their development be characterized by optimism and positive expectation? Let's take a closer look at how outdated social expectations may perpetuate the weakness fixing assumption.

In society and in schools, the belief that *fixing weaknesses leads to success* comes in part from the idea that all of us should be adept at everything. In the Animal School — and in most of our *human* schools — students take a broad spectrum of courses to be prepared for whatever path they choose to take in life. Some of them match up with students' talents and interests while others don't.

The underlying rationale is a sort of "Renaissance Man" ideal — someone who can seemingly do everything well and therefore has infinite ways to be successful. Indeed, there are some students in every school who seem marvelously talented in numerous areas — they're academically gifted, successful athletes, creative thinkers, and socially popular. But even these seemingly "perfect" students have weaknesses and strengths. The reality is that no one is perfect — but we'd all *like* to be, so the ideal lives on.

Like the Animal School, most schools are still structured so that all students learn the same subjects in the same way. This inevitably focuses students, teachers, and principals on areas in which they don't excel, in the mistaken belief that improvement in these areas represents their biggest development opportunity. Donald Austin, a high school principal in the Los Angeles area, believes that a preoccupation with weaknesses is indeed one of schools' most fundamental challenges today:

> In this new age of accountability, students' deficiencies are identified and remediated in an effort to increase test scores. Schools have become gifted at finding weaknesses, but have nearly forgotten about the strengths that students possess. Students pay the price for the constant reminders of shortcomings. They eventually grow to believe that they are defined by their weaknesses. This belief is unacceptable and avoidable.[8]

Often the attention on weaknesses stems from a lack of insight about the differences between two people and an inability to distinguish the separate dimensions along which their respective strengths lie.[9]

The next time you have a group of 10 or so people in a room, try this experiment: Ask a person at random if she sees herself as highly disciplined. Then ask someone on the other side of the room the same question. If both people claim to be highly disciplined or not highly

53

disciplined, ask another person until you find two people who give opposite responses.

Once you've identified two opposites, label the first person as a supervisor and the second as a newly hired employee. Then ask the supervisor, who, let's say, is the highly disciplined individual, "How are you most likely to describe your new employee after six months?" You will probably hear terms like "disorganized," "scatterbrained," or "a mess." Turn to the other individual, who admits to not being highly disciplined, and ask, "How are you likely to describe your supervisor?" Likely responses include "anal," "rigid," "authoritarian."

What can we conclude? Certainly, we're accustomed to using negative language to describe traits we don't see in ourselves. We didn't tell our subjects whether being highly disciplined was necessary for the new employee's job. Some positions do indeed require a very high level of discipline, but in others, it's not a key predictor of success. Regardless, our knee-jerk tendency is to: 1) see differences as weaknesses in others, and 2) believe those weaknesses should be fixed by bringing their owners around to our own way of doing things.

THE "HORATIO ALGER" EFFECT

The characteristically American view that we're all capable of achieving anything we set our minds to also feeds the illusion that weakness fixing leads to success. The notion that desire, effort, and persistence are all that's necessary to do well implies that if we try long and hard enough, we can excel at anything.

In areas where we have talent and interest, diligence and persistence do indeed pay off. That's why schools must give students more opportunities, once they've mastered core learning in all necessary areas, to concentrate on moving from good to excellent in topics for which they have demonstrated the most talent. Opportunities to grapple with high-level challenges in areas of talent are often transformative ways to learn about the subject at hand — and ourselves. Ed Hallowell, author of *The Childhood Roots of Adult Happiness*, maintains that once a student achieves that feeling of mastery, she wants to feel it again, and in the process changes from a "reluctant, fearful learner into a self-motivated player."[10]

The belief that anyone can excel at anything has a powerful Horatio Alger appeal. But beneath the surface, the presumption actually robs us of our individuality. It suggests that we're all "blank slates" with identical potential. This idea was the basis for behavioral psychologist John B. Watson's notorious claim that he could take an infant at random and "train him to become any type of specialist I might select — doctor, lawyer, artist, merchant-chief, and yes, even beggar-man and thief, regardless of his talents, penchants, tendencies, abilities, vocations and race of his ancestors."[11]

But this belief is wrong. People are *not* completely moldable through operant conditioning. In fact, current brain research suggests that the dramatic influences of both nature (genes) and nurture (our environment) mean that each of us carries unique potential when we are born — potential that is activated and developed by the opportunities we have and the choices we make throughout life.[12] If desire, effort, and persistence were all that was required to excel, the PGA tour would be impossibly crowded. Countless weekend golfers have years of desire, effort, training, and persistence under their belts. But neither new equipment nor more lessons can make most of them professional golfers. Knowledge, skill development, and better tools can take them only so far without inborn talent.

In schools, this belief leads to the implication that if a student fails to perform at high levels, he or she obviously didn't try hard enough. If desire, effort, and persistence always result in effective learning, then we can dismiss those who fail to learn the way we teach as "lazy." Discussing this harmful assumption in workplaces, the authors of the management book *First, Break All the Rules* say that in this scenario, the victim is blamed — worse, he is defined predominantly by his failures.[13]

For a struggling student, the result can be a vicious cycle. Unable to keep up with his classmates and seeing little reward for his efforts, he starts avoiding the subject whenever possible, which places him further behind. In *The Pressured Child*, Michael Thompson and Teresa Barker mark the effects of this situation on the student, saying, "It is psychologically painful for anyone to overcome frustration time and time again in order to be able to complete a task when others can do it relatively easily. Not knowing why it is so frustrating for you, or having a teacher treat you as if you were willfully malingering when you are struggling, is more than a child can bear."[14]

Unfortunately, many students faced with this situation stop trying at all. As Indiana University researchers Sasha Barab and Jonathan Plucker found in a 2002 study, "Students who are not succeeding can quickly descend into learned helplessness if they believe that they are not talented and will not succeed, regardless of their level of effort."[15]

Seeing the end result, teachers often dismiss the student as indolent or rebellious and assume that she simply needs to try harder. But no matter how much coercion is applied, students, like adults, rarely commit effort and persistence to acquiring large amounts of knowledge and skill in areas of non-interest or non-talent.[16] In these situations, persistently repeating what didn't work the first time tends to increase our frustration rather than our resolve. Eventually, that mounting frustration can threaten students' self-esteem and diminish their enthusiasm for school altogether.

MANAGING WEAKNESSES

So what *should* we do with areas of weakness — just ignore them? No. Obviously, that would leave students vulnerable and unprepared. But schools need better approaches to *managing* those weaknesses.

Let's go back for a moment to John, the student who excels at math but obviously needs to develop his writing skills to an acceptable level. Motivating John to improve his writing requires a different approach than one used for a talented writer, just as the approach to teaching John in math should be different from one used with students for whom numbers don't come naturally. We're talking not only about the *pace* of instruction, but the *method* as well. John needs teachers who understand how to help him approach writing from areas of strength that root him in self-confidence.

One size does not fit all. It is an approach that prevents John, who does very well at math, from rapidly advancing, and leaves Robert, who struggles with math, without the instruction he needs to learn the concepts. By using his existing interests and making schoolwork appear highly relevant, particularly in his area of talent, we stand a much better chance of helping John stay motivated — not just about math, but about improving his writing skills as well.

Let's look at a pair of examples that demonstrate how the weakness-fixing assumption operates in schools — and how it fails to foster excellence. We need to go no further than typical approaches to 1) student discipline and 2) teacher performance evaluations.

EXPECTING MISBEHAVIOR

The cover of the student handbook for a Midwestern middle school proudly states the school's name, the academic year, and the words "Academic Excellence." Unfortunately, when you flip through the handbook, you quickly conclude that "excellence" isn't really high on the school's agenda. Most of it is devoted to misconduct; the explanation of teacher "teams" is covered in barely 60 words. Absences and truancy, on the other hand, receive detailed passages defining the transgressions and corresponding punishments. Extracurricular opportunities get short shrift: The student council warrants four lines, intramurals receive four lines, the yearbook three lines, and student clubs two lines. An additional one-quarter of the handbook deals exclusively with what students should *not* do in school. Even in the sections describing "Computers" and "Telephones" for student use, the handbook emphasizes what students "will not" do.

Behavioral standards, and clear communication of those standards, are obviously a necessity. But do schools really generate positive outcomes by devoting so much attention to negative behavior? Probably not — but that's not the most important point. The absence of negative behaviors shouldn't be presented as students' most important common goal. Even if all of the transgressions cited in the handbook were eliminated, schools still wouldn't inspire the kind of positive behavior that leads to excellence.

Instead, highlighting the behaviors schools *want* is more likely to bring those behaviors out. As assistant principals across America can attest, some students simply look for the most obvious way to avoid being ignored. If the system or the teacher doesn't highlight *positive* ways to accomplish that goal, they may see the school's evident preoccupation with *negative* behaviors as the best available alternative.

TEACHERS AS "NEEDING IMPROVEMENT"

Traditional evaluation procedures for teachers and principals tend to suffer from one of two problems. Either they focus on the perceived weaknesses of the one being evaluated, or they are reduced to meaningless generalizations in which 80% of those evaluated fall into the "meets standards" category. In either case, the process fails to improve performance.

In the typical weakness-fixing approach, there are three steps. First, the teacher and principal prepare a set of goals. Next, the principal observes the teacher during a class session, taking notes about teacher and student behaviors, along with general observations. These notes from classroom visits — often no more than three a year, sometimes only one — form the basis for the principal's performance rating.

The third step is a conference between the teacher and principal in which the principal shares her observations of the class session. A number of positive observations may be discussed. But before the conference ends, and despite how many wonderful behaviors the teacher exhibits, principals in many cases feel obligated to identify two or three "areas of improvement." More often than not, these wind up being the crux of the feedback session.

Moreover, when goals based on the evaluation are written, they overwhelmingly focus on the perceived weaknesses, rather than expanding the teacher's knowledge, skill, and talent in areas of strength. Are the "areas of improvement" crucial to teacher performance? Not necessarily. Often, they're rather superficial, but they are the easy things to identify and record. The purpose of teacher and principal evaluations is to improve performance. That purpose can be undercut by placing undue emphasis on shortcomings that may not be the most relevant to learning outcomes.

In his 2003 book *Who Controls Teachers' Work?*, Richard Ingersoll cites a Research for Better Schools survey in which less than half of teachers in secondary schools perceived the results of their performance evaluations to be "frequently useful" to their teaching performance.[17] In fact, many good teachers dread performance evaluations because they fear they'll be subject to oversimplified or otherwise unfair criteria. Their anxiety may come in part from the likelihood that their principal feels compelled to formulate some kind of criticism — even of teachers who are doing an exemplary job — in order to justify the evaluation.

Can we find weaknesses upon which to focus in any environment? Of course, plenty of them. Unfortunately, shoring up weaknesses can at best only prevent failure. That's the trap this assumption leads us to: When it comes to human nature, failure is not the opposite of success. As Don Clifton and Paula Nelson point out in *Soar With Your Strengths*, eliminating our flaws does not guarantee excellence.[18] Usually, success comes from a different set of behaviors entirely. And the toll that dwelling on weaknesses takes in terms of time and student engagement is, in most cases, far too great.

It's a fundamental characteristic of human nature that we are energized by spending time in our areas of inherent talent. But a number of questions remain: If weakness fixing doesn't lead to success, how will a focus on talent work? Is there evidence to support that working on talents leads to success?

We'll get to those questions. But first, having identified a common hurdle in the various perspectives on improving education, let's turn to a powerful common goal.

CHAPTER FOUR

A COMMON GOAL: ENGAGEMENT IN THE CLASSROOM

"The illiterate of the 21st century will not be those who cannot read and write, but those who cannot learn, unlearn, and relearn." — Alvin Toffler, futurist

For American education to move forward, we need a common goal around which proponents of both perspectives can rally. Such a goal must have enough credibility and authority to motivate each side to play down its differences and work in concert.

In a democracy, the ultimate authority resides with the people — so let's start our search with a look at Americans' opinions regarding the goals of their schools. The Gallup Poll regularly tracks the public's perceptions of public schools and America's educational system, both independently and in conjunction with Phi Delta Kappa (PDK), the international association of educators.

Twice since 1995, Gallup presented a nationwide sample of Americans with a list of attributes and asked them to rate (a) the importance of each attribute to a school's success, and (b) how likely their local schools are to possess each attribute. Here is the question as it was asked the first time in 1995:

Schools can be successful for a number of reasons. I would like you to tell me how important each of the following characteristics is to having a very successful school. On a one-to-five scale, where "5" is having great importance, "4" is having much importance, "3" is of some importance, "2" is of little importance, and "1" is not at all important, how important is each of the following factors in determining whether a school is successful? How about . . .?

- Mastery of the basics; for example, reading, writing, and arithmetic

- Fair treatment of all the students

- Caring teachers

- Teachers with strong subject matter knowledge

- Students challenged to develop themselves to their full potential

- Positive teacher-student relationships

- A sense of safety and order

- Students provided with the technical skills needed for the world of work

- High academic standards held by the school

- Each student feels the teacher and staff care about him or her as a person

- Motivated students

- Strong preparation for future careers

- Emphasizing the strengths of each student

- Strong discipline

- Learning programs designed to fit each student

- The majority of students take upper-level math and science courses

- Above-average SAT and ACT scores

In 2004, Gallup revisited the question, modifying one survey item and adding three new ones. "Above-average SAT and ACT scores" was changed to "Students do well on standardized national tests, such as the ACT and SAT," and "Students do well on standardized state tests" was added to cover a key measurement criterion of No Child Left Behind. The other new items were:

- The school has clean and well-equipped facilities.

- Students possess a large body of facts from the social sciences, literature, and sciences.

The following graphs plot Americans' perceptions of the importance of the various items against their impressions of the likelihood that they are happening in their local schools. The further to the right an item appears on the horizontal scale, the higher its importance rating; the higher it appears on the graph's vertical scale, the more likely respondents were to think it was actually happening.

First, in Figure 1, the 1995 results:

FIGURE 1

Gallup Poll, September 1995

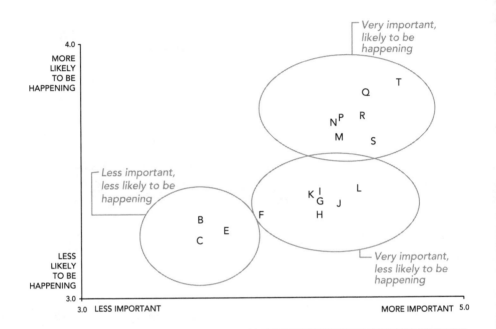

A. (2004 poll only)

B. Above-average SAT and ACT scores

C. The majority of students take upper-level math and science courses

D. (2004 poll only)

E. Learning programs designed to fit each student

F. Strong discipline

G. Each student feels the teacher and staff care about him or her as a person

H. Students provided with the technical skills needed for the world of work

I. Strong preparation for future careers

J. Emphasizing the strengths of each student

K. Motivated students

L. Students challenged to develop themselves to their full potential

M. Positive teacher-student relationships

N. High academic standards held by the school

O. (2004 poll only)

P. A sense of safety and order

Q. Caring teachers

R. Teachers with strong subject matter knowledge

S. Fair treatment of all the students

T. Mastery of the basics; for example, reading, writing, and arithmetic

"Mastery of the basics" is rated as the most important item on the list. That's typical of education surveys; Americans consistently assign the highest value to transferring the fundamental knowledge and skills all students must possess to function well in society. The concern underlying No Child Left Behind is that too many students aren't reaching that threshold.

However, even in 1995, the public seemed less certain about the importance of standardized testing as the means to address that concern. Respondents to the survey tended to place less importance on the need for students to have above-average SAT and ACT scores.

Given the high-profile dialogue about standards and accountability testing generated by NCLB since 2002, had Americans' perceptions shifted by 2004? They hadn't shifted much. In fact, there's a remarkable degree of stability in the public's ratings between 1995 and 2004 (see Figure 2), as the two graphs show. All of the original characteristics that fell into the upper right quadrant (important and likely to be happening) occupied the same status in 2004 — as did the seven items in the lower right corner (important but less likely to be happening).

FIGURE 2

Gallup Poll, September 2004

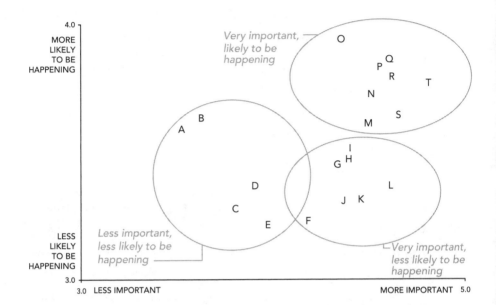

A. Students do well on standardized state tests

B. Students do well on standardized tests, such as the ACT and SAT

C. The majority of students take upper-level math and science courses

D. Students possess a large body of facts from the social sciences, literature, and sciences

E. Learning programs designed to fit each student

F. Strong discipline

G. Each student feels the teacher and staff care about him or her as a person

H. Students provided with the technical skills needed for the world of work

I. Strong preparation for future careers

J. Emphasizing the strengths of each student

K. Motivated students

L. Students challenged to develop themselves to their full potential

M. Positive teacher-student relationships

N. High academic standards held by the school

O. The school has clean and well-equipped facilities

P. A sense of safety and order

Q. Caring teachers

R. Teachers with strong subject matter knowledge

S. Fair treatment of all the students

T. Mastery of the basics; for example, reading, writing, and arithmetic

Some observations are particularly worth noting. In 1995 and 2004, "mastery of the basics" was the item most likely to be rated as having "great importance." The good news is that Americans also ranked this item highly in terms of its likelihood to be happening in both 1995 and 2004.

Certainly, school leaders should be aware that the public still sees acquiring basic academic skills as the core of a successful school. But despite the publicity devoted to No Child Left Behind since it was enacted in 2002, standardized test scores had gained no perceived importance by 2004. "Students do well on standardized state tests" — the key measures mandated by NCLB — ranks last out of 20 characteristics of importance in the 2004 survey, just behind "Students do well on standardized national tests, such as the ACT and SAT." This low priority may stem in part from the public's skepticism about capturing the quality of learning in a single test measure: In the 2004 PDK/Gallup Poll, only 25% of Americans indicated that they thought it was possible for a single test to "accurately judge a student's proficiency in English and math," while 73% said they didn't think it was possible.[1]

But that's not the most interesting point to take away from these data. Take a look at the lower right sections of the graphs. These are items that may be of particular concern to those interested in improving schools. They're the characteristics that are rated by Americans as high in importance but low in perceived implementation. Efforts to improve these factors may well garner public support. In 2004, the three items closest to the right-hand corner were "Students challenged to develop themselves to their full potential," "Motivated students," and "Emphasizing the strengths of each student."

Ratings of the item "Students are challenged to develop themselves to their full potential" appear particularly noteworthy. In both the 1995 and 2004 surveys, the item places in the top five in importance, and in both surveys, the difference between its importance rating and the likelihood of Americans to think it's actually happening ranks as the largest gap.

FULFILLING EVERY STUDENT'S POTENTIAL

The idea of fulfilling every student's potential seems like a good place to start in our effort to step back and reconsider the way we think about school accountability. It helps reorient our thinking about a simple truth: When it comes to education, the big picture is really determined by the little picture — what's best for *each individual student.* As Patricia Hersch observed in *A Tribe Apart,* her 1998 study of American teens, "Nobody is paying much attention to individual adolescents, but everyone is hysterical about the aggregate."[2] The current environment is such that policymakers and school leaders focus on averages. A school district's average ACT or SAT test scores appear in the newspaper. A school's progress is measured by averages of student scores on statewide tests.

The reality is that, in an important sense, averages mask what happens in real life, since real people exist on every point of a continuum *summarized* by the average. In education, the aggregate perspective can eclipse the specific needs of individual students. If we're serious about leaving no child behind, we should also be looking at what schools are doing to help kids capitalize on their individuality and how well they are considering what will best equip each student to lead a happy, productive life.

If parents, political and business leaders, and educators can unite behind the goal of maximizing every student's potential, their expectations will change. The need to guarantee all students a minimum threshold of knowledge will give way to the need to guarantee each student maximum opportunities for continuous growth. That goal rejects the idea that it's sufficient for all students to reach proficiency and insists instead that each student has the chance to strive for *excellence* by discovering and developing her talents.

As it's structured today, accountability testing focuses teachers and schools on students who are not scoring at a proficient level. Cognitive psychologist Jerome Bruner cautioned against this tendency as far back as 1960. "The view has already been expressed that the pursuit of excellence must not be limited to the gifted student," wrote Bruner in *The Process of Education.* "But the idea that teaching should be aimed at the average student or the low-achieving student in the hope of providing something for everybody is an equally inadequate formula. The quest, it seems to many of us, is to devise materials that will challenge the superior student while not destroying the confidence and will-to-learn of those who are less fortunate."[3]

Beyond revising curricular materials, we must revise our expectations so that schools find better ways to tap the talents of each student on a personal level. The goal is to develop *all* students, not just the elite, not just the average student, not just those failing to demonstrate proficiency. Standards that promote proficiency are insufficient. We can't afford to leave any students undereducated, but just as importantly, we can't accept "satisficing" — i.e., students' failure to realize their potential because their schools don't engage them enough to learn anything beyond what's necessary to pass the all-important test.

While being able to claim that all third graders are reading at grade level is an important objective, the underlying goal is to have all adults using their reading skills as good citizens and productive members of society. An expectation of excellence rather than adequacy better aligns America's schools with the public's hopes for them, encourages engagement and higher self-esteem among individual students, and provides greater hope that America's schools really can leave no child behind.

Fulfilling each student's potential seems like an enormous task. Is it unrealistic to expect America's schools to accomplish this seemingly larger goal when simply bringing all students to proficiency seems so elusive? No — because exploring students' potential as individuals is far more conducive to enlisting students themselves as fully engaged partners in the learning process.

ENGAGED CITIZENS

In 1990, Mihaly Csikszentmihalyi (pronounced "chick-SENT-me-high"), then a renowned psychologist at the University of Chicago, gave a name to the feeling that people experience when they're performing tasks that make full use of their abilities and completely engage their attention. He called it "flow." In his book of the same name, Csikszentmihalyi wrote that in this state, whatever activity one is engaged in — reading a history assignment, rebuilding a carburetor, writing a business proposal — literally flows. The participant is so absorbed in the task that he or she doesn't think consciously about the steps, and frequently loses track of time. Flow can be thought of as engagement at its highest level.

Csikszentmihalyi maintains that flow is one of the keys to a happy life. "[It] lifts the course of life to a different level," he writes in *Flow*. "Alienation gives way to involvement, enjoyment replaces boredom, helplessness turns into a feeling of control, and psychic energy works to reinforce the sense of self, instead of being lost in the service of external goals. When experience is intrinsically rewarding life is justified in the present, instead of being held hostage to a hypothetical future gain."[4]

Engagement on the job may be particularly predictive of happiness, because work is something most of us spend a lot of time doing. Psychologist Amy Wrzesniewski has extensively studied different types of work orientation. She sees significant differences between those who view their work as a *calling* — an activity they love that allows them to express their personal values — and those for whom work is a *career* — offering advancement and direction but largely unrelated to their core values — or simply a *job* — done solely to earn a living. Wrzesniewski found that people with callings report significantly higher job and life satisfaction than those with either of the other two job orientations.[5]

Higher engagement improves not only personal quality-of-life outcomes, but organizational effectiveness as well. In fact, customer and employee engagement have become hot topics in the business world in recent years. As the dot-com boom subsided after 2000 and the breakneck pace of technological change slowed, companies became more interested in the question of how to maximize their *human* capital to help maintain the productivity advances they acquired in the late 1990s.

Engagement represents fertile ground for development; Gallup estimates that low productivity among actively disengaged employees costs the U.S. economy about $300 billion every year. How much of that cost could be eliminated if companies were able to recruit more people who are prone to engagement because their education has given them a solid foundation of self-understanding and a thirst for experiencing flow?

Richard Florida, a public policy analyst at George Mason University, takes that argument a step further in *The Flight of the Creative Class*, noting that expanding the goals of American education is an "economic imperative" in the face of new global competition:

What's needed is, in fact, a full-scale overhaul of the way we go about teaching our children. We can no longer succeed — or even tread water — with an education system handed down to us from the industrial age since what we no longer need is assembly-line workers. We need one that instead reflects and reinforces the values, priorities, and requirements of the creative age. Education reform must, at its core, make schools into places where human creativity is cultivated and can flourish. . . . Schools need to be vehicles for enhancing and mobilizing the creative capacities of all our children so that the tinkering of today can be translated into the creative advancement of tomorrow.[6]

ENGAGING STUDENTS IN LEARNING

Promoting engagement is not just a desired *outcome* of education — it's essential to the process itself. Something terribly disappointing happens in most schools. Few observers fail to see the sparkle in the eyes of first graders who are learning something. Nearly any picture book instills rapt attention. By third grade, the enthusiasm of some students has begun to wane, and by fifth grade, there are evident differences in students' levels of involvement, behavior, and achievement.

By high school, many students have dropped out — some literally, others in terms of emotional involvement and commitment to learning. Pedagogical reforms that fail to recognize the importance of student engagement have a difficult time maintaining their impact through the teen years. Thus, while 9-year-olds showed improvement in reading and math between 1999 and 2004, according to the National Assessment of Educational Progress, results were mixed for 13-year-olds and flat among 17-year-olds.[7] Writing about the ability of American students to participate in a globalized economy, Thomas Friedman quotes an IT systems architect who taught at a local university. "Of the students I taught over six semesters, I'd only consider hiring two of them," he said. "The rest lacked the creativity, problem-solving abilities and passion for learning."[8]

Somewhere in those school years, as John Goodlad noted in his study of schools, the process of schooling — required classes, textbooks, seatwork, lectures, and tests — takes its toll. This transformation coincides with another shift, in which students become valued primarily for their ability to learn the subjects we teach in the way we teach them.[9] The emphasis moves from teaching *children* to teaching *content*.

That emphasis has been reinforced by the standards and accountability assumption, which fails to account for the importance of actively engaging students in their own learning. Students can be required to take certain classes, but their psychological commitment to an activity can't be coerced. Forcing students to do more without considering how to trigger and sustain their emotional involvement may well have the unintended consequence of lowering engagement in required courses — and in learning itself.

That consequence has the potential to lead to a crisis just as great as that put forth in *A Nation at Risk*. Indeed, some feel that in many cases, it already has. We're starting to more fully grasp the problems created as a result of teaching everyone the same way. A 2006 *Newsweek* cover story entitled "The Trouble With Boys," for example, reviews scientists' and educators' views of why, according to a variety of educational benchmarks, boys are falling behind girls at an alarming rate. The article describes how boys are biologically, developmentally, and psychologically different from girls — and notes that teachers need to recognize those differences in order to bring out the best in each student. But that's typically not happening because:

Standardized assessments have become commonplace for kids as young as 6. Curricula have become more rigid. Instead of allowing teachers to instruct kids in the manner and pace that suit each class, some states now tell teachers what, when, and how to teach. . . . These new pressures are undermining the strengths and underscoring the limitations of what psychologists call the "boy brain" — the kinetic, disorganized, maddening and sometimes brilliant behaviors that scientists now believe are not learned but hard-wired.[10]

Two weeks later, a *Time* article on the state of science education in the United States commented that "Perhaps even more important than the struggle of U.S. students to keep pace with their international peers is their failure to keep up in enthusiasm for the subject." It's hard to find talented teachers who have the kind of passion for science that keeps students motivated. And when students are lucky enough to have such a teacher, their creativity in the classroom is heavily restrained by strict content requirements. "Even teachers who are eager and equipped often face daunting curricular goals," the article notes, "U.S. science texts usually cover many more topics than international ones do. 'Compared to the rest of the world, we're a mile wide and an inch deep,' says [Gerald] Wheeler, [executive director of the National Science Teachers Association]."[11]

Let's return for a moment to the study at the beginning of this chapter. You may have noticed that the presence of "motivated students" is one of the characteristics Americans are least likely to feel applies to their communities' schools. It's also the item with the second greatest gap between "importance" ratings and "happening" ratings. As the stimulus or impulse that causes students to pay attention, be involved, and exert considerable effort to accomplish a goal, motivation is a necessary precursor to engagement.

Without doubt, higher average test scores can often be achieved through relatively short, pressure-filled periods in which teachers and students concentrate entirely on the specified content. But this can't be considered a success if it happens at the cost of leaving students with less enthusiasm for learning and teachers with less enthusiasm for teaching. Pushing up test scores with "drill and kill" tactics is a little like feeding kids hard candy just before they run a 400-meter race: It provides a burst of energy that quickly dissipates — and over the long term, makes for an extremely unhealthy training regimen.

Even "good" schools — those in which students are scoring at acceptable proficiency levels on state accountability tests and have high ACT and SAT scores — are subject to low levels of student engagement. In these situations, a significant number of students are just going through the motions. They follow the rules and do the work, but with minimal effort and little enthusiasm. The common sentiment, even among academic stars, is "What do I have to do to get the grade I want?" When students' predominant source of motivation is the need to meet expectations, the presence of "flow" in their lives becomes an afterthought — or worse, an unaffordable luxury.

It seems that from the first day of kindergarten to high school graduation, toy and game marketers are much more successful than schools at engaging the minds and emotions of students. Is that simply because selling flashy entertainment content is so much easier than selling educational content? Or do marketers really better understand how to reach young people than professional educators do?

There is a difference, as Phillip Schlechty aptly notes in *Shaking Up the Schoolhouse*. First, marketers know how to leverage active involvement, stimulating activities, and attractive end products to produce desired behaviors in young people. Secondly, those selling products and services to young people understand that students are *volunteers*.[12] They may be required to go to school every day, take certain classes, and pass a multitude of tests. But beyond all that, students cannot be coerced to actively involve themselves in learning any more than they actually *want* to. The lack of engagement in many schools is in part a result of failing to acknowledge that insight.

WHAT HELPS YOU LEARN?

Taking another cue from the marketing world, Gallup decided to go directly to students themselves for insights about the classes they feel helped them most. In a 2005 Gallup Youth Survey, students aged 13 to 17 were asked to think of the one class in which they feel they learned the most during the previous semester.

Asked to provide three reasons for their choices (Figure 3), just over half of teens — 53% — gave credit to the teacher. Those teacher-related responses fell about evenly into two general categories: 1) students like the teacher, the teacher cares, and the teacher respects students, or 2) the teacher's style makes it fun to learn. One in five students (21%) said they named the class because of its subject matter. About the same percentage (20%) said they learned the most in this class because it was challenging. And 9% said they learned the most from the class they were good at or the one that was easiest for them.

FIGURE 3

2005 Gallup Youth Survey[13]

Think about the class in which you feel you learned the most this last semester. What made you think of this particular class? Please provide three reasons.

Asked of U.S. teens aged 13-17

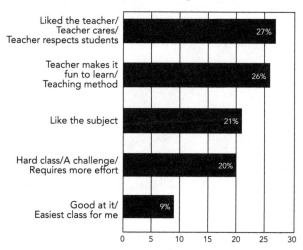

A few verbatim responses from the students in this survey illustrate the emphasis they place on the teacher:

- *"My teacher understood the way that I learned and worked. I was never criticized for my ideas or feelings, but I was met with questions and ideas that could change the way I looked at something."*
  — Jessica, 17, Waverly, IA

- *"I learned to appreciate poetry (when the teacher is passionate about it, I learned to be passionate about it). I love to write, and this is the only class in which writing assignments can be creative without the teacher docking points for 'flowery wording.' History meets creativity."*
  — Ashley, 17, York Springs, PA

- *"The teacher was AMAZING. Not only was he extremely well-informed, he'd been teaching in the subject for so long he knew what was effective and what wasn't. It's great when the teacher is so good that even in a subject I wouldn't ordinarily enjoy, it was fun to learn in the class."*
  — Michael, 17, Dixon, CA

- *"My teacher always pushed us to our limits. I have never been pushed so hard in my life to achieve. She was very fun and really took time to know each one of us. She was there after school to help when we needed it."*
  — Brittany, 16, Phoenix, AZ

Gallup also asked students more specifically whether the teacher in the class they learned the most from was different from the other teachers they had. Seventy percent said yes. When asked what set that teacher apart (Figure 4), 63% of those who said their teacher was different gave a response related to the teacher's classroom methods (good teaching methods/challenging assignments/teacher makes learning fun), while 41% offered one of a variety of responses regarding the teacher's relationships with students.

FIGURE 4

2005 Gallup Youth Survey[14]

**Was the teacher of this class different from other teachers
you had, or not? (if yes) What made this teacher different?
Please provide up to three responses.**

Asked of U.S. teens aged 13-17

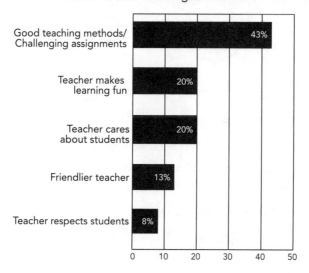

Verbatim responses to this question illustrate how the best teachers engaged their students and elevated students' sense of their own
potential:

- *"Although my outlook on most things was vastly different, we
  still connected because she was real. She's easygoing and open-
  minded. She is into pop culture and is probably the smartest
  person I know. I've had this teacher for multiple classes, and
  I've grown to love her. She was never afraid to do things her
  way and was not afraid of her flaws. She was stubborn, funny,
  and genuine."*
— Amanda, 16, Saint Johns, MI

- *"Because he taught us a new way to write and think. It wasn't the basic writing technique — he got you to open up your mind and believe in yourself."*
  — Samantha, 17, Healdsburg, CA

- *"He wasn't bland or monotone like most of my teachers, but he was full of life and made learning fun."*
  — Chris, 15, Katy, TX[15]

INTER-*ACTIVE* LEARNING

If there is a secret to motivation in the classroom, it lies in the *interaction* between a teacher and student. Motivation springs from an individual teacher's beliefs about teaching, as well as his or her capacity to build relationships and perceive each student's "starting point." No process, program, or curriculum can replace the profound impact one talented teacher makes on student learning. Finding teachers with the ability to motivate students and giving them ample opportunity to *use* that ability are the most important levers leaders can pull to influence student engagement.

As volunteers, students are motivated only when their interests and talents are part of the activity at hand. Teachers who understand this use active learning strategies that appeal to students' interests and talents and put them to work. In *The Differentiated Classroom*, Carol Ann Tomlinson describes how students' engagement levels rise when their interests determine how something is to be learned.[16] Rather than dealing with abstractions in a uniform — and passive — way, the goal, as Mel Levine suggests in *A Mind at a Time*, should be that every student is given the chance to follow his or her leanings and become an expert on something in the learning community.[17]

Students are longing for more involvement and interaction at school. In 2003, the Gallup Youth Survey asked 500 teens for their ideas about changes their school could make to help students learn. The phrase "hands-on" was peppered throughout the responses, as in the following comment from Justin, 15: "I think schools should have more hands-on activities and more fun stuff because that will help you pay attention. After awhile, just sitting makes you bored, and you pay less attention." Lauren, 16, sounded a similar refrain: "Don't just lecture to the kids; do more with activities to get the kids involved and moving during class."[18]

Richard DuFour and his colleagues took the traditional "teacher-centered" model to task in their 2004 book *Whatever It Takes*. That model, they note, would lead a visitor from Mars to believe school is a place where teachers work hard and students watch them work.[19] Recent brain research has helped us understand that education models that limit student involvement have an inherent disadvantage, because most of the learning that occurs lacks the emotional component that promotes long-term memory storage. So, for the most part, facts are stored for the test and then forgotten. But perhaps more importantly, students become accustomed to viewing time spent learning as a necessary evil rather than an absorbing exploration.

But we don't really need experts to tell us these things. Just consider your own school experience. Think of a course at any level in which you had limited individual interest. While you may have spent a significant amount of time in class sessions and reading or studying on your own, how many of the facts that were part of that subject do you remember today? If you don't use the specific subject matter in your life today, you probably remember very few of the very things about which you were tested. But if the class successfully engaged your interests, you've retained the broad concepts for use throughout your life. The trick is to provide as many moments of enthusiasm for learning as possible.

Unfortunately, the current educational system is less capable of engaging students than in decades past. As Howard Gardner has noted, a time traveler from 50 years ago would recognize the schools, but he or she would have difficulty getting a handle on much else in the lives of many fifth graders today. Away from school, students use media that border on the stuff of science fiction: MP3 players, hand-held video games, camera phones, wireless laptops, instant messages, compact videodisc players, satellite television, and movies on demand.[20]

With all this input, it's increasingly difficult for schools to maintain students' attention and engagement levels using the methodologies of the past. High-tech media and toys have accustomed kids to a highly visual, interactive, and fast-paced environment. Contrast this environment with the school setting found in too many classrooms. The teacher dispenses the information to be learned while the students sit at their desks, involved only when called upon or given assignments. All students move in lock step regardless of their abilities and interests. And all too often, minimal effort is put into personalizing what is learned or helping students connect it to their lives outside school or their personal hopes and aspirations.

ENGAGEMENT THROUGH TALENTS

Though active learning and positive, appropriate feedback are essential components, the most powerful factor in building engagement is identifying and fully deploying talents in the classroom. And not only students' talents — the talents of everyone involved in education must be leveraged, from students, teachers, and principals to parents and community leaders.

But let's start by looking at how engaged schools put student talent at the center of the education process. For many students, the most important discoveries may be the realization of where their greatest talents lie and where the flow experiences occur. Such self-awareness allows students, as well as their teachers and parents, to make better use of the resources that are currently available to them and to identify opportunities that should be sought out or declined based on the "fit" with a young person's natural gifts. It gives them a glimpse of the high road to excellence.

PART THREE

The Power of Engagement

CHAPTER FIVE

ENGAGED STUDENTS: IN PURSUIT OF STRENGTHS

"Let our children grow tall, and some taller than others if they have it in them to do so." — Margaret Thatcher, former Prime Minister of the United Kingdom

Jill was a young woman with an intellectual disability who in 2002, through her participation in Special Olympics Maryland, enrolled in a year-long mentoring program called ALPS (Athlete Leadership Programs). The program's goals included giving people with such disabilities some exposure to a business environment, helping them become better public speakers, and providing them with positive feedback about themselves.

During the first session, Jill would hardly speak in front of the group. Her shyness posed a challenge for her mentor, Alison, whose task was to help Jill become a good "self-advocate" — to see herself in terms of her abilities, rather than her disability. Early in the program, all the participants completed a talent assessment. Some of Jill's most powerful talents appeared to be in developing close relationships. Two characteristics that popped up in the assessment were "harmony," which is generally described as the tendency to look for common ground with others, and "relator," the tendency to maintain, and derive pleasure from, close friendships.

As the year unfolded, those characteristics became increasingly evident in Jill. She grew close to Alison, who regularly pointed out to Jill when she was displaying exceptionally caring, congenial behavior — when she was using her talents. Jill began to laugh and joke frequently with the other mentors and Special Olympics athletes. Reading and communicating clearly still posed a constant struggle for her, but as she learned to trust her relating skills, those frustrations began to seem more manageable to her.

By the last session, when the athletes delivered their final presentations, these relationship-oriented talents were highly evident in Jill's behavior. Her timidity gone, she stood in front of a group of parents, friends, mentors, and fellow athletes and demonstrated a variety of golf swings with obvious enjoyment. Jill's parents note that the change has carried far beyond the mentoring class. She now speaks to community groups as a Special Olympics advocate — and sings in church. "Before, she just didn't have the confidence," says Jill's mother, Nancy. "But now, every time we walk out of church on Sunday morning, she says, 'ALPS helped me do that.'"

How much of that change can be attributed to Jill's newfound ability to think of herself in terms of talents? It's hard to say — but Jill's mother points to the mentoring class as a turning point for Jill.

All students and adults should have the opportunity to learn about their talents in a proactive way, as Jill has. Focusing on talents provides an alternative to the weakness assumption and a means of fostering higher levels of engagement in the classroom.

TALENT: A CLOSER LOOK

Let's return for a moment to Gallup's definition of talent as *any recurring pattern of thought, feeling, or behavior that can be productively applied*. The degree to which these patterns *are* productively applied helps explain why some people realize more of their physical and intellectual potential than others do. As opposed to knowledge and skills, which are the tools through which schools help students cultivate and apply their talent, talent itself springs forth from genetically driven predispositions that children bring with them when they first step into a classroom. We can't take credit for our inherent talents, but we can claim credit for discovering and building upon them to create excellence.

Again, we define a *strength* as the ability, rooted in talent, to consistently produce excellence in a specific area. Developing a strength means cultivating our most naturally powerful ways of thinking, feeling, and behaving through the addition of pertinent knowledge and skills. The ability to consistently and nearly perfectly close a tough sale, manage a geographically dispersed team, or detect patterns emerging from complex scientific data — these are all examples of strengths.

In this chapter, these terms are used in the context of students, but they are germane to each of the groups discussed in the remainder of the book. We must learn how to better use the talents and strengths of *everyone* involved in the education process.

That's tougher than it sounds, because while talents come naturally to us, our recognition of them often doesn't. Because our greatest talents are so natural to us, we often assume they're commonplace. Whether it's an innate ease in learning mathematics or the inherent need to take action when confronted with a problem, it's just what we do; we've never known anything different. While others may marvel at our ease in an area of talent, we often fail to see our own talents as very special. The areas of our lives in which we use those talents tend to go smoothly; thus, we spend little time consciously thinking about them.

Further, our preoccupation with what we *can't* do well often clouds our ability to see what we *can* do well. Child psychologist Mel Levine echoes Jill's story in pointing out how this occurs in children with attention deficit disorder:

> Parents and teachers should never lose sight of all the good things that come packaged with attention deficits like the extras you purchase with your new automobile. So many children with deficit attention controls reward their parents with such redeeming features as creativity, compassion, and perceptiveness. They may also shine as wheeler-dealers, entrepreneurs in their own right. Many possess specialized talents and rugged independence.[1]

Talents are everywhere. We just need to look for them. One key to more fully appreciating our talents is better understanding their origins. Where do talents come from? In recent years, neuroscience has provided some new insights into that question.

FINE-TUNING THE BRAIN

At birth, a baby's brain is comprised of a rapidly expanding group of neurons. Some of these have been wired for specific purposes, but far more are not yet differentiated. For decades, the "nature vs. nurture" debate led to competing hypotheses about whether it was a child's heredity or environment that determined which connections would coalesce to form the adult brain.

Today that debate appears largely irrelevant, because both nature and nurture play a crucial role. Recent breakthroughs in MRI technology have led biologists to a better understanding of the active interplay of genetic signals and environmental stimuli through successive stages of a child's development.[2] Environmental conditions trigger latent genetic influences, causing certain neurons to fire more frequently and in repeated configurations with other neurons. This solidifies certain connections and creates patterns where the brain performs with greater ease. Just the opposite occurs to neural connections that fire infrequently; they eventually atrophy.[3]

In this way, every child's development is composed of a set of opportunities for his or her environment to determine which genes will be expressed, and in what ways. During critical periods, the brain goes through a cycle in which neural connections proliferate rapidly and are then "pruned" to the ones that are used most often. One such phase occurs in the womb. Recently, scientists have determined that another occurs later in childhood and another in early adolescence. By adulthood, many connections have dropped away — but those that remain are faster and more efficient. Once they're wired and insulated, neuroscientists say, those pathways become very difficult to redirect.[4]

That neural pruning process makes it possible for the human brain to function. In effect, it fine-tunes the brain much like we tune a radio when a number of stations are grouped on similar frequencies. If too many signals are received at once, all we hear is noise. Less is more in this case, as the brain's most frequently used connections become personality characteristics. These connections give us talents, the naturally recurring patterns of thoughts, feelings, and behavior that make us unique individuals.

NATURE AND NURTURE

The cycle of interaction between our genes and our environment implies that talents such as learning languages or singing rely on both nature and nurture. Talent shows up partly as a strong affinity for an activity. A potential concert pianist, for example, naturally gravitates toward the keyboard. In his 2003 book *Nature Via Nurture*, Matt Ridley describes how genes establish an "appetite for practice" in a certain area. In one case, identical twins reared apart both grew up to be outstanding basketball players. Must be genetic, right? Ridley maintains that even in this instance, the role of the environment is critical. Both twins began with a similar inborn talent that resulted in an appetite for basketball. That appetite led the twins to similar experiences in the form of initial success, additional practice, and greater refinement of their talent. Thus, the interaction of nature and nurture, rather than genes alone, was the key to their success on the court.

Ridley goes on to suggest that the genetic differences resulting in varying levels of talent may be relatively small. But they're amplified by the fact that they lead one person to invest more time in practicing the piano while another does chemistry experiments in her spare time. Ridley describes it as a quiet whisper in our ear that says, "Enjoy doing what you are good at; dislike doing what you are bad at."[5] Child psychologist Sandra Scarr describes the resulting tendency for each person to be drawn to environments in which their talents are more likely to be used, thereby augmenting our genetic starting points.[6]

The authors of *Now, Discover Your Strengths* note that specific behaviors that reflect talents, such as making sure people feel included or considering all the aspects of a problem before acting, "feel just right" while other behaviors seem "stilted and forced" even after repeated attempts.[7] In the final analysis, they conclude, talents explain "how well and how often" we engage in certain behaviors.[8]

CLUES TO TALENT

So how do we go about identifying our greatest talents — and those of our kids? Most people don't have a clear idea of how to pinpoint those "intangibles" that made them successful. While there are more and more research-derived psychometric tools to help identify talents, they all tend to rely on three basic indicators. These markers are *yearnings*, *rapid learning*, and *satisfactions*.

Yearnings are the relative appeal of one activity over another. They often manifest themselves after you observe a performance or an activity, when you may find yourself thinking, "I'd like to do that." The fact that the activity resonates with your strongest synaptic connections draws you back to it. The tense in which you find yourself thinking provides another clue to your yearnings. If you're thinking in the future tense, with the anticipation of repeating an activity, you may be operating in an area of exceptional talent.[9]

Rapid learning is another strong indicator of talent. Gallup's studies of top-performing salespeople have shown that many of the most successful prefer to meet with prospects early in their training and learn by doing, rather than in a class setting. But the biggest differentiator wasn't their favored learning strategy. No matter what training program was used, the top performers simply *learned faster*.[10] You've probably experienced rapid learning yourself. With certain new activities, the instructional steps disappear quickly — as opposed to areas of slower learning, in which you must repeat each step slowly and deliberately to internalize the process.

However, the best indicator that an activity represents an area of exceptional talent is the pleasure that results from the experience. Feelings of emotional satisfaction heighten the motivation to repeat the activity again and again. We have a built-in reward system for developing our talents. We very easily become engaged when working in these areas, and when the work is complete, we are often left with the powerful gratification of having accomplished something at a level of excellence.

THE MOVE-FROM-TALENT PRINCIPLE

For each of us, our most powerful talents represent the best developed neural pathways in our brains. When we use these solid connections, we tap into the best of our natural selves. What's more, these pathways have the greatest potential for further development and refinement. The move-from-talent principle maintains that those dominant connections should be leveraged as much as possible. Using our most natural talents makes learning easier, increases the probability that what is learned will be retained, and provides greater satisfaction. In short, it fosters engagement.

Talent in the Business World

The management book *First, Break All the Rules* culls insights from interviews with 80,000 outstanding managers from all types of organizations, including school principals. Reviewing the interview data, the authors note that outstanding performance in any role requires an individual to display uncommonly deep understanding or great efficiency in certain aspects of thought, feeling, or behavior. The greater the match between a person's natural patterns and the demands of his role, the greater the likelihood that his performance will reach the highest levels.[11] In addition, the authors found that top managers reject the idea that their employees' performance can be improved through attempts to develop in weaker areas. Instead, these managers accept their employees' differences. In fact, they capitalize on those differences and try to "help each person become more and more of who he already is."[12]

Three recent Gallup studies demonstrate how engagement rises and performance increases when managers concentrate on matching talent with task:

1. The first study included performance numbers and survey data for 2,000 managers. The objective was to examine productivity differences between workgroups with managers whose strategies leaned more toward leveraging employees' greatest talents and those with managers who leaned toward bolstering "weaknesses." Managers who used a strengths approach were 1.9 times more likely than those with an approach more focused on remediation to be above the median on a composite measure of organizational performance. Conversely, managers whose teams ranked above the median were far more likely to work with their best performers, align dominant talents and tasks, and choose strengths over seniority when making personnel decisions.[13]

2. The second study compiled data from 10,885 work units, 309,000 employees, and 51 different companies — a huge sample spanning nearly two dozen industries. The work units reporting above-average agreement with the item "At work, I have the opportunity to do what I do best every day" were 1.4 times more likely to score above their company's median on productivity, customer loyalty, and employee retention measures.[14]

3. Finally, a 2004 Gallup survey sampled 1,000 American workers' opinions regarding their managers' style (Figure 5). Respondents were asked if their managers focused on "weaknesses or negative characteristics," on "strengths or positive characteristics," or whether they simply ignored team members' individual characteristics altogether. A separate set of questions was asked to determine each respondent's level of engagement at work. As is true in the classroom, engagement levels are crucial in the workplace because they are closely linked to productivity, profitability, safety, and retention of employees across industries. Engaged employees typically contribute the most to a company's

performance. *Actively disengaged* employees, on the other hand, tend to be not only unproductive at work, but disruptive as well.

The survey results, which follow, show the engagement levels of the groups, broken down by how they identified each of the three management styles.

FIGURE 5

2004 Gallup Workplace Poll — Manager's Focus

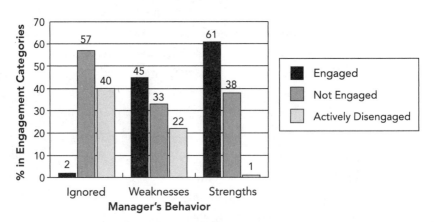

Interestingly, when the manager was seen as simply ignoring individuals' characteristics, the team members were even more likely to be actively disengaged than when the manager focused on weaknesses. Among those who felt their manager focused on strengths, 6 in 10 were engaged, and just 1 in 100 were actively disengaged. Among those who indicated that their manager focused on weaknesses, just over 4 in 10 respondents were engaged, while 2 in 10 were actively disengaged. But among those who felt their manager simply ignored their individual differences, just *1 in 50* were engaged, while a full 40% were actively disengaged.[15]

What does that tell us? Remaining oblivious to the differences between individuals sends the worst message of all when it comes to building engagement: "I'm not really interested in who you are." Acknowledging and working with employees' individual talents, on the other hand, boosts the number of engaged and productive workers.

These general and cross-industry studies are helpful in ensuring that the move-from-talent principle works in a broad range of settings. But more dramatic are the specific examples of companies that have reaped huge dividends by identifying employees' talents and refocusing their efforts on them. Let's briefly touch on two of those stories:

St. Lucie Medical Center

At St. Lucie Medical Center in Florida, the staff was treating record numbers of patients due to the aging population in the surrounding county, but the hospital was in trouble. Employees were chronically unhappy, and annual staff turnover was an alarming 35%. Physicians were also growing increasingly discontented, which threatened their long-term support of the hospital.

In response, the medical center leadership began with examining the talent and responsibilities of existing staff. Talent inventories were conducted with the leadership team and a group of 50 "role model" employees. The results helped identify whether job responsibilities had been assigned to people who were best suited for them and provided ideas for aligning and building teams. Two years later, St. Lucie's employee attrition rate had declined significantly. Among nurses, turnover declined almost 50%. Employees became strong advocates of the hospital, with record numbers agreeing with the statements, "I plan to be working in this organization one year from now" and "I would recommend my facility as a place to work." At the same time, patient satisfaction rose 160%

relative to that of peer hospitals, and physician satisfaction improved by 72% in the same period.[16]

Toyota

Initially established with a Japanese-style team culture, Toyota's North American Parts Center in California found itself slipping back to a more traditionally Western supervisor-employee culture within 18 months of opening. To correct the orientation among its 400 workers and 54 teams, managers attended a four-day training session in which they identified their own dominant talents and learned strategies for working from talents as individuals and in teams. Warehouse associates also identified their most natural talents and attended "Learn at Lunch" sessions in which they learned how to best leverage those talents in conjunction with those of their teammates.

Within a year, these efforts paid off. In each of the three previous years, per-person productivity at the center had fluctuated by no more than ±1%, but in the year following the strengths intervention, it rose by 6%. In the two groups selected for intensive team training about strengths, productivity rose by 9%.[17]

DOING WHAT YOU DO BEST

Such stories are becoming more commonplace. The idea that successful companies build engagement through strengths gained a big boost with the 2001 bestseller *Good to Great*, in which author Jim Collins showed how moving from strength at the corporate level helps successful companies outperform their peers. In describing what he calls the "Hedgehog Concept" (the name comes from a Greek parable that states, "The fox know many things, but the hedgehog knows one big thing"), Collins suggests that the "good-to-great companies" first determined what they can do better than any other company, what drives their profitability, and what creates a passion within the organization. In explaining how the Hedgehog Concept works for a person, Collins wrote:

> Suppose you were able to construct a work life that meets the following three tests. First, you are doing work for which you have a genetic or God-given talent, and perhaps you could become one of the best in the world in applying that talent. ("I feel that I was just born to be doing this.") Second, you are well paid for what you do. ("I get paid to do this? Am I dreaming?") Third, you are doing work you are passionate about and absolutely love to do, enjoying the actual process for its own sake. ("I look forward to getting up and throwing myself into my daily work, and I really believe in what I'm doing.") If you could drive toward the intersection of these three circles and translate that intersection into a simple, crystalline concept that guided your life choices, then you'd have a Hedgehog Concept for yourself.[18]

As Collins implies, putting our greatest efforts into activities, at work and elsewhere, for which we have exceptional natural talent leads to not only greater productivity, but greater fulfillment as well. It leads to engaged workplaces — and more broadly, to engaged *lives*.

Of course, schools are different from for-profit companies, and it has often been observed that reform initiatives inspired by management principles will fail dismally in schools. So it's time to carefully consider how the move-from-talent principle can affect the future of America's *students*.

TALENTS IN EDUCATION

In a 1981 article, Benjamin Bloom, the education researcher best known for classifying levels of intellectual behavior in Bloom's Taxonomy, outlined the difference between talent development and conventional schooling. Bloom was disturbed that the notion of talent development seemed so radically at odds with what normally takes place in America's classrooms. He concluded that conventional schools not only were failing to encourage talent development — they were actively *discouraging* it:

> In the talent field the individual becomes fully engaged. There is a major commitment to learning and development in one field, while other activities are given lower priority. In school, the individual is expected to put equal effort and time into the different academic and other major activities. An individual who becomes too preoccupied with some aspect of the school is persuaded to do it in a more moderate way. The school does not encourage or permit many students to become fully involved in any one part of the curriculum.[19]

As Bloom noted, heavy focus in any given area has historically met with skepticism as schools strive to ensure that graduates emerge "well-rounded" — in other words, that they've thoroughly covered all the academic bases.

In the past, universities have encouraged that emphasis on well-roundedness, but prestigious institutions are increasingly looking for excellence in a specific area. In her 2001 book *Admissions Confidential*, former Duke admissions officer Rachel Toor said it's increasingly difficult for BWRKs ("bright, well-rounded kids") to get into their first-choice universities without a distinguishing talent, because there are so many of them. Selective universities have begun to acknowledge that students who've spent a significant portion of their time on intense development of one or more "signature" talents — those whom Toor termed "angular" students — have the most to offer.[20]

Bloom's concern that schools discourage the pursuit of talent is becoming all the more relevant as teachers narrow their curriculum in response to accountability testing. The thinking behind standardization is that the differences between students' educational experiences should be minimized, with the hope that disadvantaged inner-city kids will then be learning the same basic content as those in affluent suburbia. But in doing so, the process squeezes out the idiosyncratic experiences that excite students by resonating with their individual talents. The idea that we need to compensate for differences in students' *extrinsic* advantages — e.g., income level and parental support — threatens to blind us to the fact that in the classroom, teachers must play to students' *intrinsic* differences to make the learning process meaningful. Rather than whitewashing over those differences, the system should help teachers leverage them to keep students fully engaged.

Given the limited amount of time students spend in the classroom, schools appear to have two choices. Students could invest more time in reaching specific standards in a broader range of topic areas, at least some of which they don't care much about. Or they could focus on a more limited range of topics of higher interest, exploring each in greater depth but possibly creating "blind spots" in the areas to which they are less exposed.

The options aren't necessarily mutually exclusive. Essential core content should always be considered first, although even here personalization pays dividends. Particularly in the early years of schooling, students need exposure to a broad range of different subjects and ways of thinking in order to explore possible areas of high interest and talent. But as those proclivities are discovered, students should be given greater opportunity to pursue development in those areas rather than being diverted too quickly to other topics.

Can we learn subjects for which we have no inherent yearning? Of course — but we don't *enjoy* the learning process as much. Lacking that genetic "starting point," the learning process takes greater effort and generates less natural curiosity. The learning comes more slowly, and we tend to do only what is required. Does that mean students should take only courses that interest them or that they like? No. There's obviously a baseline of knowledge and skills that students must have, even in areas where they have little interest. What's more, I agree that students need to explore a broad range of topics early in their academic lives in order to identify their interests and talents.

In practice, the level of knowledge and skill required of adults in their areas of lesser talent isn't normally as extensive as the college pre-paratory curriculum currently being suggested as the minimum in *all* areas for *all* students. If you've found your calling as an attorney, how of-ten do you find yourself recalling theorems from that trigonometry class you were required to take in your senior year in high school? Wouldn't the opportunity to take a college-level civics class or spend more time with the debate team have served you better in the long run?

Moreover, the memorization of specific curricular content so highly stressed from elementary school through college isn't nearly as impor-tant in the adult world as knowing how to learn, how to work with other people, how to communicate well, and how to apply critical-thinking skills.

Responses to a 2005 Gallup Panel survey (Figure 6) reflect the idea that being successful in high school is about more than just getting good grades. When respondents were asked in an open-ended question to name the "single most important thing" they learned in high school, the largest percentage gave answers related to "social skills" or "get-ting along with others." Academic pursuits were also on the list — 12%

mentioned various academic subjects — but the frequency of responses related to ethics, self-reliance, and self-confidence indicates that many Americans reflect on the value of high school in terms of character formation first and foremost.[21]

FIGURE 6

March 2005 Gallup Poll

What was the single most important thing you learned in high school?

Asked of U.S. adults

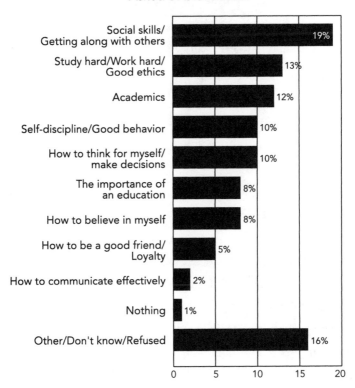

"WELL-ROUNDED" IS OVERRATED

Jim Hawkins, now superintendent of the Killeen, Texas, Independent School District, shared with me the following story about his son's school experience:

"When Chris was in junior high, we couldn't get him to read, and he didn't like to write. His penmanship was horrible! English, reading, and literature were a challenge, and we were always on him. Math, science, and music were different. He loved those areas, practiced, and was involved in everything. But, it was a constant battle at home because Mom was a great English student, a poetry writer, and dad was a school district administrator. We had a lot of family fights over homework and assignments in English and literature. It was pretty bad.

"Then I attended a seminar on building talents. It was a professional development opportunity for me, but all I could see was the personal application because it was so timely. My wife and I talked about the ideas. When Chris was a sophomore going into his junior year in high school, we started taking a totally different approach.

"We told Chris that we wanted to help him do as much as possible in the areas in which he excelled — math, science, and music — but he had to manage English. At first, Chris seemed to be asking, 'Is this a trick or something?' But we explained exactly what we were doing, why, and what we expected of him. He understood working in his areas of strength. In dealing with English, we told him some things can't be ignored. You must pass English to graduate, and you need to have a certain minimum level of competence. So, manage English: Learn as much as you can, and pass the course. My wife and I backed off.

"We were fortunate that Chris had some teachers who would work with him. I think they felt he was a good student, but they understood — and could accept — that he didn't care for either the content or the activities of what they were providing in English classes. With their help, he managed the English classes and got through them.

"In music, physics, and math, Chris would soar. He really enjoyed the work. He would persist when the work got hard, and he would do things on his own. His junior and senior years, he loaded up on all those subjects and opportunities. In his senior year, he took a zero hour so he could take physics during lunch, enabling him to be in choir, band, and jazz band. He was in an AP English class and ended up making a three on the AP exam [the cutoff score to qualify for college credit]. But he just barely passed the course.

"By allowing Chris to concentrate on his strengths, our relationship changed. During his sophomore year, our relationship had become pretty adversarial. Taking a different approach changed how we viewed each other. I think he figured out that we — and especially dad — cared for *him* more than we cared about what he was doing.

"When we started looking at a program and a college, we approached it from a strengths perspective. The counselors provided some search software that enabled us to say, 'If these are your interests, those are the programs, and here are the colleges and universities that offer the programs.' So, with Chris' strengths in music, science, and math, what's the program? The idea was that we wanted his avocation and vocation to be identical. We found a program called music engineering at the University of Miami.

"Chris went to UM. As a result of scoring a three on his AP English exam, all he had to take for his program at UM was a six-week online research course in the library that met all of his English requirements. He would have never graduated college if he hadn't gotten those three hours of credit in English. It would have never happened.

"Chris graduated from the University of Miami with a bachelor's degree in fine arts with a minor in electrical engineering that combined his music and math strengths. He's now a sound engineer in Coral Gables, Florida. He's very successful, making a living doing what he loves to do."

The emphasis on academic well-roundedness, on striving to do well across the board by working the hardest on problem areas, reduces students' ability to investigate potential strengths. What's more, it can also create a rather hostile educational environment both at school and at home, as Hawkins' story illustrates. Pediatrics professor Mel Levine describes the difference between school and adult life this way: "When [students] grow up, they will be able to practice their brain's specialties; in childhood they will be evaluated ruthlessly on how well they do everything."[22] More opportunities to practice the brain's specialties earlier would be healthier, in terms of both cultivating talent and elevating student engagement.

What if students miss out on specific content that they discover is needed for a job in the future? If they have the talents required for the role, they will learn the requisite knowledge and skills relatively easily. In practice, we learn very efficiently when a need is apparent and the new learning can be immediately applied, particularly in an area of strong interest.

It's far more critical that students become accustomed to getting excited about learning, because the knowledge required for specific career paths is far less predictable than it once was, and it is changing far more rapidly. Young people entering the workforce today must be more prepared than ever before to be creative, to engage in lifelong learning, and to adapt to conditions as they arise. Most of all, they need a profound self-understanding that guides them in making decisions about the job opportunities for which their most natural talents best suit them.[23]

Former Harvard President Lawrence Summers said, "It will not be enough for us to just leave no child behind. We also have to make sure that many more young Americans can get as far ahead as their potential will take them. How we meet this challenge is what will define our nation's political economy for the next several decades."[24] But the task of fulfilling each student's potential is different from that of guaranteeing proficiency, and the goal will be achieved only by adopting assumptions and behaviors different from those that have held sway in the past.

Helping students realize their full potential means helping them discover and apply their distinctive talents to the fullest extent. Those talents not only serve as the key to keeping students highly engaged in learning, but they will also be the source of each individual's greatest contributions. Successful companies mine the creative niche in which they can best compete. Our goal should be that each student leaves school with the ability to do the same. That will happen only if schools are retooled to search out and emphasize the best in students.

IMPACT ON STUDENT PERFORMANCE

Talent assessment isn't yet as influential in educational settings as it is in the workplace, but it is gaining ground. Differentiated instruction techniques have become more widespread. A number of recent studies have demonstrated the impact of discovering and using talents on student performance. First, consider two from higher education:

1. Two freshman expository writing classes at a private, faith-based university were selected at random. At the beginning of the semester, the students in the two classes were statistically equivalent in terms of ACT scores and high school grade-point averages (GPAs). The study class of 32 participants completed a talent assessment and went through two presentations to review talent theory and discuss their individual assessment

results. They also received one-on-one advisement with a trained coach on how to use their particular talents in class and extra-curricular activities. The contrast class of 40 students received none of this instruction.[25]

Two achievement standards were used to compare the classes: 1) a cumulative GPA of 2.0, and 2) a minimum of 12 semester hours earned. In the group receiving talent instruction, 2 of the 32 students (1 in 16) failed to meet both standards; in the contrast group, 8 of the 40 students (1 in 5) failed to meet both standards. Moreover, at the end of the semester, the class receiving talent instruction posted a higher average GPA than the contrast group.[26]

Jeff Williamson, the researcher who oversaw the study, conducted exit interviews with students who had gone through the intervention. "Without exception, they said something like, 'I feel like for the first time it's OK to be me,'" Williamson said. "That sense of affirmation alone is powerful."

2. At another university, two introductory public speaking classes that were taught by the same instructor were chosen at random; this instructor had received training in working with talents. Pre-tests given at the outset of the semester found no significant differences between the two classes on three measures to be tested: 1) speech delivery abilities as measured by blind raters using the Speech Communication Association's performance instrument, 2) course content tests, and 3) students' engagement levels as measured by a self-report instrument. The instructor was videotaped in each class session for both groups. Six videotapes were selected at random, and a blind rater independently scored the instructor's behaviors to ensure that similar content was presented.

    However, the *approaches* used to present that content differed between the two classes. Students in the experimental class completed a talent assessment and received written feedback on their talents and additional class instruction on talent theory. During the semester, the instructor shared her strongest talents with the students and described how she used them in preparing for the class. She also provided positive feedback about each student's most natural talents during class sessions, stimulated discussions about how those talents contributed to excellence in the students' speeches, and encouraged students to provide feedback on each other's most prominent talents following the speeches and in class discussions.

The class that included the talent component performed substantially better than the contrast group. Their average exam scores and final speech ratings were significantly higher. And self-reported engagement levels were found to be significantly higher in the study group than in the traditionally taught class.

By the end of the semester, students in the two classes also displayed remarkable differences outside the bounds of the study's formal outcome measures. The instructor found that members of the talent-based class arrived on time more frequently, had fewer absences, and displayed fewer class disruptions than the traditionally taught group.

Teaching assistants kept logs of other behaviors and found that students in the study class asked three times as many questions and voluntarily contributed in class three times as frequently as those in the traditionally taught class. They also turned in a higher percentage of assignments on time, made more appointments to see the instructor, more often requested suggestions on their speeches, and more often attended prep sessions prior to exams. Lastly, no members of the talent-focused study class dropped out of college, while 4 of the 30 students in the traditionally taught class dropped out prior to the end of the term.[27]

In their 2002 book *StrengthsQuest*, Chip Anderson and Don Clifton call for a "strengths revolution" in higher education as a means of increasing motivation and reducing dropout rates. "Far too many students who enroll in college never graduate, and many of those who drop out do so in the first year," they write. "Why? Quite frequently, the reason is that they have selected classes that do not suit their talents. As a result, they do not experience the success they expected, and then they become frustrated and disillusioned and eventually give up."[28] As these examples from different campuses demonstrate, making students more aware of their talents can boost their sense of achievement — and their likelihood to stay in college.

WHAT ABOUT HIGH SCHOOL STUDENTS?

But college students are adults, you may be thinking. They're fully formed people whose talents have already matured. Can the move-from-talent principle work as well with high school students? Two studies involving incoming freshman classes in high school settings provide further evidence that a focus on talent does indeed produce powerful results.

1. In one Chicago high school with below-average attendance and student achievement, half of the freshman class' homeroom teachers were trained to administer and score a structured talent assessment. Early in the school year, these teachers gave one-on-one feedback to their students based on their assessment results. The other half of the freshman homeroom teachers — the contrast group — performed no such intervention. In all classes, student attendance, tardiness, and grade point averages were tracked and analyzed annually.

    Over the course of their four years, the 807 students who completed the talent assessment and received feedback from their freshman homeroom teachers demonstrated higher performance on all three measures than the remaining 841 students. Over four years, the grade point averages of students who received feedback on their talents was 8.7% higher than the contrast group. Additionally, the students in the study group were tardy to class 47% fewer times and absent from school 28% fewer days, when compared to the contrast group.[29]

2. About 500 students who enrolled in a required, six-week freshman seminar course at La Sierra High School in California were randomly assigned to study and contrast groups. No statistically significant differences were found between the two groups of students on the basis of ethnicity, parents' education, gender, free and reduced-cost lunch participation, or grade point average at the beginning of the semester. The study group completed a talent assessment, received written feedback on the results, and participated in teacher-designed activities to help them use their talents in academic settings; the contrast group did not.

At the conclusion of the six-week course, all students completed the Self-Perceptions of Academic Ability instrument. Students in the study group, who received the talent assessment and follow-up activities, scored higher than students in the contrast group on five subscales of the instrument. In doing so, the study group students expressed more:

- belief that they could handle difficult courses
- confidence in their ability to master content
- desire to be viewed positively as students
- desire to do well and receive good grades[30]

"Across the board, for both adults and kids, this idea that we have a positive language to talk about our differences is incredibly powerful," says Leigh Anne Taylor Knight, school-to-career director for the North Kansas City Public Schools, which has integrated a talent-based approach into their culture. "Themes of talent can appear in so many different ways, and they can help connect kids to a bigger picture."[31]

TALENTS AND INTERESTS CANNOT BE IGNORED

Research on talent-based development continues, but the preponderance of evidence thus far is that performance improves most, and most rapidly, when the developmental focus is on strengths rather than on remediation of weaknesses. Schools can't afford to ignore that evidence, particularly when it's clear that they can be better structured to help students discover and explore their natural inclinations and to expand their talents into real areas of expertise. These case studies demonstrate that it's within our reach.

Already, those concerned about America's competitive future are focusing on the recognition and development of high talent. Smaller schools and schools-within-schools are becoming more common. Many are explicitly geared to meeting individual students' needs and allowing them to fully explore areas that appeal to them. Deborah Meier helped advance this idea with the development of the Central Park East schools in New York City and Mission Hill in Boston.[32] The Bill and Melinda Gates Foundation has been among the leading supporters of "theme-based" and "student-centered" high schools that are designed to engage students based on their interests.

Those specialized schools are doing amazing work. But enabling each and every child to explore, identify, and use his or her talents is within the reach of any school.

But where to start? The most important factor in using *student* talent to boost classroom engagement is *teacher* talent. That's where we'll turn next.

CHAPTER SIX

ENGAGED TEACHERS, PART 1: HEROES OF THE CLASSROOM

"Teachers are more important than buildings and things."
— *John Portman, world-renowned architect*

My daughter Elizabeth has always been gregarious and confident, seemingly able to bend the world to her will. One of the few times during her childhood I can recall her outgoing self-assurance being shaken was when she was seven years old and she decided to learn to water-ski.

Elizabeth's two uncles and I agreed to help her. Her uncle Dwight expertly drove the boat, throttling just the right amount of speed to lift her little body out of the water without pulling her over. Uncle Larry provided clear, concise instructions on how to get out of the water: "Keep your knees bent; sit on the skis; keep your arms extended; stay in a crouched position until the boat picks up speed." I was in the water helping Elizabeth with her skis and providing reassurance.

Even with an expert driver and excellent instruction, Elizabeth experienced the inevitable difficulties. In her first few attempts, she fell, lost her skis, and choked on lake water. After half a dozen tries, she began to doubt her ability to learn. As Dwight brought the boat around again, Elizabeth said, "I'm tired. My legs aren't strong enough." But Dwight replied in a positive tone, "Let's try it again." Larry's constant chatter and humorous antics from the boat kept the tone light, and he tapped into one of Elizabeth's talents, a natural desire to compete, when he challenged her to ski past the dock to impress her older cousins. I continued to point out Elizabeth's successes in following her uncle's instructions after each attempt.

Finally, Elizabeth skied past the dock on wobbly legs, with her cousins yelling and jumping up and down. She learned to water-ski partly because of the technical know-how of her two uncles. But more importantly, she succeeded because her teachers displayed patience, humor, and encouragement — and because we knew her well enough to tap into her competitive nature.

Those inherent components represent the missing link that the knowledge and skills assumption fails to acknowledge. As applied to schools, the third assumption maintains that *selecting and developing teachers and principals on the basis of their knowledge and skills is the most reliable way to promote student success.* In reality, success is far more likely to hinge on the innate talents of the teacher, such as his or her ability to build strong relationships with students.

Knowledge and skills form the basis of most school districts' hiring decisions and training programs. Knowledge and skills also serve as key salary determinants for teachers in all but a handful of school districts, with salary increases driven by additional college coursework and years of teaching experience. Moreover, a bachelor's degree, a state license to teach, and tested or demonstrated competence in a subject area constitute the criteria for "highly qualified" teachers under No Child Left Behind.[1]

The message seems clear: Subject-matter knowledge is the primary driver of any teacher's effectiveness. That assumption implies that great teachers are made in college classrooms, mostly by learning content and, to a lesser degree, pedagogical techniques.

As with the previous assumptions, there's a justifiable basis for this belief. The problem is that it ignores a very important component of effective teaching. Certainly the knowledge and skills are necessary, but they should be treated as prerequisites rather than the primary basis for declaring teachers "highly qualified." Such a classification should be reserved for teachers who display the *talents* necessary to promote student engagement.

WHAT, HOW, WHY, AND WHO?

In *The Courage to Teach*, educator and activist Parker Palmer presents four questions commonly associated with teaching. They create a useful framework for examining the knowledge and skills assumption.

Palmer suggests that the most commonly asked question is "What?" As in, "What are the subjects and what is the content within those subjects that we should teach?" This is the *knowledge* component. Asking "What?" would seem to provide a good basic starting point. But reaching consensus on the correct answers has proven extremely difficult. The drive to make the "what" consistent in grade levels across a district and between school districts in a state was the major impetus for standards-based reform in the 1990s.

The second question is "How?" This question considers the methods and techniques — the *skills* — required to teach the content. Skill development is the focus of the teacher preparation courses required in college. Traditionally, schools have sunk a significant portion of their professional development efforts into boosting teachers' instructional skills. But despite the millions of dollars spent annually, there have been relatively few attempts to measure the effects of these efforts on student performance.

The two remaining questions are much less frequently considered. "Why" asks us to justify the specific content and methods used to impart it, and to define the desired outcomes. Asking the "Why?" question allows the education system to adapt in response to social and technological change, instead of simply repeating what has been done in the past.

But the most important question is the last one: "Who?" As in, "Who is the teacher as an individual, and what level of teaching talents does he or she bring to the role?" The three preceding questions — What? How? and Why? — are all driven to some extent by the characteristics of individual teachers. As Palmer suggests, "We teach who we are."[2] No matter how much educators try to standardize responses to those questions, the teacher remains the prism through which all other decisions about the educational process are filtered.

Working definitions of knowledge and skills will be helpful as we consider the assumption that the "What?" and "How?" questions are the most critical to student success.

Knowledge can be acquired through direct life experience or through the kind of learning process we undertake in school. Knowledge refers in part to the various objective facts associated with a content area. For a first grade teacher, this would include the framework of the reading text, the vocabulary needed for success in the reading series, and the specific reading theory associated with the textbook. Knowledge can also refer to the lessons people have acquired from experience, the patterns they've noticed, and connections they've made between disparate events.[3] For our first grade teacher, this more experientially derived knowledge would include understanding when and how to respond to students when they begin to experience difficulties in reading, or recognizing the most helpful response to a parent who is anxious about his daughter's reading progress.

Skills can be thought of as the ability to perform, at a basic level, the steps required in any activity.[4] Skills are learned by breaking down a task into a teachable sequence leading to its accomplishment. Practice normally improves skill levels. Skills enable individuals to perform more effectively because they eliminate trial and error with regard to a given activity. But while skills enable people to reach average or acceptable performance, rarely do they alone lead to excellence.[5] In teaching, skills often include proven techniques about how to teach. A first grade teacher, for example, acquires questioning skills — the steps involved in framing a question for the class, calling on a variety of students, and allowing enough wait time for a response.

My point in challenging the knowledge and skills assumption is not to diminish the importance of either knowledge or skills. Nor am I ignoring the evidence that students achieve more academically when their teachers have degrees in their subject areas. No teacher can effectively teach material that she doesn't know well.

The fallacy is in the idea that such knowledge is *enough*. We've all had teachers who were considered knowledgeable or even experts in their fields. But some — perhaps many — of these people weren't especially gifted at synthesizing and communicating their knowledge in ways that made it understandable or interesting to the non-expert.

What about skills? Great teachers use a diverse repertoire of acquired instructive techniques. But they alone aren't what make these teachers outstanding. Classroom management is a classic example. The most daunting task for many beginning teachers — as well as quite a few veterans — is maintaining an orderly classroom in which learning can occur. But acquiring specific skills doesn't do the trick. If it did, unruly classes would be a thing of the past, because there has been no shortage of skills training on a wide variety of disciplinary strategies.

Gaining the skills involved in a method is only the first point of progress. Each teacher must then *adapt* the method, using it in a way that works best for that person. The approach must be tested, tried, and in some cases, modified or even rejected because it doesn't mesh with that teacher's instinctual beliefs or behaviors. The teacher internalizes those approaches that do fit. An elementary school art teacher in one of our focus groups said of this selective process: "The best advice that I ever heard from one of my fellow workers was this: You go, and you listen, and you find out what you need to teach, and then you close your door and you do what you know you need to do to reach your kids."

When it comes to a task as complex as engaging a roomful of 13-year-olds, skills work only up to a point. The successes that great teachers accomplish are not rooted in a skill set acquired in a college course or a school in-service. As Palmer suggests, "Technique is what teachers use until the real teacher arrives . . ."[6] Teaching excellence may move *through* acquired skills, but it springs more fundamentally from talent. Skills may prevent failure, but they can't move teachers from average to outstanding performance.

KNOWLEDGE + SKILLS + TALENTS = STRENGTHS

Now that all the components have been discussed, we can turn back to the idea that pertinent knowledge and skills combine with talents to form *strengths*. The advantage in defining a strength this way is that it forces us to conceptually distinguish what can be easily learned from what is much more difficult, or even impossible, to learn.

Explicitly recognizing the three components of a strength helps avoid confusion between knowledge, skills, and talents. We tend to use phrases such as "interpersonal skills," "skill set," "work habits," and "competencies" interchangeably, with little thought about the specific thoughts, feelings, or behaviors involved. This is not just careless language but "careless thinking," as the authors of *First, Break All the Rules* point out.[7] When looking at the requirements of a complex task like teaching, career counselors and human resource directors should consider which consist of teachable knowledge and acquirable skills, and which are more fundamentally tied to innate characteristics. The latter should be accounted for first and foremost.

People can discover and develop their talents, but it's very hard to progress toward excellence in areas for which they lack any inherent starting point. You probably know someone who naturally feels comfortable walking into a hotel ballroom full of strangers and enjoys every moment of the meet-and-greet activity. For those to whom socializing doesn't come naturally, it's possible to learn how to meet new people and gain networking skills, but it requires constant work. It's more time-consuming and less satisfying. The same activity that is exhilarating for one person is exhausting for another.

While knowledge and skills tend to be comparatively similar from one person to the next, talents are the wild card necessary for consistently near-perfect performance in nearly any role.[8] Talents are the "intangibles" that lead certain people to perform better than others with similar backgrounds. It's a common misconception that the accumulation of knowledge or skills can compensate for lack of talent. *Nothing* can compensate for a lack of talent.

In *Good to Great,* Jim Collins notes that the leaders of the outstanding companies he studied paid an extraordinary amount of attention to hiring the "right people."

> In determining "the right people," the good-to-great companies placed greater weight on character attributes than on specific educational background, practical skills, specialized knowledge, or work experience. Not that specific knowledge or skills are unimportant, but they viewed these traits as more teachable (or at least learnable), whereas they believed dimensions like character, work ethic, basic intelligence, dedication to fulfilling commitments, and values are more ingrained.[9]

The good-to-great companies looked for talent. They understood that once an individual with the right talent was found, he or she could obtain the specific knowledge and skills needed for a particular role relatively easily through training.

The most successful companies avoided two interrelated pitfalls regarding knowledge, skills, and talent. One is simply the weakness-fixing assumption, the idea that adding more and more knowledge and skills can make an outstanding performer out of anyone in any role.[10] The other is confusion between acquired attributes — knowledge and skills — and genetically based attributes, talents. Some people never really grasp that distinction and have to learn the same lessons repeatedly. The two pitfalls result in a similar false conclusion: We can "fix" individuals in areas where talent is required but not present.

Professional development opportunities available to teachers and principals provide a case in point. Most of the training in schools falls into one of three major categories: (1) orientation training for new teachers or teachers new to the district, (2) training about curricular requirements, which forms the biggest share of these activities, and

(3) pedagogical training, built around specific methods for teaching the content.

As you might expect, the most successful classes tend to be those in the first two categories. Attempts to impart specific teaching methods tend to be problematic, because the abilities that drive student engagement — such as building relationships and infusing the classroom with a sense of creativity — are so complex that they require talent first, knowledge and skills second. This third type of training deals with such areas as teachers' relationships with students and parents, classroom discipline, individualizing instruction within a classroom, and assorted programs to assist teachers experiencing difficulties. While there's value in relaying such techniques, for those teachers or principals without the underlying talents necessary to effectively and consistently apply them, it's unlikely the training will "stick."

For example, a teacher may enroll in a seminar intended to improve interpersonal skills. The teacher might be instructed on the importance of smiling, greeting people by their names, looking directly at the speaker, leaning forward toward the speaker, and understanding the other person before replying. These are pieces of knowledge about personal interactions that are good to know. But in any given class of 25 teachers or principals, some of them will use this information far more effectively than others. That's the talent part; people tend to fully internalize new information — or not — based on who they are.

In many cases, when training fails to improve an employee's performance, the supervisor's reaction is simply to try again. So, the teacher or principal is sent to another class or workshop with the assumption that she "just didn't get it" the first time. Naturally, the re-teaching rarely results in a dramatically different outcome.

You may have run into similar problems in your personal life. Have you ever tried to fundamentally change a spouse, child, parent, or best friend? Most of us have. The real question is, how successful were you? If you're like most people, you'll have to admit that you were marginally successful at best. Can people change? Certainly. Human beings have a marvelous ability to adapt if we're highly motivated to do so.[11] The success of rehabilitative programs like Alcoholics Anonymous demonstrates that people can make significant changes in their lives. But these changes largely represent movement in the individual's goals and self-perception, rather than his or her basic personality traits.[12] And rarely does even this type of change happen quickly or easily.

Citing a study of 80,000 successful managers, the authors of *First, Break All the Rules* discussed these managers' "secret" for changing team members. In short, they don't try. Attempting to do so, many managers said, wastes precious time and effort and frustrates the employees. The task of helping people more effectively use what they already have is in itself a difficult one — but it carries the potential for a much higher return on investment.[13]

A client of mine once said that training is like brewing tea: You never know for sure whether it's good until you add hot water. When under pressure and forced to choose between behaviors in the moment, we tend to rely on our natural dispositions — and any training at odds with those dispositions is often forgotten. In the case of the relationship seminar, if the knowledge and skills it offers don't resonate with a participant's talent for creating quality interpersonal relationships, they will easily become lost amid the hundreds of daily decisions that a teacher or principal must make.

Again, there's no "either-or" when it comes to acquired versus innate attributes. Both are important to building strengths and achieving excellence. And given the new challenges and expectations facing America's schools, excellence must become a more realistic standard. Poor or mediocre teachers and principals may have gotten by in the past, but as the bar continues to rise, they will find it increasingly difficult to do so.

Hopefully that means we will come to more fully recognize and value high talent among educators. "There are countless opinions and myths about teaching, but I believe the most erroneous ones are that teaching is easy and that anyone can do it well," says Fred Stephenson in *Extraordinary Teachers: The Essence of Excellent Teaching*. "No doubt, many people have the ability to teach, but doing it superbly is an entirely different matter. What this nation needs, what it is demanding, is exceptional teaching, not average performance."[14]

SEARCH FOR THE PERFECT CURRICULUM

The idea that teacher talent is central to student engagement leads back to another of the faulty assumptions. It's the fourth assumption that has been given undue credibility by the current emphasis on consistent standards: *There exists a perfect curriculum that can help solve student achievement problems in a way that works for all students and teachers.*

In effect, this assumption devalues teacher talent. It implies that all students can learn any subject as long as they're presented with the right content using the right methodology. It casts the teacher as a mere conduit. Taken to its logical conclusion, the assumption implies that the education process can be made "teacher-proof" — i.e., immune to variations in teacher quality. Despite the fact that the basic academic subjects have changed little over the last 100 years, many reform efforts have been driven by the pursuit of answers to the "what" and "how" questions that work for everyone. It's an article of faith for those who believe in such a curricular "holy grail" that for each subject, there is a right way and a wrong way for teachers to teach and for students to learn.[15]

The phonics and whole-language debates in reading instruction illustrate the problems created by this assumption. Successful reading teachers will attest that one approach rarely fits all students. Some approaches work better for some students than others, while still other students require a mix of strategies to succeed. Yet the controversy over which approach was the "right" way to teach reading spilled from education into the media and, inevitably, the political arena.

The assumption that a single ideal curriculum can be found generates cynicism among teachers and principals in two ways. First, many come to see the pursuit of a quick curricular fix as a "flavor-of-the-year" approach, resulting in much superficial change but little in the way of sustained, substantive progress. In many cases, administrators attempt to implement the latest, greatest instructional idea without careful regard for how well it fits with the history, culture, and overarching strategy of the district or its individual schools. In addition, schools are under such pressure to show improvement on state tests that they're often forced to implement curricular changes to align more closely with the state's standards in the hope that doing so will move the numbers.

But schools have not been good at gauging precisely how such changes affect student learning. Some districts never bother to measure whether new curriculum improves performance or to track the specific ways in which it is or isn't better than the old curriculum. In the absence of meaningful measurement, the organization drifts from one idea to another as interest wanes or the leader initiating the change moves on. The cycle takes a toll in the form of extensive effort by teachers who must learn and re-learn the successive curricula, not to mention the expense in new materials. But by and large, little sustained growth has resulted locally or nationally from this "musical chairs" approach to school improvement.

Secondly, as we've already noted, the search for the perfect curriculum implies that ideally, the teacher would make little difference — that any teacher would be successful with the correct process. This results in ever more limiting controls on what is to be taught, how it is to be taught, and when it is to be taught in order to mitigate any "X factor" introduced by variations in teaching quality. In some cases, teachers are already handed "do and say" curricula that specify how they must execute each step of a lesson.

Intentionally or not, this assumption turns teachers into assembly-line workers. And it grossly underestimates the importance of teacher talent in shaping learning. As Peter Temes put it, "Teaching with method A instead of method B makes much less of a difference than having a teacher who cares about and questions all her teaching methods, who teaches thoughtfully and constantly tries to make her classroom practices better."[16]

Undervaluing their role can significantly reduce teachers' engagement levels. This issue often arose spontaneously in our interviews and focus groups with teachers. In Virginia, where two of the focus groups were conducted, a number of teachers said that the expectations impair their ability to do what they do best. Stifled by the state's detailed Standards of Learning curricular requirements, they felt that they no longer had the freedom to use their creativity and talent to fully engage students in the learning process. Here's what some of them had to say:

- Amber, instructional assistant: *"It's a factory production line. I'm bored in there. And I know if I'm bored, the kids have got to be bored out of their heads. I think that's the most idiotic thing to do, because kids, we all know, do not learn the exact same way. And your creative energy is just sucked out of you. You know, it just sucks the life out of you because you, yourself, are bored teaching it."*

- Debbie, middle school teacher: *"Standards are good to have as a framework for understanding, but standardization puts a stranglehold on teachers and students. Why do we spend four years in college and two years in grad school to not be a professional?"*

- Leonard, high school teacher: *"As [teachers] move on in experience and comfort level, they should be given more freedom. I consider it a truism that you will never have a situation where the student will be more enthused about a lesson than you are. So if you're not really that interested in it, if it just doesn't do anything for you, I would venture to guess that not a single student is going to be above whatever engagement level you're at."*

- Tammy, high school teacher: *"Teachers are not in a position to take risks anymore. The idea used to be that if the student could at all learn in a particular environment, you moved her or him into that environment and gave her or him that opportunity. Now you have to ask yourself, 'Are they going to pass the test at the end? And if they don't, what's that going to do to me and the assessment of my performance?' And so now students are being kept back and kept in this cycle of mediocrity."*

- Aaron, a middle school history teacher, complained that he wasn't able to use the resources available to bring his topic to life — such as allowing students in his hometown of Pittsburgh to spend more time investigating local steel baron Andrew Carnegie. Noting that his day-by-day lesson plans are PowerPoint presentations given to him online, he says, *"It's like I can honestly teach an entire year without having an original thought."*

Some teachers said they feel intense pressure from administrators who want to raise test scores as well as parents who want to make sure their child gets good grades. The obvious irony here is that current education reforms make it a priority to find highly qualified teachers, even as they establish conditions that make teaching less attractive to such creative individuals.

It's not that choices about curriculum and technique are unimportant. Clearly, asking questions regarding the "what" and "how" of teaching can result in better learning, and schools need to build on these understandings. What's more, curriculum alignment and curriculum mapping avoid senseless duplication on the one hand, and gaps on the other.

But such choices alone can't determine educational excellence. A good curriculum in the hands of great teachers results in excellence for students, just as a good recipe in the hands of a great chef results in an excellent dish. At the same time, poor teachers will fail to execute a good curriculum, just as a poor chef can ruin the best recipe.

The idea that teachers are interchangeable parts in a curriculum-driven machine inevitably weakens the drive to find and retain individuals with a gift for engaging students. The implied belief is that if we lose a teacher, we can just go find another one with similar credentials, and student performance shouldn't vary greatly as a result. The unintended consequence is that school leaders see themselves as responsible for filling empty teaching slots, rather than for attracting the best possible teachers to their schools. But the reality is that every single teacher-selection decision significantly changes the overall quality of the school, either for better or worse. Failing to appreciate that means undervaluing the most critical link in the learning chain: that between student and teacher.

TEACHERS ARE KEY

Jessica, now a student at the University of Southern California, recently told me about her favorite high school teacher. Mr. Franklin, she said, taught French in a way that made students want to take his classes again and again. "He wanted to make the French language and culture a part of our lives. So, every other week, we had a French meal, and as we were walking in to class, he'd play a popular French song. He would talk to us about French current events on top of teaching us grammar and the language in general. Class wasn't ever boring."

Mr. Franklin also had a gift for building relationships conducive to learning. "He was very personable and one-on-one with people. He found an interest in students, and he talked to them about it," Jessica said. "Since I was an art major, he had me paint murals on his walls. Students would go talk to him outside of class. A lot of times, we'd carry on a conversation in French. He had a really good relationship with everyone in the classroom versus just teaching to a crowd."

Mr. Franklin's enthusiasm paid off in the extra effort he was able to elicit from students like Jessica. "I definitely have more respect for a teacher, and take more interest, when the teacher lets you know that they want to be there, and they want to teach you something," Jessica said. "I worked harder in his French class than in other classes. I actually cared about him being disappointed. I just kind of felt disrespectful if I didn't put effort into work for his class because he was doing so much for us." Since she was in Mr. Franklin's class, Jessica has visited France twice.

How important are talented teachers? If stories like Jessica's aren't evidence enough, survey data from students and the general public, as well as piles of research data, all point to the idea that the people invited to teach in our schools are the X-factor that invariably makes the difference in student learning.

View From the Classroom

The Gallup Youth Survey has been tracking the opinions of 13- to 17-year-old students for more than 25 years. In August 2003, teens were asked, *"Thinking now about your high school/middle school, do you have any ideas for changes your school could make to help students learn better? What are they?"* Responses varied greatly, but by a wide margin, the most frequent response involved the quality of teaching. Approximately one in six teens communicated dissatisfaction with their teachers.[17] Many of the comments involved teaching methods and relationships between students and teachers. Here are a few examples:

- *"Some teachers just lecture, which gets boring. The teachers who demonstrate what they are teaching and come up with creative ways to get it into our heads are much more popular, and we enjoy going to their classes and learning."* — Sarah, 13

- *"Teachers should treat the students as people and not just as 'stupid kids' — then the students would want to learn more."* — Matt, 17

- *"The teachers should be more caring and less judgmental. They should make things fun so people will think it's worth paying attention to."* — Josh, 16

In another Youth Survey completed in March 2004, teens were asked, "Would you say you work harder for some teachers than others?" Seventy-six percent of the teens responded "yes." When those students were asked why that was so, they most often said that they liked some teachers better than others, worked up to the teacher's level of expectation, or worked harder for teachers who seemed to care about them.[18]

- *"When teachers don't want to be there, they give off a bad vibe that I will not respond to in a positive way."* — Susan, 17

- *"Teachers that actually put their soul into what they are doing are going to get a better response out of students. The teachers who just assign worksheets and slap a grade on them are getting what they are asking for — uncaring attitudes and disobedience."* — Stephanie, 16

- *"Some teachers motivate certain students more than others. Sometimes you can sense teachers that are there just to gain enough experience to move to a higher paying school system. Different teachers bring out different patterns in me."* — Jennifer, 14

The Public's Viewpoint

Survey after survey has shown that Americans view teacher quality as critical to the education of their children. In 1999, for example, a Phi Delta Kappa/Gallup Poll asked respondents to rate the importance of various factors in selecting a school for a child; 97% felt the quality of the teaching staff was "very important."[19] Three years later, a national survey sponsored by *Education Week* and the Public Education Network found "Raising teacher quality" to be Americans' most common recommendation for improving the overall quality of education. Twenty-nine percent of the participants selected that option, while 16% chose the next most popular item: "Equalizing funding between rich/poor schools."[20]

In a 2002 Educational Testing Service (ETS) study titled *A National Priority: Americans Speak on Teacher Quality*, 4 in 10 participants chose "Improving the quality of teachers" as the federal government's biggest challenge in improving schools. As Figure 7 indicates, when asked to select the factors that define quality teaching, educators and the general public alike were most likely to choose "Having the skills to design learning experiences that inspire/interest children." The next two most commonly selected characteristics of quality teaching included the teacher's enthusiasm and caring attitude toward students.[21]

FIGURE 7

"What is quality teaching?"

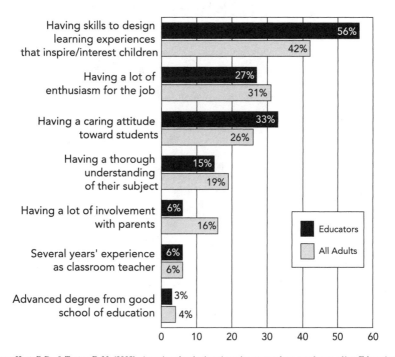

Source: Hart, P. D., & Teeter, R. M. (2002). *A national priority: Americans speak on teacher quality*. Educational Testing Service.

"Overwhelmingly, Americans believe that knowing *how* to teach is more important than knowing *what* to teach," states the report. "Teaching quality is not about formal academic degrees, but rather about the degree to which a teacher can engage his or her class. When it comes to quality teaching, it is not about what you know, but how well you convey what you know to students."

The study included focus groups that were conducted with parents to discuss their definitions of teacher quality. Here are a couple of sample comments from the parents:

- *"Teacher quality would mean somebody that can relate to everyone in the classroom. They can understand each student, where they came from. If one is far behind or has a problem, they can take them to the side and deal with it instead of pushing them to the side whenever they just didn't make it, or give them a bad grade."*

- *"You've got to love [teaching], too. If you're not enthusiastic and you're dealing with a bunch of kids who inherently have more energy than you do anyway, they're just going to plow right over you."*[22]

In an August 2004 Gallup Poll, Americans again cited better teachers as the best way to improve public education. Respondents were asked the following open-ended question: *"Just your opinion, what would be the best way to improve kindergarten through 12th grade education in the U.S. today?"* After the widely varying responses were grouped, the top category was "Quality teachers/better educated/more involvement/caring."[23]

The Research Perspective

There's no shortage of research to support the public's perception that teacher quality is central to student achievement. Dan Goldhaber, a senior research associate at the Urban Institute, studies the factors that influence student performance. The majority of the variance in achievement, Goldhaber maintains, can be attributed to individual student and family differences. But of those factors that *are* under the schools' purview, teacher quality is the most important. "In fact," Goldhaber notes, "most research suggests that the benefit of improving the quality of the nation's teaching workforce is far greater than other policy interventions, such as lowering class size."[24]

Goldhaber estimates that a very small proportion of the teacher's contribution to student achievement — about 3% — comes from "teacher experience, degree attained, and other readily observable characteristics." The remaining 97% "was associated with qualities or behaviors that could not be isolated and identified." Referring to these characteristics as "intangible attributes," Goldhaber describes them as things like "enthusiasm and skill in conveying knowledge."[25]

Perhaps the most compelling evidence of teachers' paramount importance to student learning comes from William Sanders' team at the University of Tennessee. Until 2000, Sanders was the Director of the University of Tennessee Value-Added Research and Assessment Center. His duties included managing research efforts across the university and overseeing the processing of accountability test data from schools across the state. The Tennessee accountability testing program is similar in many ways to those of other states across the country, but it was one of the first to gauge students' *progress* over the course of the school year.

Instead of measuring all students against some proficiency standard — for example, students must read at a nationally normed fourth-grade level and satisfactorily answer 75% of the math items — the Tennessee Value-Added Assessment System (TVAAS) computes a student's individual annual progress from one year to the next. This "gain score" represents the value added by that year of instruction as a percentage of a national norm for student progress. Thus, a less successful student

133

could make 90% of the anticipated gain from one year to the next, while a more successful student might post a 125% gain in that year.

The system is neither simple nor without its critics. The next step is, in fact, the most controversial: The gain scores for individual students can be combined to represent the total progress made by all students who have a particular teacher. It's by no means a perfect indicator of teaching effectiveness. Nonetheless, TVAAS scores have been recorded since 1992, and they provide a wealth of information about the effect that having one teacher versus another can have on student learning.

Sanders and Sandra Horn used the unique TVAAS student progress data to conduct a variety of studies. They first found that the relative effects of different teachers on student outcomes could be reliably measured. They then established that school effects and the effects of individual teachers are relatively consistent from one year to another and that students' gain scores for the year were relatively unrelated to the level of ability or achievement they demonstrated at the beginning of the year. Lastly, higher or lower gain scores could not be accurately predicted simply by knowing which school the students attended — even when a school in an affluent area was compared to a school with many more disadvantaged students. Given these conclusions, the source of the gain-score variance appeared to be driven more by the students' particular teacher than by the socioeconomic variables widely thought to drive achievement.

Teachers in the study were assigned to quintiles based on the average gain scores of their students over a period of time. In subsequent years, students at statistically comparable levels were tracked to determine the impact of top-quintile teachers versus those in the other quintiles. As you might expect, students with top-quintile teachers in three successive years achieved significantly more than students who had three teachers in the bottom quintile. But the size of the difference was startling — between 52 and 54 percentile points — the equivalent of a placement in an accelerated versus a remedial program in the classes studied.[26]

It will come as no shock to parents or students that different teachers achieve very different results with students who start out at similar levels in a given subject area. But this study also found that over the long term, teacher quality may be even more important than most people think. Sanders and other researchers found that the teacher effects are both *cumulative and residual*. That means: 1) the presence of a good teacher as opposed to a bad one results in gains that are increasingly larger than expected with each year, and 2) an individual teacher's effect — whether it's a big gain, no gain, or backward movement — can be seen in an individual student's performance up to *two years later*.[27] Researchers in the Dallas public schools similarly found a residual effect of teacher quality lasting three years.[28] Moreover, when highly effective teachers followed highly ineffective teachers, students made gains, but at a reduced rate.[29]

In addition, Sanders and other researchers confirmed that the impact of a highly effective teacher on students' gain scores was several times greater than that of a number of other factors, including individual students' socioeconomic levels, class size, heterogeneous or homogeneous ability grouping, the racial or ethnic mix of the classroom, and the suburban or urban context of the school.[30]

A final conclusion from the researchers in Tennessee focused on the levels of teacher effectiveness. The researchers found that teachers in the bottom two quintiles failed to make the targeted gains with most of their students. Moreover, the best students in those classes tended to make the smallest gains. In fact, only teachers in the top quintile consistently helped high-achieving students achieve or exceed their anticipated gains.[31]

Drawing conclusions from these data, Sanders issued the following imperative: No student should be placed in an ineffective teacher's classroom more than once and only then when preceded by a highly effective teacher and followed by a highly effective teacher. In an interview for *Teacher Magazine*, Sanders said that excellent teachers help all students because "They've got kids working at different paces and at different places." Of ineffective teachers who tend to focus disproportionately on students at the lower achievement levels, Sanders said, "They may be sincere and conscientious, but they're holding back the others."[32]

In fairness, let me be clear that there is considerable disagreement among researchers as to the relative importance of some of the tangible characteristics. Linda Darling-Hammond and Peter Youngs of Stanford University, for example, cite compelling evidence that teacher education, certification, and subject-matter knowledge are important contributors to student achievement.[33]

But the most important point is not whether teacher quality comes more directly from training or talent. It's that developing strengths requires *both* — knowledge and skills of the kind cited by Darling-Hammond, in combination with the more innate qualities hinted at in the student comments and the ETS study, and explicitly referred to by Goldhaber. As you will recall, when knowledge and skills are used to develop a talent, the result is a strength. Identifying talent and developing strengths in teachers — not finding the perfect curriculum or ratcheting up accountability sanctions — should always be the first and foremost consideration in strategies to improve education quality.

FOCUSING ON WHO SHOULD TEACH

Neither major camp in the school reform debate spends enough time talking about teacher talent. But it's not that either side fails to recognize the importance of teachers, just that they're distracted from this most fundamental consideration by less decisive concerns. Focusing on who should teach, how to make the profession more attractive to those people, and how to help them build upon their talents to create strengths has more potential to drive up student achievement than any other approach. What's more, recruiting and developing great teachers is another focus around which proponents of both perspectives in the education reform debate can rally.

Let's turn back to the matter of what great teachers are like. How are they different from less effective teachers? Can we reliably identify teachers with strong potential to help students exceed expectations? These are the questions we'll explore next.

CHAPTER SEVEN

ENGAGED TEACHERS, PART 2: WHAT DO THEY DO DIFFERENTLY?

*"If there is any magic in education at all,
it is in its people, not in its process."*
*— James M. Moudy, former chancellor
of Texas Christian University*

The following sequence of events was related to me by the assistant superintendent for human resources in an Ohio school district:

Nearing completion of her student teaching and soon to graduate from a state university, Janice was eager to work with her own group of elementary school students. Armed with excellent grades and outstanding recommendations, she applied to a number of school districts in her state. But one district emerged as her first choice, partly because it had a reputation for supporting teachers in important ways, but also because the opportunity to teach its diverse range of students appealed to her.

After submitting her application and recommendations, along with the required certification and teacher test results, Janice completed a Web-based assessment and an initial interview. Soon, she received a telephone call from the district's human resources office saying that she would be contacted for interviews with principals. Janice knew this was the make-or-break step because the principals would make the final hiring decisions.

Janice was interviewed by three elementary school principals, and in all three cases, she felt the interviews went very well. During each, she tried to communicate her excitement about teaching and explain how she could help all students succeed. But each of the three principals selected another applicant.

The school district's human resources administrator, who kept results from the Web-based assessments and initial interviews for all of the applicants, saw a great deal of potential in Janice. She decided to follow up with each of the three principals. They all responded similarly: Janice was a very enthusiastic, warm person with many positive attributes that would serve her well as a teacher — but her preparation for reading instruction seemed weak compared to other, more experienced applicants.

After the interviews failed to result in any job offers, Janice asked for an opportunity to meet with the human resources administrator. Fortunately, the administrator was candid with her. After reviewing Janice's positive attributes, she summarized the feedback from the school principals that indicated that they saw Janice's weak background in reading instruction as an impediment.

Once she got over her hurt feelings, Janice went to work. First, she communicated to her university advisor the principals' judgment that her reading preparation wasn't sufficient, despite the fact that she had completed all the required and suggested courses with good grades. More importantly, she began a study program to learn more about reading instruction and about the specific reading program used in the district. She was determined to be ready the next time she interviewed there.

That opportunity arrived sooner than expected. A late resignation created an unexpected vacancy, and the human resources administrator submitted Janice's qualifications to the principal along with those of other applicants. After interviewing them all, the principal expressed some reservations about the breadth and depth of Janice's reading background but said he saw potential in Janice's other qualities, including her eagerness to learn. He recommended Janice for the position, and she got it.

Fast-forward to the end of the first semester, when the human resources administrator followed up with principals about each teacher who was new to the district. Janice's principal was enthusiastic about her performance: "She knows everything there is to know about reading, and I can hardly keep up with her. She wants to learn more!"

Fortunately, the principal looked beyond Janice's experience and training, realizing that reading programs can be learned, but that no training could have resulted in the positivity, the relationship-building ability, or the motivation to learn that Janice brought to teaching. Building on those talents, Janice added the knowledge and skills she needed to make reading instruction a strength.

DIFFERENT ROUTES TO GREATNESS

Strengths are essential to great teaching. Knowledge and skills are critical to the formation of strengths. But our ability to effectively apply these assets is rooted in our genes. Talents explain why one person excels in a given role, while another person with similar knowledge and skills does not. Great teachers share knowledge and apply skills through the lenses of their dominant talents.

The idea that the effectiveness of outstanding teachers is driven by innumerable combinations of talents, knowledge, and skills immediately leads to the realization that such teachers are not cookie-cutter versions of one another. On the contrary, when you start considering specifically *why* great teachers are effective, the differences among them become clear. They certainly achieve similar ends with students, but they get there by pursuing widely disparate routes based on who they are.

But all outstanding teachers are similar in one respect: They leverage their natural talents. Often through trial and error, they have become aware of where their greatest potential lies and have added knowledge and skills in those areas to great effect. Others may carry strong potential, vaguely feeling the "tug" of talents but never really developing them. Given the country's shortage of great teachers, that wasted potential is tragic. And there's no reason for it — these days, psychometric tools can help teachers, students, and anyone else identify probable areas of high talent.

YOUR BEST TEACHER

The concept of talent becomes less abstract when applied to real people. Think, if you will, of the very best teacher you ever had. What did this teacher do to make you remember him or her as special? Take a few moments to make a list of characteristics that you would use to describe to another person why you feel he or she was your best teacher.

There is little doubt that this teacher knew his or her subject matter. You may recall specific insights that this person conveyed about the subject or simply his or her depth of knowledge in the field. You may have applied yourself more in this teacher's class because you took him or her seriously as an expert.

Similarly, this teacher probably exhibited a skillful grasp of contemporary teaching methods, using techniques like essential questioning and differentiation to draw students in. The activities in this class may have been expertly planned to dovetail with one another so that they led you to the discoveries intended, and the presentations and stories may have been rehearsed many times to achieve polish and flair.

But if you look at your list again, you're likely to realize that many of the items refer not to the knowledge and skills involved in great teaching, but to the *natural* qualities of the teacher. Your list may include words like *enthusiastic, funny, caring, stimulating, challenging, fair, friendly, positive, innovative, creative, inspiring, interested,* and *passionate.* Regardless of the specific words, it's a safe bet that this teacher's greatness was defined in large part by the innate talents that separated him or her from other teachers in your experience.

Take one more look at your list and mark those items that you feel one person can effectively and efficiently teach to another person. Again, the likelihood is that a significant number of items remain unmarked. Is enthusiasm a teachable quality? How about a sense of humor, or positivity? On the other hand, if those characteristics are already present, they can be leveraged through self-awareness and conscious application.

The knowledge and skills assumption, you will recall, would imply that talents are secondary concerns — that they can be taught after the teacher is hired, or that they have little impact on performance. Yet 40 years of Gallup research — involving teachers; nurses; doctors; salespeople in a variety of industries; stockbrokers; hockey players; basketball players; orchestra conductors; and leaders in business, education, government, and the military — indicates just the opposite. In all of

these roles, innate talents make the difference in performance. And trying to teach them is not only resource-consuming, it is at best impracti-
cal — if not impossible.

STUDYING SUCCESS

In the late 1960s, Don Clifton, then a University of Nebraska professor, decided to devote his career to studying success across a variety
of roles. Clifton found it odd that the conventional approach to studying success in a role was (and typically still is) to begin with a group of
randomly selected individuals in that role. The process involves drawing as large a sample as possible, calculating a mean for the group, and
rating each individual on the basis of how far they fall above or below
the mean. This approach assumes that everyone along the spectrum of
performance — from the most successful people to the least successful
— has a consistent set of characteristics. The difference between the average performers and the stars is simply a matter of how much more or
less of those characteristics an individual possesses.[1]

Through his research, Clifton found something different: Top performers typically rely on an entirely different set of characteristics to
achieve excellence. Over decades of study, Dr. Clifton established that
"Success has its own rules, and highly successful people look at the
world in a different way."[2]

Another common — if somewhat mystifying — tendency is to study
failure, which also often takes us in the wrong direction. Here's a typical
example: A group of teachers is having trouble with student discipline.
Sent to training sessions, they study cases in which teachers have had
to deal with severe discipline problems in the past. The instructors conclude that clear initial statement of the rules and consequences along
with consistent and immediate enforcement is the best solution. As a

result, the teachers learn an approach that will make the atmosphere in their classrooms more overtly control-oriented from the outset, with greater distance placed between teacher and students. The possibility that using a defensive strategy might have contributed to the study classes' unruliness in the first place isn't even considered.

Outstanding teachers, on the other hand, tend to give responses more consistent with child psychologists, who argue that the secret of success in student discipline is establishing rapport and concentrating on helping students succeed, rather than emphasizing heavy control.[3] The point is that the best teachers — as is true of the best performers in any field — intuitively know something different. Just as weakness fixing leads to an unproductive dead end, studying average performance or failure usually results in a wrong turn. If we want better teachers or principals, we should study the best in these roles.

THE CORNERSTONE OF TEACHING — A THEORY

Before further examining what great teachers do and the talents that enable them to be effective, I'd like to describe a theory by renowned psychologist Carl Rogers that is applicable to teaching and a number of other fields. The theory was Rogers' attempt to distill his learning and experiences in psychotherapy into a set of general principles.

The resulting concepts are of interest to teachers and principals because Rogers' focus in psychotherapy was "constructive personality change." He defined this as a profound change in the personality of a person that creates "less internal conflict and more energy utilizable for effective living," a shift away from behaviors generally regarded as immature and toward those regarded as mature.[4] While the definition is aimed at psychotherapy, it also applies to goals of education, as Rogers himself pointed out. Such goals include promoting self-discipline, self-motivation, and academic engagement in students, turning them into lifelong and independent learners as well as involved citizens.

Rogers identified and explained several conditions that were "necessary and sufficient" to bring about constructive personality change. The first is that a *relationship* must exist before change can occur. More broadly, this means that personal development occurs only in relation to another person. The next condition is that the therapist be in *congruence* — that is, genuine in the sense that her words and actions are aligned with her belief structures — while the client is experiencing an incongruence — i.e., a discrepancy between his beliefs on the one hand and his words and actions on the other. In addition to congruence, the therapist or teacher must demonstrate *unconditional positive regard,* an accepting warmth and respect for the client or student as a person and an *empathic understanding* of the client's world.[5]

At the risk of oversimplifying Rogers' theory, the general idea is that high levels of genuineness, understanding, and unconditional acceptance are most likely to bring about constructive personality change. Translating that conclusion to the educational setting, the more teachers exhibit genuineness, understanding, and unconditional acceptance for students, the more successfully they can encourage the beliefs and behaviors that lead to engagement and maturity. Applying the same ideas to the relationships between principals and teachers helps create an environment in which teachers are free to use their talents more effectively. We'll return to this idea in Chapter 9.

Rogers' theory assumes importance as a cornerstone in understanding effective teaching. Keep it in mind as we delve into what great teachers do differently as identified by Gallup's research and the work of other researchers and observers.

WHAT DO OUTSTANDING TEACHERS DO?

Gallup's research on teachers follows Don Clifton's principle of studying success. Over the course of 40 years, numerous public school districts have partnered with Gallup to identify the talents of their best teachers. School principals identified those teachers by using any hard data that was available and selecting those teachers they would seek out first if they were hiring a new staff from scratch. These teachers participated in initial focus groups with Gallup researchers, after which larger groups of teachers nominated by their principals took part in quantitative surveys, along with randomly selected teachers, to contrast the characteristics of the two groups.

The teacher and parent comments quoted in this chapter come from focus groups held in 2000, 2001, and 2005. Their insights resulted in hypotheses that were further tested in more widespread studies completed in 2001 and 2004. As we explore the broad patterns of talent that consistently appear in outstanding teachers, it helps to think of them in terms of three general categories:

- *Motivation* describes what causes outstanding teachers to choose the profession initially and remain in teaching over the course of their careers. Note that we're talking about the teacher's drive to teach here, rather than how they motivate students. Teachers' level of motivation is critical, given their considerable daily challenges and typically low pay. It is a strong indicator of whether or not new teachers will stay in the profession.

- *Relating* explains how outstanding teachers create relationships — with students in particular, but also with colleagues and parents. It describes how teachers express themselves as individuals and connect with others in the school environment.

- *Activating learning* addresses how teachers motivate students and initiate the learning process. This category describes what teachers do to make learning happen for their students, regardless of the curriculum or subject area.

AN INNATE MOTIVATION TO TEACH

There are myriad specific reasons why people become teachers, but many of them boil down to this: The idea of teaching others is innately appealing to some people. That urge is fulfilled in a variety of ways. People volunteer to teach in churches, on athletic fields, in gymnasiums, or in tutoring programs. In focus groups and interviews, Gallup researchers often hear participants say longingly, "I always wanted to teach, but . . ."

For their ironically titled book *Teachers Have It Easy*, Daniel Moulthrop, Nínive Clements Calegari, and Dave Eggers interviewed many highly educated professionals who were making significant financial sacrifices so they could teach. In a chapter entitled "So Why Do They Bother?" the authors offer teachers' responses to that question.[6] Simply put, the opportunity to share understanding or skills with another person is a source of enormous psychological gratification for many.

Earlier, I referred to psychologist Amy Wrzesniewski's studies identifying the three predominant ways people regard their work:

1. As a *job*, done solely for financial reasons.
2. As a *career*, in which advancement in status and financial return become personal goals.
3. As a *calling*, in which the individual derives personal satisfaction from the nature of the work itself.

Wrzesniewski's findings demonstrate that people with "callings" find meaning in their jobs even when they are doing low-status or stigmatized work.[7] Great teachers almost invariably approach their work as a calling. That orientation is evident in the sense of altruism that drives great teachers to remain committed despite typically low pay and limited advancement opportunities. Many possess a fervent desire to make circumstances better for young people through teaching.

In its 2000 survey of beginning teachers titled *A Sense of Calling*, Public Agenda documented this attraction to teaching. Beginning teachers and college graduates under the age of 30 (who were not teachers) were surveyed about their attitudes toward teaching. The nonteachers were asked, *"If the opportunity were to present itself, which of the following statements do you think would best describe how you would feel about becoming a public school teacher?"* Eighteen percent of the respondents indicated that they would "very seriously consider it," 50% indicated that teaching was one of the jobs they would consider, and 32% responded that they "could never imagine being a public school teacher." However, many of the 68% who said they would at least consider teaching also pointed out the negatives, including poor career advancement, low prestige, and low pay.[8]

On the other hand, 96% of the beginning teachers surveyed by Public Agenda (Figure 8) said that they love teaching, and 80% indicated they would choose teaching if they were to choose careers again.[9]

FIGURE 8

Survey of Beginning Teachers

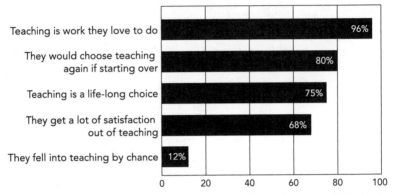

Source: Farkas, S., Johnson, J., & Foleno, T. (2000). *A sense of calling: Who teaches and why.* Public Agenda.

It's not that the non-teachers were less likely to feel that teaching fulfills a critical social need. The young non-teachers who were interviewed for *A Sense of Calling* were also asked, "Which do you think provides a more important benefit to society — your current job or being a teacher?" Eight out of 10 respondents chose being a teacher, 9% cited their current job as more important, and another 10% said their job and that of a teacher were equally important.[10]

But non-teachers don't express the highly emotional attraction to the profession that teachers have. As a parent in one of Gallup's focus groups said about great teachers, "When you love what you do, it comes through in their mannerisms. It comes from their pores. You feel the energy and the excitement. You can see the difference. Other teachers can do their job, but there is not the light, the passion." A parent of a high school student, when asked to think about the very best teachers her son experienced, said, "They are all qualified. It comes down to whether they want to be there. Did teaching fill their expectations? If they don't like it, they won't be good at it."

Let's hone in a little more specifically on the psychological rewards that teachers who have participated in Gallup's research over the years have described.

The Students

The single reward most commonly mentioned by teachers is working with students. Effective teachers often describe a degree of reciprocity with their students. Students respond to teachers who enjoy their work. "When teachers want to teach, I want to learn," said Susan, a 17-year-old Gallup Youth Survey respondent. A participant in a focus group of parents said, "My son's kindergarten teacher goes through this litany. She tells them that she believes in them. Their obligation is to do the best they can do. It's a partnership. My son doesn't want to let his teacher down. He wants to do his best, and it's important to him to do quality work."

Seeing children learn is an innate motivational influence for some people. It's the same thrill avid gardeners get from seeing a patch of dull earth bloom into vibrant color — in fact, Clifton used that analogy often, saying, "Great teachers have a green thumb for kids." They see potential that lies beneath the surface, whether they're coaching basketball in a YMCA after-school program or overseeing a group of papier-mâché sculptors in a middle school art class. They're strongly motivated by the desire to grow that potential into strengths.[11]

Let me share one of the best stories I've ever heard about that inherent longing to see students succeed. On her very first day as a teacher, Maria Figueroa, now a retired 30-year veteran of the New York City school system, was told by a fellow staff member, "Don't knock yourself out; these kids are on their way to jail soon." Located in a tough neighborhood, Maria's new school was known as a "dumping ground" for all kinds of challenging students.

During that first year, Maria noticed a boy in her class, Francisco, who seemed really bright, but didn't turn in his homework and sometimes fell asleep in class. When Maria asked him what was going on, Francisco's response was straightforward: "I have to take care of my four brothers and sisters at home. I'm the oldest, so I have to take care of them while my mother works."

Maria's daughter Maribel related this story to me. As she tells it, "My mom made a deal with this kid. She promised to help him catch up if he would come in over his free periods. To protect his 'rep,' they agreed that she would be making him 'stay after class.' Francisco more than made up his deficiencies by the end of the year and turned around his attitude for the remainder of his time at school. Then he went on to high school and mom lost touch with him."

Many years later, Maria and Maribel were walking down Fifth Avenue in Brooklyn on a Saturday afternoon when a tall, good-looking gentleman flagged them down. "Do you remember me?" he asked Maria. "It's Francisco. I was one of your students." He gave Maria a big smile and a hug. When Maria asked how he was, he said, "I'm great. I'm finishing up my residency at St. Vincent's Hospital in Manhattan. I'm a doctor in part because of you. I remember you telling me that I was smart, and that you believed I was a good kid. And I just want to thank you, after all these years."

"We were bawling on the street for 10 minutes," Maribel said.

Maria saw potential where others saw only problems. Few of her students became doctors like Francisco, but Maria was proud of every student who graduated from high school. Over time, she developed her own "rep" — for helping students complete applications for work or community college.

The Subject

Passion for a particular subject also contributes to many teachers' motivation. In a study of secondary mathematics teachers in Great Britain, for example, Paul Andrews and Gil Hatch found that their most common specific reason for teaching math was love of the subject. Thirty-eight percent of the teachers in their study indicated that they chose to teach — and teach mathematics in particular — because of their learning experiences in math classes. Moreover, those experiences were more likely to have occurred in elementary and secondary school than at the university level.[12]

Paul Richardson and Helen Watt of Monash University in Australia studied individuals who had left established careers in other fields to earn a teaching credential. They found that most of the participants had considered the move for some time and that they saw teaching as a better career fit for them.[13] In many cases, participants taught about the field they had entered, combining their attraction to that field with a deep-seated conviction that they should be helping people learn and grow.

Jim, now the chief financial officer of a consulting company with $250 million in annual revenue, understands the life-altering effect of a great teacher with a passion for his subject. For him, high school was mainly about sports and friends until a great accounting teacher was able to focus his attention. "I was lucky," Jim explains. "The subject matter could have been very dry and functionary. While it would be stretching it to say that Mr. Benson made accounting fun, he did make *learning* accounting fun. He enabled me to connect some dots to what could be. For once, I was learning something that I could relate to things outside school and use math for something that was relevant."

Role Models

Great teachers are often motivated by the impact of other talented teachers in their lives. Many of the participants in Gallup's focus groups with outstanding teachers had family members who were also teachers. Some of these participants said they yearned for the satisfaction they saw these family members deriving from their work.

A majority of the participants in the focus groups with teachers nominated as outstanding by their principals said they chose teaching as a profession largely because their own teachers made such an impression on them. Most spoke of how they identified with or were inspired by a particular teacher. But a few simply felt they could do better. One said: "I had some pretty bad teachers and thought, 'If I were up there, this is how I would do it.' When it was time to make a choice in career, I thought, 'I can do this. I can make it interesting for kids; I can make it where they want to learn.'"

Do we take teachers' inner drive for granted?

What do all these forms of motivation have in common? They are all derived from a deep-rooted urge to experience the intrinsic rewards associated with teaching. Participants in Gallup's outstanding-teacher groups suggested that the incentive for devoting large amounts of time to the job came from an "internal drive." They viewed themselves as willing to work hard, to give and then give some more. Putting a significant amount of "extra" time and effort into teaching was a foregone conclusion for them. "If it is better, and it will take me an hour," one teacher said, "so what? I do it." As another teacher put it, "There is no peace until you figure out what to do for a child who is not succeeding."

Those around them — students, parents, fellow teachers — are likely to recognize which teachers are strongly motivated. Participants in our parent groups were certainly able to identify which of their children's teachers were the most dedicated. "She gives herself to the job — goes the extra mile with us," said one parent. "She lets us know that she will do whatever we need her to do." When asked in a recent Youth Survey why he worked harder for some teachers than others, one 17-year-old boy said simply, "Because some teachers work harder for me."

Their innate passion serves as a wellspring that great teachers can call upon, when disheartened or weary, to remind them of how significant their work is. It also pushes them to levels of excellence by forcing them to impose high expectations upon themselves.

But it's not limitless, and it can't be taken for granted. The drive and energy of talented teachers should be recognized as an invaluable national resource. Instead, it's given mostly lip service. Realizing that talented teachers are willing to make great sacrifices in order to fulfill their sense of purpose, we routinely require them to do so. But as we'll discuss further in Chapter 9, even those special teachers whose motivational fire burns the brightest can be — and too often are — ground down by years of feeling undervalued thanks to low pay and little recognition. When this happens, engagement among even the most dedicated teachers can plummet — taking student engagement along with it.

A GIFT FOR BUILDING RELATIONSHIPS

Sue, a colleague of mine, told me a story about her daughter Alyssa that I think vividly illustrates talented teachers' inherent knack for activating student learning:

"We faced a very hard decision for our family in moving to another city, knowing how Alyssa, our second grader at the time, adapted to new situations. She likes to know her surroundings, and so anything that takes her out of that is intimidating and uncomfortable for her.

"The move made third grade a tough year for Alyssa. She had a teacher who was pretty structured, not much of a relator, high discipline. She challenged the kids and was a good teacher academically. But because the relationship was not there for Alyssa, all it did was intimidate her. The thrill and excitement of learning and the confidence to take risks, both personally and academically, were missing.

"By February, it was a challenge for all of us. I called the school and asked to meet with the principal. I said, 'I'm a parent who will always make the best of a situation, and this year has not been a horrible situation. But I think it could have been a lot better.' The principal asked questions to learn more about Alyssa. Finally he said, 'I know exactly who she needs — Mrs. Paul.'

"We were anxious about the day we got to meet the teachers that next fall. We walked in the room, and immediately, Mrs. Paul physically embraced Alyssa and welcomed her. She connected Alyssa with Kylie, who shared her table, and gave her a relationship to then build from. Now Kylie is one of Alyssa's best friends. That was the beginning of a phenomenal fourth grade year.

"When I think about how Mrs. Paul was different, it seems that she really understood Alyssa. She drew upon Alyssa's reading and writing talents and helped Alyssa think about math concepts in a way she hadn't before that made that light bulb click for her. Mrs. Paul is a huge learner herself and very strategic. She can take concepts that are difficult to teach, break them down into smaller components, and put them in a way that reaches the individual child, while making it exciting and fun.

"Mrs. Paul made Alyssa feel included and part of something. She wanted to know about the kids' lives. She asked, 'What are you doing for your birthday? Oh, you had a slumber party!' Her students couldn't wait to share those stories with her. So, the relationship was encouraging and supportive. She really fostered diverse relationships within the classroom by partnering students with different individuals so that they had that experience of really knowing other students. She could say, 'Hey, this person's really good at this; I'm going to match you guys together, and let's see what you can do.' She really valued what it was that people brought to the table, and then built relationships and success around that.

"When we think about those two years for Alyssa, they were very different experiences. In third grade, we saw a very insecure little girl who came to a new school, frightened, and had a hard time building relationships. Alyssa wasn't excited to learn and grow, to take challenges and risks. But fourth grade was different. Alyssa completely turned around because of a teacher who believed in her, encouraged her, cared about her, and supported her. Alyssa has confidence now that 'I can figure this out; I can learn it' and to not give up. I know that having Mrs. Paul as a teacher will positively influence Alyssa's life forever."

Reflecting on the massive amount of data collected for his widely regarded book *A Place Called School,* John Goodlad observed in 1984 that though classrooms differed, schooling itself looked pretty much the same from one classroom to another. He meant that students' day-to-day activities were strikingly similar across the majority of classrooms he studied. In the rare cases in which the learning process stood out from the pack, it tended to do so because of the positive relationships developed by the teacher.

In the vast majority of cases, Goodlad noted, the interaction between teachers and students appeared neutral in tone. Goodlad describes the overall impression of most classrooms as "neither harsh and punitive nor warm and joyful; it might be described most accurately as flat."[14] Kris Bosworth described a similar type of relationship — neither "caring nor uncaring" — in her year-long study of two middle schools in which researchers observed more than 300 classrooms and interviewed more than 100 students. "We observed too many classes," Bosworth said, "in which the teachers rarely smiled, said anything positive to a student, or used a student's name other than for a reprimand."[15]

Whether they intend to or not, teachers create relationships of one kind or another in their classrooms. Today, many students and parents still describe the kind of detached — or even defensive — student/teacher relationships that Goodlad and Bosworth documented. But highly talented teachers at all levels spontaneously create positive, supportive classroom environments.

In his 1983 study of American high schools, Ernest Boyer maintains that "When we think of a great teacher, most often we remember a person whose technical skills were matched by the qualities we associate with a good and trusted friend."[16] Thinking back to the characteristics of the best teacher you have known, you will likely agree with Boyer's observation.

The concept of "professional distance" is one that schools have unfortunately adopted from the business world. The threat of lawsuits has fed into it, as teachers have become increasingly wary of any closeness that could be interpreted as "inappropriate behavior." Scandals involving improper situations between teachers and students — lightning rods for media coverage — prompt warnings from legal advisors to keep your distance. But in both business and school settings, the resulting neutrality represents a missed opportunity. It leads to lack of trust and reduced productivity in workplaces, and less effective teaching in schools.

Great teachers show they care by treating students with respect and dignity, even as they maintain their authority. This is the congruence required by Rogers' theory of constructive personality change. It's undoubtedly easier to pull off these positive relationships at the elementary school level than at the secondary school level, as middle school and high school teachers typically see far more students than elementary school teachers. What's more, elementary school students are more open to and desirous of close relationships with teachers as "parent substitutes."

At the secondary school level, positive student-teacher relationships typically more closely resemble respectful mentor-mentee relationships between adults. But the *need* for close relationships doesn't fade as students get older, despite the moodiness of adolescence. If students' interactions with teachers grow dramatically more distant and impersonal as they get older, their engagement levels will tend to suffer as well.

The tendency of great teachers to develop close positive relationships is connected to the sense of altruism that helps motivate them. Such relationships encourage individuals to think in terms of what is best for the other person, requiring nothing in return. That's the kind of focus truly effective teachers need to earn the trust and enthusiasm of their students. "Kids are like animals," said a teacher focus group participant whose classes consistently outperform others in her school. "Kids know who likes them — who's in education because they like kids as opposed to getting a check."

Indeed, students tend to be highly attuned to those teachers who initiate and cultivate positive relationships with their students, as opposed to those who deem it sufficient to make themselves available. A parent in one of Gallup's focus groups described her son's response when asked why he liked his favorite teacher: "He said, 'Because she knew I could do good, but it wasn't just the grades I got.' He had value to her regardless of his grades." Andrew, a 15-year-old Gallup Youth Survey respondent, described his attitude this way: "I want to make different teachers happy. Some care more about me than others, and I want to make them proud." As one parent told us, "Students start to learn when you establish rapport."

Important research conducted in the late 1970s by David Aspy and Flora Roebuck supports that view. As reported in the book *Kids Don't Learn From People They Don't Like*, their work is one the most comprehensive studies to date regarding the impact of students' relationships with teachers. The study's initial goal focused on whether there were measurable outcome differences "when the teacher is able to show the students that he or she really likes them, understands them and wants to help them."[17]

The title of Aspy's and Roebuck's book came from a student's comment, which was borne out by their data. Over a three-year period, 500 teachers and 10,000 students were involved in a training program to encourage closer, more trusting relationships between them. Aspy and Roebuck found that students whose teachers participated in the training program posted significantly higher average achievement test scores, better attendance, and better self-concept assessments than students whose teachers didn't participate. In other words, students whose teachers were more likely to cultivate strong relationships learned more, came to school more often, and felt better about themselves as learners.[18]

Following in the footsteps of Aspy's and Roebuck's research and Goodlad's large study, more researchers began to investigate the specific effects of caring environments in schools.[19] In a three-year study of middle school students, Kathryn Wentzel demonstrated that perceiving their teachers cared about them elevated students' level of academic effort — in eighth grade significantly more so than in sixth grade. In describing how they could tell whether or not teachers cared, students in the study mentioned open interaction with students, an enthusiasm for their own work as teachers, and useful feedback about work and behaviors.[20]

When thinking about student motivation and engagement, we typically consider instructional and curricular approaches without giving equal consideration to the quality of relationships in the classroom, which is at least as important. Emphasis usually falls to the "what" and "how" of teaching — but it's the "who" that provides the cement that holds everything else together. The presence or absence of close relationships has an effect on the way students think about learning, and eventually how they will think about work. It's part of what is often referred to as the "hidden curriculum."[21]

HOW DO GREAT TEACHERS BUILD RELATIONSHIPS?

As we did in the previous section, let's look a little more specifically at this consistent characteristic of great teachers. How do they overcome severe time constraints, adolescent hormones, and the fear of litigious parents to build positive relationships with as many as 150 students in a semester?

First, keep in mind that the specific ways in which individual teachers develop rapport with students vary greatly, depending on a teacher's dominant talents. There is no magic formula to follow. But there are a few broad consistencies in the ways outstanding teachers establish relationships.

Helping

Outstanding teachers naturally go out of their way to help students, constantly sending a signal that they are allies rather than enemies. After a yearlong study of two middle schools in the mid-1990s, Kris Bosworth found that students almost always described caring teachers as those who went out of their way to help them with their schoolwork and personal problems. Bosworth noted that though such behaviors are often considered "good teaching," they actually depended on the personal qualities of the teachers.[22]

Similarly, a 1995 study of two highly effective elementary school teachers suggested that helping is a key relationship-builder when conducted appropriately. Effective teachers provided help "but did not demean [students] for needing help."[23] Again, this may seem to simply be a good teaching technique, but considering the pace of everyday classroom life, these behaviors don't represent conscious decisions on the part of great teachers. They're intuitive; they are *talents*.

Showing Respect

Great teachers display respect for students in all situations, not just when they need extra assistance. They refrain from embarrassing students in front of peers, constantly recognize students' accomplishments in class, and listen carefully to students' ideas and comments. Bosworth quotes one seventh grade male student as saying, "They treat you the way you want to be treated." That's much easier said than done when it comes to relating to 25 or more students at a time.

More fundamentally, great teachers establish respectful relationships by being non-judgmental and accepting students as they are — a stance closely aligned with Rogers' criterion of unconditional positive regard — even as they maintain clear expectations and encourage the best in them.[24] They then follow up on that respect with a willingness to help, thereby building within students a feeling of trust in the relationship.[25]

Inescapably, the feelings of students and teachers play an important part in establishing the type of close rapport that breaks down educational barriers. Rogers cited empathic understanding as one of his necessary and sufficient conditions for constructive personality change. Their talent for empathy leads some teachers to naturally and easily grasp the perspective and emotions of the students and act on this understanding. Bosworth found that the students in her study tended to value the ability of caring teachers to understand their feelings second only to those teachers' willingness to help.[26]

Working with an inquiry group of seven exceptional high school teachers in the Boston public schools over the course of a year, researcher Sonia Nieto was surprised to hear them openly talk about their love for their students and the subject matter they teach.[27] Despite the climate of paranoia created by high-profile lawsuits, love and caring are emotions most parents want their children to experience as often as possible. Summing up the strongest components of her kids' education, a parent in one of Gallup's focus groups said, "My kids have felt loved by their teachers."

Setting the Right Expectations

The tendency to set high expectations is frequently cited in discussions of effective teachers and effective schools. But it's a little off the mark. Teachers who build strong relationships set the *right* expectations, academically and behaviorally, for each student. They carefully devise expectations that maximize students' engagement levels by stretching them without unduly frustrating them. Only by developing insight about the potential of each student — insight that can come solely through relationships with students and parents — can great teachers be confident they're setting the right expectations.

In turn, those expectations strengthen the relationship because they show the student that the teacher has thought about her best interests. Elizabeth, a 16-year-old Gallup Youth Survey respondent, described students' reactions to relationship-based expectations this way:

> Because some teachers expect more of you and believe
> in you, you don't want to let them down, so you try hard-
> er for them — especially if you like that teacher and that
> class. If a teacher is mean, then a lot of times you don't
> want to make them happy by doing what they ask. You
> want to just do enough to get by.

Simply setting high expectations isn't enough to foster engagement. In fact, expectations that are too high and are repeatedly unmet have the opposite effect. Perpetually frustrated students eventually become chronically disengaged and are at high risk for dropping out. Setting expectations too low, on the other hand, makes students bored and restless. Great teachers know each student well enough to set the bar at the right level to sustain his or her interest and maximize his or her growth.

Rogers' observations from psychotherapy suggest that communicating a high level of genuineness, understanding, and acceptance to students would improve education. Is the translation of his ideas from psychotherapy to schools a stretch? Not at all. Everyone searches for a place to belong and for people who can be counted on to provide caring and acceptance. It's no surprise that students look for those things in the place where they spend so much time during childhood and adolescence. Their need to trust teachers brings to mind the saying "I don't care how much you know until I know how much you care."

AN UNDERSTANDING OF HOW TO ACTIVATE LEARNING

Rosemary Travis became an English and journalism teacher because of a teacher in Indiana who focused on individual students. She shared with me her memories of Ms. Christiansen: "A petite woman of five feet one, thin as a pencil, who walked fast and didn't smile much. But she filled the room with an air of certitude, a presence. She really knew her material, and she was tough."

Rosemary vividly remembers the first day of fourth quarter in senior English class. "Ms. Christiansen rolled a cart filled with books into the classroom just before the bell. She gave me a historical fiction novel about Lincoln and his wife, Mary Todd. It was a 500 page book. Huge! The girl across from me got a thin book. What an injustice! I challenged her. Ms. Christiansen simply replied, 'Read two chapters. If you don't like the book after two chapters, I'll give you a different book.' Well, that was the first book I ever read counting the number of pages to the end because I didn't want the book to end!"

Ms. Christiansen maintained a personal connection with each student through her comments on their papers. "The margin notes showed that she really read my paper and cared," Rosemary recalls. "She had an amazing way of framing those notes on the edge of my writing that made me think and learn something from them. It sounds crazy, but the notes meant everything because they were just for me.

"Other English teachers gave pop quizzes of details, like 'What was the color of Johnny's hat?'" Rosemary says. But Ms. Christiansen's questions "always made you think about the characters, their personalities, how the setting complemented the storyline. She opened up literature and made it vivid. As I think back to that class, it's as if she taught the class just for me. She didn't, obviously, but it was a very personal experience because she really pulled out the best in me.

"Two summers ago, I was with some classmates, and we went on and on about Ms. Christiansen," Rosemary continues. "One of the people was more of a jock for whom English was not her thing, and she talked about Ms. Christiansen giving her a book. It was a perfect book, and it turned her on to reading. I guess she gave each of us what we were ready to do."

From the foundation of their own motivation and their positive relationships with students, great teachers work to keep students as actively involved in their education as possible — to keep them fully engaged. Extraordinary teachers regularly use "active learning" techniques to stimulate higher order thinking in their classes.[28] They acknowledge that students can learn content in different ways, and they seek any number of innovative means for bringing it to life. The constant is that these methods actively involve students in learning rather than allowing them to be passive observers. Thus, the emphasis naturally shifts from memorizing facts ("What happened during the Industrial Revolution?") to analyzing and synthesizing the concepts underlying those facts ("How does the Industrial Revolution continue to affect our lives today?").

Students and parents tend to become enthusiastic when active learning methods are used effectively. David, a 13-year-old respondent to the Gallup Youth Survey, described how evolution comes to life this way: "In language arts class, we just did a debate on evolution versus creationism, and my teacher made us get on teams and research it and argue for and against it. It really made me and my friends think about it and talk about it even when we weren't in class." A parent describes similar activities in a high school mock trial by saying, "They love to argue, and they put a lot of energy into it. It creates teamwork. It wasn't just memorizing. It strikes me how kids like to participate in their own learning."

Adopting New Techniques

Many specific active learning methods and other good pedagogical techniques are taught — in college, training seminars, mentoring sessions, and the like. But outstanding teachers bring talents to the classroom that enable them to apply those lessons easily and in exceptional ways.

Take questioning skills of the kind used by Ms. Christiansen as an example. Barry Croom of North Carolina State University studies how to improve teachers' questioning techniques. Typically, teachers ask too many "call out" questions of the class at large and don't wait long enough after asking the question for students to respond (the average wait time is one second). If no immediate answer is forthcoming, they grow impatient or uneasy and ask another question. According to Croom, directing more questions at specific students for particular reasons improves student learning, as does increasing the wait time for a response.[29]

All teachers can be taught that idea, but some will incorporate the technique immediately, while others will have to learn it more than once with minimal impact on their long-term performance. As we discussed in the last chapter, this occurs not because some teachers refuse to accept the idea, but because it doesn't align well with their talents. For teachers who are patient, trust in their students' abilities, and genuinely like to learn students' views, the idea will resonate and be easily incorporated into their toolkit, to be customized and fine-tuned over time.

Spreading a Love of Learning

In *The Elements of Teaching*, James Banner and Harold Cannon maintain that "Teaching requires more than knowing how to learn, although that is important. Above all, teaching requires learning itself."[30] Just as great writers love to read, outstanding teachers love to learn. In many cases, this love is the stimulus for originally considering a career in teaching.[31] Since the process of learning is natural for these teachers, they believe deeply that learning can be just as enjoyable for their students.

Participants in Gallup's focus groups with teachers discussed the resiliency that their love of learning brings in terms of openness to a variety of methods. As one teacher explained, "When something doesn't work, you just go back and try something else. That's why you have to be a learner." Another noted that the best teachers "don't have their lesson plans laminated." On the contrary, the participants expressed a need to keep expanding their repertoire, to do things differently every year, and, in some cases, from class to class. Even small additions can boost the delight teachers and students get from the education process. Sue, an elementary school teacher in a Virginia focus group, provides an example:

> I'm almost always reading a biography. I love learning nuggets and bringing them into class. In reading a biography of Winston Churchill, I learned the origin of the word posh. When rich people sailed to India, they got to sit on the port side of the ship on the way there, and on the starboard side on the way home. So Port Out, Starboard Home: P.O.S.H. I just loved that!

For many great teachers, their love of learning combines with their innate motivation and relationship-building skills in a chemical reaction that generates high energy levels. Banner and Cannon underscore the importance of this quality, saying, "It is a teacher's infectious enthusiasm for learning itself, as much as the student's curiosity about the teacher's subject, that is apt to captivate a student."[32] A participant in a parent focus group suggested that she could tell a great deal about teachers from "the enthusiasm that children come home with. [For example], they want to read more about penguins!"

Asked how teachers motivate their students, a parent participant responded, "Some is by their personal enthusiasm on a topic. Learning what is a trigger in the kids. My oldest had some very special interests, and they allowed him to research them." The enthusiasm expressed by these teachers allows their students to "feel" the subject. But such excitement can't be faked — teachers have to genuinely experience that love of learning.

As with their innate passion for seeing students develop, the power of great teachers' infectious curiosity should not be undervalued, but it too often is. When the push for standards becomes too focused on specific processes rather than outcomes, it threatens to rob great teachers of perhaps their single greatest asset — the simple love of exploration. After all, if teachers aren't fully engaged in what's going on in the classroom, what chance do students have?

Teacher engagement is a necessary precursor to student engagement. As with students, engagement among teachers depends on their freedom and opportunities to use their greatest talents as frequently as possible.

Tapping Students' Talents

Finally, let's go back to our fundamental goal for American education in the 21st century: helping each student tap his or her true potential. As Stephenson comments in *Extraordinary Teachers: The Essence of Excellent Teaching*, "Effective instructors recognize that *all* students have ability and that teaching involves finding ways to nurture these talents."[33]

Gallup's focus groups with teachers whose students consistently outperform those in similar classes provided some insights on developing potential. These teachers clearly structure their teaching so students can learn — and "learn how to learn" in the process. They do this by actively looking for areas of high potential. Instead of dwelling on students' weaknesses, they constantly ask themselves, "What does the student do *well*?" As one parent told a Gallup researcher, "[It is important] for the child to begin to *realize* their own potential, to help the child come to *understand* their potential." Referring to a teacher from the previous year, the parent continued, "She helps children be proud of their abilities."

Parents seem to recognize this talent in teachers more easily than teachers perceive it in themselves. A parent in one focus group talked about a high school teacher who walked around the room and said something to each student individually about his or her capabilities nearly every day. His comments always began with something like, "You have the ability to . . ." Another parent noticed that great teachers are able to remove specific obstacles facing particular students: "The ones that I really admire identify when he learns the best. In second grade, a teacher identified that he wasn't doing well when there were distractions. They figured out the learning environment that worked best."

In *Shaking Up the Schoolhouse*, Phillip Schlechty suggests that the "art and science of teaching" emerges as the ability to create learning activities that not only reflect what adults think students need to learn, but that students actually *want* to complete.[34] Parents and teachers suggest that teachers accomplish this when they look to the individual. In her middle school study, Bosworth found "valuing individuality" to be a quality students commonly associated with great teachers. A seventh grade female student in her study says her teacher "doesn't see you as a unit."[35]

Outstanding teachers constantly apply this innate capacity for individualized perception to monitor two things: each student's natural ability and each student's needs. They then use that information to optimize their resources and methods, instinctively operating according to Rogers' and Renard's assertion that "We must understand the needs and the beliefs of our students as they are, not as we think that they ought to be."[36] Or, in the words of a high school parent describing one of her son's best teachers, "The quality teacher is one who sees that children are different."

A HIGH DEGREE OF SPECIFIC TALENTS

Intrinsic motivation, relationship-building talents, and a rich toolkit for activating learning are three core areas that Gallup has consistently found distinguish highly effective teachers. Obviously, not all great teachers do all of the things described in this chapter, but they consistently tend to do more of them than other teachers do. In essence, they possess talents that promote student learning, and they constantly seek opportunities to develop and apply those talents as teaching strengths.

The bottom line is this: Effective teaching, like outstanding performance in other demanding professions from athlete to surgeon, requires a high degree of natural talent. Not everyone can learn to do it, and schools should focus far more effort on identifying and developing those individuals who can.

As Tony Bagshaw, an elementary school principal in Ohio, told me, "What you can't teach teachers is what really matters." I asked Tony about the best teacher he ever knew, and he immediately began telling me about a second grade teacher who he said builds the most profound relationships with students and has the deepest commitment to the profession that he's ever seen.

"It makes me emotional just thinking about this lady; she's just so incredible as a teacher," Tony said. "I first met her right after I got the job. As I was walking in the building, this lady was out in front pulling weeds. I said, 'Hi, I'm Tony. It's nice to meet you,' and she said, 'Oh hi. I teach second grade here.' I thought, 'Why is this lady out front pulling weeds?' But that was her level of devotion. If every teacher in the country was like this one, the world would be a different place."

How do we find more teachers with that level of engagement? We place a priority on selecting teachers with the innate potential to perform at excellence. Instead of simply filling vacancies, we hold out for talent. Then we focus and supplement that talent by helping those gifted teachers attain the knowledge and skills they need to perform at excellence. Anything less does a disservice to our students.

But in order to ensure that those priorities are in place, we'll first have to scrutinize the uncomfortable discrepancies between our beliefs about the importance of teachers and the behaviors of principals, district leaders, parents, business leaders, and the community. We clearly recognize the importance of teachers to the success of our students in school after school across this country. But here are the questions everyone concerned with the success of their community's schools needs to ask:

- Do we treat teachers as the important people they are in our children's lives?

- Do we give them the time they need to be professionals?

- Do our teachers have the things they need to move our children to achieve to the standards and demonstrate it on the accountability tests?

- Does the job of teacher look more like assembly-line work?

- Do we pay them what they are worth to our community or just what we must to keep classrooms filled?

- Do we demand that all teachers have the talent, knowledge, and skills to teach our own children?

Once we feel good about the answers to these questions, we can begin to feel better about our community's — and our country's — capacity to maintain a position of global leadership.

For example, economic prosperity in the global marketplace currently depends on graduates who have shown talent and enthusiasm for careers in math and science. There are thousands of outstanding math and science teachers in our schools, but we need many more. That fact can put enormous pressure on schools to just hire the best candidates available, rather than holding out for individuals who have the talent, knowledge, and skills to fully engage their students. In most cases, recruiting such individuals is incredibly difficult because we don't have satisfactory answers to the questions above.

The result is that many students don't pursue math and science as careers because they are left with the impression that the subject is flat and uninspiring or because their teachers don't have the capacity to recognize the spark of talent within them. This leads to a shortage of math and science graduates emerging from college to teach or to become the engineers and scientists we need to compete globally.

So, what can be done? We can make hiring the right teachers a priority and view the process of hiring the same way pro football teams view the NFL draft, with the recognition that our future depends on the right talent. In addition to focusing on the questions above, for teachers in high-demand areas — and for math and science teachers in particular — we should pull out all the stops, with compensation, developmental, and advancement opportunities that make these positions particularly attractive.[37]

CHAPTER EIGHT

ENGAGED PRINCIPALS: HELPING THE HEROES

"If your actions inspire others to dream more, learn more, do more and become more, you are a leader."
— *John Quincy Adams*

In one Midwestern school district, all of the schools are ranked annually on the basis of student test scores. Not surprisingly, the schools with the highest scores usually have the *lowest* percentage of students on free and reduced-cost lunch plans (i.e., the fewest low-income students).

One school, however, stands out as an exception to this rule. Sixty-three percent of the students at Washington Elementary are on free and reduced-cost lunch plans — one of the highest percentages in the district. Yet, each year, Washington's students rank in the top half of 36 elementary schools on standardized tests. The success at Washington didn't come easily, and there's a story behind how it was achieved.

Jim Wilson became principal of Washington Elementary in 1997. At that time, Washington served one of the poorer sections of the city, with a very diverse student population. Its staff was jaded, and student achievement was low. These problems were apparent to Wilson when the superintendent asked him to become the school's principal, but nonetheless, he accepted the challenge of turning it around.

Wilson found it to be a bigger task than he had anticipated. The community has a large immigrant population, which meant that learning English was the first step for many students. Beyond this hurdle, the staff seemed resigned to assume that low achievement would be the norm. There were remedial classes at every grade level; in fact, in the majority of classrooms, more students were in the remedial reading groups than the "regular" groups, and very few were identified as "gifted." Four counselors and a social worker worked furiously to handle student problems.

Wilson's approach at Washington turned the school around. He began to change the attitudes of staff members and parents by focusing on: 1) a powerful vision of what the school could *become*, rather than what it was, 2) an emphasis on getting the right people in place, and 3) a determination to develop the capacity of the school's staff and create a new culture to deal more effectively with its problems.

As a matter of fact, the school's preoccupation with its own problems was one of the first hurdles it had to overcome. Wilson first reduced the four counselors' positions to one. "Having four counselors simply meant that we were identifying more problems," he explains. The three other counselors became reading teachers, and reading became the primary focus of every teacher at every grade level.

The second step was to focus the staff on *teaching*. It wasn't that the teachers didn't care about students. To the contrary, they frequently used their own resources to provide coats, boots, and even food and shelter for some students and their families. But looking out for their students' basic needs took a physical and emotional toll that sapped the teachers' energy. "The counselor, social worker, and I had to concentrate on providing what students needed in and out of school," Wilson says, "so that teachers could focus on teaching reading and math."

Wilson quickly found that although many teachers bought into the idea of higher expectations for students, others simply wouldn't. Some, in fact, voiced outright opposition. For those teachers, Wilson suggested transfers. Others failed to live up to the heightened expectations for teachers. In response, Wilson began challenging and documenting poor performance, which usually led to the departure of those teachers as well. The increased turnover meant the process of selecting new teachers took on major importance each spring, and Wilson established a process for identifying the right talents in new teachers.

Making it clear that he alone didn't have all the answers, Wilson constantly reiterated the common mission of promoting student achievement to all staff members and offered them a bright new picture of their students' potential. Asking for staff members' ideas and involvement, he encouraged them to take ownership of a variety of new initiatives.

Perhaps most importantly, he acted on their suggestions regarding the school's budget. Wilson listened, for example, to the concerns of a core group of staff members who felt that to learn new ways to approach students, they would need more development opportunities. Schools in this district are allowed to distribute their total budget dollars to meet their needs, so Wilson and his staff took advantage of this flexibility by dedicating a larger percentage of the school's budget to staff development than other district schools did. To this day, Washington invests more in staff development than most schools its size.

Washington's success sprang from the efforts of a uniquely talented principal and an equally talented teaching staff. Wilson, like other outstanding principals, was able to unify teachers and administrators around a common vision of what the school and its students could become. The result was a climate of success that sets Washington apart from other schools. And Washington's students have become the winners that the school's staff knows they can be.

THE ROLE OF KNOWLEDGE, SKILLS, AND TALENTS

As with teachers, there is a widely held assumption that the primary criterion for excellence in the principal role is the right combination of knowledge and skills. To be sure, every principal must possess a great deal of knowledge and many skills these days, perhaps more of each than ever before. But the critical attributes that set truly outstanding principals apart from the rest stem from innate qualities like their beliefs, motivation, ways of relating, adaptability, and orientation toward continuous improvement. These talents, *combined* with knowledge and skills, create strengths that lead to outstanding performance.

Because these talents are so natural to them, in many cases, outstanding principals don't fully recognize their role in making them successful. Nevertheless, great principals intuitively distinguish between those aspects of running the school that play to their strengths and those that are better left to others. They delegate the latter tasks and activities whenever possible, refining over time their own sense of self-awareness and surrounding themselves with staff members who possess complementary talents.

We can teach someone like Jim Wilson what principals need to know, but we can't give him the talents required of an outstanding principal. At the same time, while broad lessons like those listed above can be drawn from the turnaround at Washington Elementary, its success can't be exactly reproduced in other schools. Excellence comes from using knowledge and skills in unique ways based on the particular blend of talents present in the school, starting with those of the principal. Another outstanding principal may achieve the same outcomes, but the processes she uses to get there will look a little different.

A person whose natural talents match the demands of the principal role will grow in the position. On the other hand, the single most common mistake regarding professional development is the attempt to "teach" innate qualities to someone for whom they are simply not present. Attempts to compensate for a poor selection decision with additional training are rarely successful. New demands on principals have raised the bar for necessary knowledge and skills — but they have also raised the bar for principal *talent*.

MANAGERS AND LEADERS

The experience at Washington Elementary demonstrates how most principals' jobs have changed in recent years and what is expected of principals today. The extent of this change varies by individual schools and districts. But for many current principals, their role earlier in their career was very different than it is today. It consisted largely of managing the building, which meant supervising the curricular and instruction program, the staff, the students, budgets, food service, transportation, and extracurricular activities (although not necessarily in that order).

In many schools, principals were evaluated entirely by procedural criteria: the degree to which staff and students followed the rules, the cleanliness of the school, the efficient operation of buses, and the availability of extracurricular activities for students' participation and parents' enjoyment.[1] The fact that principals were usually judged on such measures meant that's where most of them placed their emphasis.

Improving instruction was an important goal, but few principals lost their jobs over it.

Today, all of those traditional expectations remain, but the priorities have changed. Students' performance on statewide accountability tests has become increasingly important to the success of the principal, the school, and the school district. Pressure to improve test scores requires that principals be more involved in analyzing student performance data with teachers, coordinating teacher efforts, arranging for staff development opportunities, and working with an expanded array of community members and business partners. Education researchers Joseph Murphy and Philip Hallinger describe this shift in terms once reserved for the business arena: "bureaucratic accountability (compliance with rules and regulations) gives way to accountability for outcomes (student performance) and customer satisfaction (parents choosing to enroll their children in a given school)."[2]

In most schools, principals play two competing roles, simultaneously acting as managers and leaders. Management most frequently involves efficiently and effectively maintaining the status quo by making the organization run smoothly.[3] Stability is often considered a hallmark of good management. Leadership, on the other hand, implies doing what's necessary to keep an organization moving forward, constantly developing to meet shifting demands. Hence, leadership occurs primarily in a context of change.[4]

Many labels are used to describe different forms of leadership, but they all have a similar goal: to supply direction within an organization and spur individuals to move in that direction.[5] Fundamentally, leadership requires influencing the "goals, motivations, and actions" of others.[6] Previously, the role of principal was primarily that of an overseer, requiring the talents of a good manager. But the increased emphasis on accountability has shifted the role further toward the domain of "leader" — and the talents required to be an excellent principal have changed accordingly.

The pressure to improve students' learning outcomes has led many principals to take on new responsibilities, but principals still must balance their management and leadership roles. That's partly why the position demands high levels of talent in a number of specific areas. One East Coast principal described the management and leadership demands she faces and the difficulties those expectations create: "Every single day you make a choice. Do you [focus on being] the instructional leader of the school, or do you make a dent in the paperwork, take care of things like stocking toilet paper, fixing leaky faucets, and all of that? I go home sometimes feeling very guilty that I did not spend enough time with the kids and teachers."

Principals as Managers

Principals serve as managers by their very position. Their job entails mediating the differing demands of students, teachers, parents, community members, district administrators, and state policymakers. A principal who is a good manager makes the school run smoothly, creating an orderly environment in which learning can take place and ensuring that the basic needs of the school community's members are met. Good management is evident to students, teachers, parents, and supervisors in the substance *and* the image of the school. Without it, there is an unsettling feeling that the school is constantly on the verge of chaos.

But truly *great* management requires principals to know and understand each staff member in ways that relatively few principals do today. The authors of *First, Break All the Rules* summarize Gallup's study of 80,000 great managers by pointing to four fundamental activities common among them: They know how to 1) select the right person for the job, 2) set the right expectations for that person, 3) motivate her, and 4) develop her. Great managers are described as "catalysts" who promote heightened performance by "speeding up the reaction between the employee's talents and the company's goals, and between the employee's talents and the customers' needs."[7] Great managers help each person find a talent-to-role fit and understand what's required of them. They also make sure each employee receives regular recognition and is growing within his or her role. And they do all of this one employee at a time.

If any particular group of employees is especially in need of that kind of support, it's teachers, with their mission-driven mindset and physically and mentally demanding jobs. But too often, teachers indicate that those aspects of great management are conspicuously absent from their schools. As we'll see, outstanding principals build a positive environment by constantly communicating to teachers and other staff members that they are valued.

Principals as Leaders

Most principals — and *all* great principals — have always to some extent been leaders as well as managers. Effective principals introduce many changes to the organizational structure and processes in their schools in response to new student, employee, or community needs. These innovations require influencing the goals and behaviors of staff members and community leaders.

It's not surprising that the focus of principals' leadership activities is on student learning — it is, after all, the goal underlying every aspect of effective schools. Reform efforts intended to improve learning depend on the principal's success in building constituencies by helping teachers and parents understand, accept, and support changes, wherever those changes originated. The principal must then establish the conditions for successful implementation, assisting staff members as they acquire the pertinent knowledge and skills and use their greatest talents in new ways to make the changes work.[8] None of this is easy; the principal must be a highly effective consensus builder and motivator if such change is to succeed.

The balance between management and leadership activities is just one example of the growing complexity of the principal's role. Never an easy position in which to succeed, its demands seem to grow with each subsequent year. "[Principals] are pulled in so many different directions," said Patty, a teacher in one of Gallup's focus groups. "I would never consider going into administration because I see what types of conditions they're working under." Recognizing these pressures, some observers have even suggested that the job has become too big for one individual.[9] But so far, there have been few serious efforts to implement alternatives to traditional staffing structures in public schools. Most principals continue to live with a job that is as complex and demanding as any in education.

ARE PRINCIPALS IMPORTANT?

Do principals make a big difference in the success of schools? In 2001, Gallup asked 1,000 American citizens essentially that question. They replied with an emphatic "yes." Specifically, the survey asked: *Using a five-point scale with "5" as extremely important, "4" as very important, "3" as fairly important, "2" as of little importance, and "1" as not important at all, how would you rate the importance of the principal to your neighborhood school?* Eighty-five percent of the respondents said "extremely important" or "very important," the two highest categories."[10] A 2003 survey by Public Agenda found that 62% of the superintendents surveyed said that moving a successful principal to a struggling school was "an excellent way to turn around a school with proven talent."[11]

That perceived importance probably stems in part from the fact that so much that happens in schools requires the inspiration, communication, leadership, and support of the principal. Researchers typically agree with the public's view and cite principals as second only to teachers among the school factors central to student learning.[12] Moreover, the impact of a talented principal is greatest in difficult situations. Recent research suggests that it's almost impossible to turn troubled schools around without a talented and skilled leader.[13] Data that studied the relationship between student and principal performance in one district suggested that "The quickest way to change the effectiveness of a school, for better or worse, is to change the principal."[14]

PRINCIPALS AND STUDENT LEARNING

Research studies investigating the effect of principals on student learning go back almost 30 years. In the late 1970s and 1980s, these efforts concentrated on "effective schools," and the data suggested that the quality of the principal as an "instructional leader" was related to the effectiveness of the school. The term *instructional leader* gained widespread use, even though these studies failed to identify a definitive group of leadership behaviors common to effective principals.[15]

It became commonly accepted that school principals needed to be experts in curriculum and instruction.[16] Researchers looked for evidence indicating that principals directly affected teachers' behaviors in the classroom through practices like clinical supervision.[17] This approach called for the principal to serve as a "master teacher," frequently visiting classrooms to monitor teachers and give them specific suggestions for improving their instruction.[18] It bolstered the assumption that teaching strategies could best be improved by exercising control over what teachers did in the classroom.[19] In other words, principals should closely supervise teachers' use of a prescribed curriculum and specific instructional techniques.

By the mid-1990s, researchers had begun to question that assumption. A sizable number of increasingly sophisticated research efforts turned up little evidence that the principal had a *direct* effect on students' learning outcomes. In fact, the most recent review of such studies notes that "Rarely does this form of research find any effects at all."[20]

The earlier research had gotten the true nature of the principal's contribution wrong. Indeed, there is a link between the work of the principal and student success — but it occurs predominantly via principals' support of and collaboration with talented teachers.[21] Researchers found a much better fit to productive schools using models that more heavily incorporated collaborative activities and staff participation in school improvements.[22]

Chain of Student Success

The idea that principals drive student success by supporting teacher talent makes intuitive sense. As Richard Ingersoll notes in *Who Controls Teachers' Work? Power and Accountability in America's Schools*, no matter how much administrative authority they are subject to, teachers alone exercise real control over what happens in their classrooms.

In other words, while teachers have very little influence on many of the key decisions that determine what they do, they have a great deal of responsibility for implementing those decisions. Because the task of teaching represents such a complex mix of clients, products, and technologies, schools are unusually dependent on the cooperation, motivation, and commitment of those actually entrusted with the work — teachers.[23]

Steven Bossert and his fellow researchers at the Far West Laboratory for Educational Research and Development were a decade ahead of their time when they suggested in 1982 that principal effects occur indirectly through teachers. In "The Instructional Management Role of the Principal," Bossert and his colleagues suggested that principals affect student learning by influencing two major elements: "Instructional Organization" and "School Climate." The model Bossert and his colleagues proposed (Figure 9) has served as a basis for research from the mid-1990s through today. Further refinements of that model have resulted in a more sophisticated and complete theory,[24] but the original model provides an overview:

FIGURE 9

Bossert's Framework for Examining Instructional Management

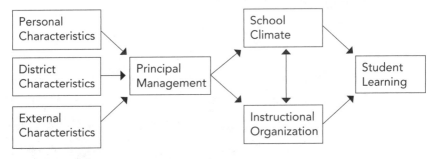

Source: Bossert, S., Dwyer, D., Rowan, B., & Lee, G. The instructional management role of the principal. *Education Administration Quarterly, 18* (3), pp. 34-64, copyright © 1982 by Sage Publications. Reprinted by permission of Sage Publications, Inc.

Bossert and his colleagues theorized that three types of contextual characteristics influence the range of a principal's behavior. *Personal characteristics* refer to the principal's training and experience (though not characteristics indicative of talent). *District characteristics* include factors imposed by a principal's district, such as whether innovations at the individual school level are encouraged or whether all schools must introduce district-mandated innovations. *External characteristics* describe aspects such as state funding, parental involvement, and the socioeconomic makeup of the student body.

In Bossert's model, principals affect student learning by continuously improving the climate and instructional organization of the school. School climate includes the essential "intangibles": the values and expectations of the staff, the presence or absence of supportive relationships, and maintenance of an orderly environment focused on learning. Instructional organization includes more overt policy-oriented elements such as class size, student grouping practices, curriculum, and systems for ensuring that teachers get regular feedback. Bossert theorized that the background, beliefs, and behaviors of principals are key determinants of all these factors. Their cumulative effect influences teachers' performance in the classroom, thereby affecting students' learning outcomes as well.[25]

A New Model

In their comprehensive review of research for the Learning from Leadership Project, Kenneth Leithwood and his colleagues created a similar but more sophisticated construct. Their model represents a growing consensus among researchers. The major difference between it and Bossert's model from two decades prior is a more direct recognition of the degree to which differences in students' backgrounds and family situations produce differences in learning outcomes.

Leithwood and his colleagues suggest that there are three essentials for effective leadership at the school or district level. The researchers caution that these basics "are necessary but not sufficient in almost all situations," but they do point to key areas in which principals can assess their efforts. The three areas are: setting direction (establishing

187

goals and expectations), developing people (suggesting new ideas and instructional approaches), and redesigning the organization (promoting collaborative change).[26]

Leithwood and his colleagues build on this foundation to identify areas in which principals' efforts have the greatest potential return. Principals should focus, they say, on "school mission and goals, culture, participation in decision-making, and relationships with parents and the wider community" as potentially powerful determinants of student learning.[27]

HIRING THE RIGHT PEOPLE

Both of these important perspectives on the principal's role underscore the idea that principals foster student learning by supporting other people, primarily teachers. The idea that the most important goals of schools must ultimately be carried out by teachers brings us back to the importance of hiring great teachers. The authors of *First, Break All the Rules* summarized the position of managers — including principals and other school administrators — this way:

> As a manager, you might think that you have more control, but you don't. You actually have less control than the people who report to you. Each individual employee can decide what to do and what not to do. He can decide the hows, the whens, and the with whoms. For good or for ill, he can make things happen.

> You can't. You can't make anything happen. All you can do is influence, motivate, berate, or cajole in the hope that most of your people will do what you ask of them. This isn't control. This is remote control. And it is coupled, nonetheless, with all of the accountability for the team's performance.[28]

All principals understand what it's like to bear responsibility with a sense of only "remote" control, but this is the lot of any manager, whether in schools or the private sector. Outstanding principals understand the need to focus on areas in which they exert a high degree of influence and are most likely to foster a great working environment.

The hiring of talented teachers is one of those areas. Participants in Gallup's focus groups with outstanding principals noted a number of times that their school "is not for everyone." What they meant was that teachers who failed to embrace and progress toward the vision put forth by the school community, and in particular those who would not raise their expectations for students, could not be overlooked, because only with everyone working toward it could that vision be attained.

Tony Bagshaw, the Ohio principal I mentioned earlier, described five core values that he shares with his staff. "This is what this school is about," he said, "and we will never give on these under any circumstances.

"Number 1 is love children. As a parent, I am sending you something that is precious to me. Care about those kids so deeply that you view them just like you view your own.

"Number 2 is take care of parents. They pay the bills. We have to understand that parents are our partners, and when we lose them, it creates havoc for the district from that point forward.

"Number 3 is be artful in your practice. Make sure that in year 28, you're better than you were in year 27. I expect all of us to continue to learn and grow in the science of teaching.

"Number 4 is be a positive contributor to our school culture. We're all in this boat together, and we're all equally accountable for our culture. If there are concerns or quarrels, let's talk and resolve them.

"Number 5 is be loyal. I am fiercely loyal to the people that work with me, and I expect the same from them. We are like a family."

In his study of Dallas Public Schools, Robert Mendro discovered that principals in the higher achieving schools were similarly unwilling to hire or retain teachers who didn't meet certain non-negotiable criteria for quality: "Ineffective teachers were expected to change, or they were removed."[29]

But not all principals commit to such a policy; some are constrained by a lack of resolve, others by external circumstances such as minimal district support. A Public Agenda survey in 2003 found that only 36% of teachers rated their principals "excellent" or "good" at "moving ineffective teachers out of their building."[30]

In *Good to Great*, Jim Collins describes an interesting sequence that occurred in companies that moved from being good to great in their fields. Collins and his researchers fully expected the good-to-great leaders to begin their changes by establishing a new vision and set of goals for the company. Instead, they found that the companies' leaders "*first* got the right people on the bus, the wrong people off the bus, and the right people in the right seats — and *then* they figured out where to drive it. The old adage 'People are your most important asset' turns out to be wrong. People are not your most important asset. The *right* people are."[31]

Discussing the cultural makeover at Adlai Stevenson High School in suburban Illinois, Kent Peterson and Terrence Deal describe how the new principal changed the school's recruiting standards to match its renewed emphasis on student success:

> Now the school hired only teachers who had a clear sense of what they were trying to accomplish, who connected their purpose with the experiences and interests

of their students, and who motivated and inspired students to believe in themselves and their ability to be successful in school. Above all else, a school truly committed to every student's success needed teachers who were willing to accept responsibility for students' learning.[32]

Gallup's research clearly indicates that outstanding principals place a heavy emphasis on finding the right people to work in the right places with students. That usually means looking for specific talents. "I look for people that, when they say 'teaching,' their eyes light up," a principal in one of Gallup's focus groups said. "I think you can teach teachers to teach, but you can't teach people to be caring."

STUDYING SUCCESS

Once the right people are part of the school, how do great principals maximize their contribution? Gallup's principal research follows the same principle of studying success as the teacher research described in the previous chapter. Over nearly 20 years, school districts from across the United States and Canada have participated in a number of studies to identify the talents that are consistently found in outstanding principals. Gallup's standard research processes include both listening to what the best principals have to say about their work and analyzing statistics on the relationship between particular talents and overall principal performance.

The qualitative studies include focus groups with principals nominated as "outstanding" by district supervisors, university professors who work with principals, and award-winning principals. Several such studies were conducted in Alabama, California, Illinois, Nebraska, New Jersey, and Virginia in 2001. The focus-group principals represented a variety of backgrounds, including differing district and school sizes (school sizes ranged from 100 to 3,500 students), school types (elementary, middle, and high school), and community settings (rural, suburban, and urban). The participants were also diverse with regard to gender, experience level, age, and race. But despite all these differences, they shared many similar beliefs, attitudes, and approaches.

Input from the focus groups assisted Gallup researchers in developing hypotheses to be tested with a broader sample in a 2003 study. Gallup's research interest focuses on the greatest talents of outstanding principals — their most naturally recurring patterns of thought, feeling, and behavior that can be productively applied. Our experience with outstanding performers, both in education and in the private sector, underscores an observation made by Leithwood: "Our interest in leaders' cognitive and affective states is based on the simple premise that what they do (leaders' practices) depends on what they think and how they feel."[33] In other words, those practices that *feel* most comfortable and intuitive — i.e., those that are best aligned with their most natural talents — are the ones principals and other leaders are most likely to use.

Three broad categories similar to those applied to teachers in Chapter 7 help organize Gallup's findings on the consistencies in what outstanding principals do:

- *Motivating* describes how principals inspire themselves and their staff members to constantly strive for improved student outcomes.

- *Relating* encompasses the ways in which outstanding principals establish relationships with and garner support from teachers, students, parents, and community members, and the ways they foster teachers' growth and development as professionals.

- *Empowering the staff* explains how principals provide
  resources for growth and ensure that staff members
  have the opportunity to participate in the school's ongoing
  development.

All three dimensions affect the emotional engagement of students, parents, and staff members with the school.

MOTIVATING

Nancy Oberst is a wonderful example of a principal who motivates her staff through a powerful vision of what their school can accomplish. By all accounts, Oberst and her staff have created a truly outstanding learning environment at Liberty Elementary in inner-city Omaha.

They didn't start with much. When the prospect of starting a new school in the neighborhood arose, it met with a great deal of skepticism due to the area's high crime rate and high proportion of non-English-speaking families. But Oberst had a powerful vision of the school as a center of inclusiveness and positive change, which she shared with prospective new teachers right from the start. "I would kind of spin my vision for them during the interview," she remembers. "And I could kind of tell just by the conversation if they had ever thought about this before, if it was something they found intriguing, if they loved children and diversity and all the things that go with an urban situation. I told them there would be some obstacles to overcome, but that it was going to be this safe, great place, and that we wouldn't even be able to kick the kids out of here at night."

Oberst's vision strongly appealed to teachers who wanted to make a difference, resulting in a highly dedicated staff. "I even tried to discourage some people who wanted to transfer in from other schools," she recalls. "Truly I said, you know, I was as bleak as I could be about what might be, and I could not deter them. And as it worked out, they are what they said they were, you know?" And they're succeeding: despite the fact that 78% of Liberty's students are classified as "economically disadvantaged" and many live in homes where English isn't spoken, they're not far behind the district averages for student performance. In 2005, 63% of Liberty's fourth graders met or exceeded standards on state reading tests, and 82% did so on state math tests.[34] But more importantly, the faith and resolve of Oberst and Liberty's teachers have infused fresh optimism to a neighborhood badly in need of it.

Sustaining high levels of motivation in the face of all the demands placed on America's schools requires inspiration. Schools can't improve to the extent that we need them to unless those working in them feel a deep, emotional commitment to that change. That inspiration begins with a simple, compelling purpose. In the case of schools, the natural altruism of most talented teachers both increases the importance of that clearly communicated purpose and amplifies its effect. If it taps into and expands on their personal sense of mission, a principal's message can inspire many teachers to unusual levels of achievement.

The research literature on principals is rife with references to the need for creating a shared sense of purpose within the school. But three studies are particularly noteworthy because they examine the degree to which that consistent message affects learning outcomes.

- The earliest, a 1987 study of elementary schools, found that the largest gains in reading and math occurred in schools where teachers felt that the principals communicated a vision for instructional goal setting, planning, and performance standards.[35]

- A 1996 study of elementary schools found a relationship between student learning outcomes and the degree to which a school's mission expressly emphasized two things: 1) students' opportunities to learn, and 2) high expectations for student achievement.[36]

- Most recently, an eight-year study that culminated in 2000 cited among the key factors influencing student achievement principals' ability to describe a "vision in outline" as a way to inspire staff members while still giving them room to participate in the formation of school-wide goals.[37]

Let's look a little more closely at how effective principals motivate teachers and other staff members with a compelling mission, a vision of the future, and a clear set of goals.

Mission to Vision to Goals

The words "mission" and "vision" are often used interchangeably, but the concepts are more usefully seen as separate but related. *Mission* refers to the purpose of an enterprise, the core values that it serves. *Vision* is communicated as a verbal picture of the future state of the organization and those it serves once that mission is fulfilled. *Goals* are the mile markers along the way to that envisioned destination. They are the concrete steps needed to carry out the mission.

Dr. Martin Luther King Jr.'s historic "I Have a Dream" speech offers a good illustration of the distinction between mission and vision. The *mission* behind Dr. King's efforts is working for social justice, for the idea that members of all races should be given equal opportunities. The *vision* Dr. King so vividly described was an American society that accepted little boys and girls, white and black, on the content of their character. It was a better future exemplified by his final line, "Free at last!" Dr. King's specific *goals* at the time of his famous speech were an end to segregation laws in the South and a federal voting rights act.

Now let's look more closely at how the mission to vision to goals progression can foster engagement in schools. Effective principals use mission and vision to establish important values that are general enough to be embraced fully by everyone but that are also action-oriented and adaptable enough to have an effect on the learning process every day in every classroom.

Mission

Mission is the engine at the heart of any successful organization. It allows workers to identify with the organization, justifies their sacrifice and commitment, and infuses their work with lasting meaning. Usually altruistic in some respect, an effective mission sparks employees' pride and gives them a reason to show up every day beyond their own self-interest.[38] A general mission for schools might be to provide all students with the knowledge and skills necessary to be productive citizens.

But great principals often highlight more specific elements of mission, galvanizing their staff around a defining belief. For Nancy Oberst, that belief was the value of diversity and inclusiveness; she and her staff used that belief to turn what was formerly seen as a liability into an advantage. For Stephen Hockett, an award-winning principal we'll meet a little later in this chapter, it was a commitment to a level of collaboration among teachers, administrators, and the community that is rarely seen in America's schools.

Finding ways to bring the school's mission to life is a hallmark of outstanding principals. Using it as the basis for a compelling vision is one way they commonly do that.

Vision

While mission describes why we do things, vision is a vivid picture of the results of our efforts. A compelling vision engages employees' emotions and resonates with their deeply held beliefs. "What kind of place do you think you should help create for the kids?" said a principal in one of Gallup's focus groups. "I think that commitment to kids starts from the vision piece."

Developing that vision typically starts with the principal, but it doesn't end there. As with a school's mission, once the principal and (usually) a small group of staff members express a vision for the future, it must be fine-tuned by input from teachers and parents so that it truly resonates with those who strive, day by day, to achieve it.

A school's vision tends to pull the individuals within it together. Penny Bender Sebring and Anthony Bryk found in their study of Chicago schools that involving others in forming the school's vision contributes to an overall feeling of participation and inclusiveness within the school.[39] Sharing a vision creates a bond among group members because of its emotional appeal. A group really doesn't function as a team until the individuals who make it up are deeply committed to a common end and understand the goals needed to get there.[40] Once that point is reached, the school community may truly function as a team for the first time.

Goals

If a vision refers to the organization's ideal destination, goals are the practical road map that makes that destination seem reachable. A given school's goals might include the number of students achieving at a higher level this year than last year. These goals can then be broken down further to student success in a particular classroom. At that point, the vision ceases to be abstract for a teacher, taking on the faces of her students. But it's up to the principal to make the connection between vision and goals by regularly calling attention to it.

Expectations

Mission to vision to goals is a path that invariably leads to elevated expectations. One point of commonality between the perspectives of educators and opinion leaders on school reform is the idea that for schools at any level to improve student learning, teachers must maintain high expectations of themselves and their students. A West Coast principal in a Gallup focus group said this about expectations: "What we believe about people is what they will become. If we believe that our staff will be successful, if we believe that our children will be successful, then they will aspire to reach that level."

It's rarely easy to do, but the more effectively the mission of a school (or any organization) is integrated into its day-to-day expectations, the more effectively it will drive engagement and other positive outcomes. A 1996 study of Tennessee elementary schools found that there is a chain leading from clear and constant communication of mission, to more time devoted to instruction, to higher teacher expectations, and finally, to higher student achievement.[41]

The translation of a school's vision to more specific goals is where the principal and other administrative staff should allow ample room for the unique contributions of teacher talents. A 2000 study of Chicago's public schools, for example, concluded that effective principals "set high standards of teaching" while simultaneously supporting innovation and risk-taking.[42] Each teacher will see the vision slightly differently and come up with his own set of specific goals on the path toward it. This lack of uniformity may make mediocre leaders uneasy, but great principals understand that the development of such diverse approaches means staff members have internalized the vision and are committed to attaining it.

RELATING

Outstanding principals successfully relate to a variety of constituencies, including teachers, students, parents, and community members, in myriad ways. The most obvious is simply by not being afraid to show they care. Great principals typically show a great deal of personal concern for staff members and students. This builds trust and breaks down barriers to communication.[43] "Nobody tells you that 99% of the job is dealing with relationships," said one Midwestern principal. Said another from the West Coast: "A lot of being principal has to do with relationship building and being able to connect at a personal level with students and teachers." That ability isn't something that can be taught or gained from experience.

Caring and Trust

Teachers often describe genuine caring as the single most important quality of a good principal. In Gallup's focus groups, teachers from elementary schools or smaller secondary schools tended to feel that the principal had a huge impact on their feelings about the job. Those in larger secondary schools usually interacted more often with a vice principal or department head. Elementary school teachers were more likely than secondary school teachers to agree with the statement, "My principal, or someone at my school, seems to care about me as a person."

But almost all the teachers we spoke with noted that having a close, trusting relationship with an administrator made a dramatic difference in their day-to-day lives. "I came from a small school setting in Louisiana where there were less than a hundred teachers, and the principal, every holiday, handwrote us a letter saying how important we were and got gifts specific for us," said Tammy, a middle school teacher. "I moved — otherwise I think I would have retired with her, just because I felt like she was a confidante. . . . I have friends that stay in the poorest parish in Louisiana and take the lowest pay just to stay with her."

Two research studies highlight the importance of personal relationships between teachers and school administrators. In the previously mentioned study of Chicago schools, the researchers found that higher performing schools exhibited a sense of "social trust" between staff members, parents, and the principal. That trust, they observed, nurtured cooperative relationships among the adults in the school community.[44] Secondly, in their effort to test the influence of relationships, David Aspy and Flora Roebuck found positive and significant links between the quality of principals' relationships with teachers and the quality of teachers' relationships with students.[45]

Finally, caring relationships between teachers and administrators make communication of needs more likely. Maxine, a high school art teacher, said, "[In] my first year at [my current school], the principal actually came in and sat down and just observed what was going on, not taking notes or anything like that, not evaluating me, but just seeing me as a person and how I interacted with kids. As a result of that one visit, I received quite a few supplies that I used throughout the year. And I received a personal thank you at the end of the school year from that particular principal."

Encouraging Development

Making a priority of helping staff members learn and grow is another powerful relating tool essential to great principals. In *The Differentiated Classroom*, Carol Ann Tomlinson calls attention to the importance of this form of relating. "It is a curiosity of teaching that no two days are alike," Tomlinson notes, "but, if we are not careful, all the days can take on a deadening sameness. We must remember that we have every opportunity to transform ourselves and our practice, just as we have every opportunity to stagnate, remaining much the same teachers we were when we began."[46] As noted earlier, great teachers are avid learners. They need intellectual stimulation and opportunities to explore to remain fully engaged in their jobs.

Outstanding principals understand that helping provide teachers with such growth opportunities is important to ensuring that their students will grow as well. In their 2004 report "How Leadership Influences Student Learning," Kenneth Leithwood and his colleagues maintain that developing people is the second basic task of leadership. They suggest that student learning benefits when principals stimulate teachers' thinking and reflection, individualize support, and suggest instructional models.[47] Similarly, in summarizing studies of Chicago schools, Penny Bender Sebring and Anthony Bryk found that schools in which principals invested significant time and resources in teachers' professional development were more likely to see improvements in student learning outcomes.[48]

Promoting staff members' development obviously helps expand their repertoire of skills and knowledge. But the point here is that it also elevates the teacher-administrator relationship to a highly personal partnership. Most of us can think of a time when someone saw a spark of talent in us even before we did and helped fan it into a flame. In challenging us, this person offered insight and a high level of respect — and created an expectation that we *wanted* to meet.[49] Many of our successes in life can be traced back to these pivotal relationships.

Outstanding principals create these opportunities for teachers, sometimes without knowing it. For them, it's just part of the job. Often, we see certain schools in a district move disproportionate numbers of people to all kinds of leadership roles within the district. When this happens, we know that there is a principal at that school who is functioning as a talent scout and development partner.

In a qualitative study of 800 teachers from the Southeast, Midwest, and Northwest, Jo and Joseph Blase identified two major themes that teachers tend to associate with effective principal leadership. "Talking with teachers to promote reflection" prompted self-examination by teachers and made them more aware of the effectiveness of their teaching practices. Principals provided teachers with ideas, feedback, models, opinions, and recognition as part of these discussions. Secondly, "promoting professional growth" meant ensuring that teachers routinely had the opportunity to learn new methods, talk and share with other teachers, and create new programs.[50]

Unfortunately, just as many teachers fail to differentiate instruction for students, many principals and district leaders make the critical mistake of assuming that all teachers can arrive at student outcomes in the same way. Consequently, they believe the right development opportunities should produce similar improvement in all teachers. As a result, much training for teachers comes from a single model, shaped by district goals, and delivered in group settings with little or no assessment of whether the knowledge and skills they offer are aligned with an individual teacher's particular talents.

A 2003 Public Agenda study asked more than 1,300 teachers whether their school's professional development program helped them be a better teacher. Responses were about evenly split between yes and no. The authors of the report noted that in focus groups, many teachers described the programs they'd been to as "one-size-fits-all." One veteran teacher said, "We've been victims of the cookie cutter for several years now."[51]

Gallup's research on successful managers in the private and nonprofit sectors[52] indicates that these managers understand and use the differences in employees to build their organizations. They try to help each person become more and more of who he already is. Furthermore, modifying the Golden Rule in an important way, they're careful to treat each person as *that person* would like to be treated, according to who he or she is. Beyond the general expectations and standards that must apply to everyone, these managers approach each employee differently based on his or her talents and needs.

Outstanding principals are no different. They realize that it's virtually a guarantee that two great teachers will use different approaches, styles, and talents to achieve similar outcomes. The best explanation of one teacher's success may be her sheer dedication, the sense of calling that causes her students to work harder for her. But another's success may be more directly linked to his talent for creating unconventional new learning strategies that foster student enthusiasm and performance.

Great principals are sensitive to these differences. They take the time to understand them and then work differently with each teacher. It's not an easy task given the current demands for standards and conformity. "There are some days when I'm feeling that pressure more than others," says Liberty Elementary's Oberst, "but I try to keep it off the backs of my teachers. And I try to keep it away from our day-to-day operation because that kind of feeling that my kids can't get to the 74th percentile on all the tests is something that will erode the learning that can take place and overshadow what is really important, which is the real broad learning, not the specific learning for the test. It makes us small is what it does."

EMPOWERING THE STAFF

It's doubtful that schools can dramatically improve without strong leadership, but principals can't change schools by themselves. Positive and enduring change occurs when the principal gathers a critical mass of teachers committed to a new future for students and provides those teachers with the support they need to achieve it. This support comes in large part in the form of encouraging collaboration throughout the school, keeping everyone focused on teaching and learning, and providing the resources teachers need.

In the mid-1990s, the area served by Hunters Woods Elementary School outside of Washington, D.C., was becoming very racially and economically diverse, with a growing number of low-income, minority, and non-English-speaking students. In 1997, the school board decided to turn Hunters Woods into a magnet school to try to attract high-achieving students from other neighborhoods as positive role models for the school's disadvantaged students.

Stephen Hockett joined Hunters Woods as an assistant principal in 1996; then he became principal in 1999. He estimates that in its first year as a magnet school, fewer than 100 parents applied for their children to attend, but by the 2004-2005 school year, that number had grown to more than 800. What's more, despite the challenges inherent in a school with such a diverse student population, Hockett never had a hiring problem. Quite the opposite — experienced and new teachers alike were scrambling to transfer to Hunters Woods.

Why? The school is highly innovative, with multi-age groupings and constant collaboration between teachers and classes. It is also a community school, with a high level of involvement from parents, local artists, and the surrounding business community. But Hockett feels the biggest reason is that Hunters Woods was set up to allow talented teachers to elevate their game, to collaborate and innovate to a degree not possible in more traditional schools.

"It sounds so corny, but I think it was really about creating a vision and having staff on board that supported that vision," he says. "I think it was all about relationship building; it was about trust and professionalism. It grew to be filled with teacher leaders. It was a staff of teacher leaders."

Hockett describes himself as the conductor of a symphony; he provides overall vision and guidance for the group, but its quality and vitality rely fully on the virtuoso talent among those he's conducting. With that in mind, he was committed to hiring teachers who: 1) had a great deal of energy and initiative, 2) were themselves inquisitive learners, and 3) had the innate capacity to see the whole child — to consider all the aspects of a child's development in their approach to teaching.

That means finding a very special kind of teacher, one capable not only of powerful insights, but the ability to act on those insights. Teachers at Hunters Woods are constantly asked to balance innovation and diversification with the need to meet basic standards — and they embrace the challenge. "The staff understands that the same key doesn't unlock learning in every child and that it's going to take a plethora of different opportunities," Hockett says. "We tried to give the students the most enriching, extended type of education possible. We would look at it and say, 'What can we do to this to make it more exciting and more engaging without losing the core purpose?' We understood that by tapping in to all of those different areas, we would have a greater chance of hitting that nerve, that one thing that's going to light a fire in a kid."

Though he defers virtually all of the credit for the school's success to its teachers, Hockett was named Principal of the Year for 2006 by the Fairfax County Public School District, the 12th largest in the country. He has moved on to apply the same formula for success to a nearby elementary school. Hockett and other great principals understand that the best way to drive success in a school is to set teachers and other staff members up to use their talents and creativity as much as possible.

Teamwork

Teachers' sense of their own significance is vital. Outstanding principals foster this by asking staff members to be directly involved in decisions that are important to the type of learning environment at the school. As Richard DuFour and his colleagues observe in *Whatever It Takes*, "Ultimately, what will make the difference is not the standards themselves, but the self-efficacy of the staff — their belief that it is within their sphere of influence to impact student achievement in a positive way."[53] Regardless of the current level of student achievement in an individual school, the prevailing belief that it will improve can become a self-fulfilling prophecy.

A number of recent studies have extolled collaborative leadership in schools. In their review of studies investigating the impact of leadership on student learning, for example, Leithwood and his fellow researchers cite the importance of learning communities in which staff members collaborate on ways to improve student outcomes.[54] Likewise, a 2002 study of eight elementary schools in Chicago found that the distinguishing characteristic of higher-performing schools was teachers' active participation in instructional decisions.[55]

Greater teacher involvement builds a sense of confidence in staff members that enables them to meet new demands. As a teacher in one of Gallup's focus groups said, "There's got to be a whole lot more leadership than just coming from the office." A principal in another group said, "Empowerment can't be emphasized enough. If you are going to be successful as a principal, the teachers have to take things and go with them. You have to be the guide; you have to be the catalyst; but if you empower them, they will take off." Great principals take it on faith that, rather than diminishing their authority, involving teachers in critical decisions empowers teachers *and* principals by improving the performance of the whole school.[56]

Teaching and Learning

How great principals prioritize their time and efforts directly influences students' learning outcomes. In California elementary and secondary schools, Ronald Heck and George Marcoulides found differences in student performance according to the amount of time principals devoted to supporting teachers' instructional efforts, as well as the quality of that support.[57] The Chicago studies mentioned earlier also stressed the importance of principals' focus on instruction (as opposed to other management issues) and their involvement in teacher development as key factors in student learning.[58]

Providing Resources

Outstanding principals understand that top priority must be given to ensuring that staff members have the resources they need to teach effectively and progress toward the school's vision. This is a tricky task given budgetary constraints, and too often, teachers are forced to spend their own money on necessary classroom supplies. Richard Andrews' and Roger Soder's study was one of the first to demonstrate that principals' effectiveness at providing necessary resources contributed to student achievement. When the principal provided the tools teachers needed, teachers and parents saw the school as a place where "Things get done."[59]

In some cases, ensuring that teachers have all they need means addressing students' basic necessities as well. "We've got to make sure that our kids come prepared for school," said a participant in a principal focus group. "Some of my kids do not get their inoculations. So, we get nurses to give shots right here. In many cases, students don't have glasses. So, we have to find money for glasses. Otherwise, some students aren't prepared to learn." Whether we're talking about equipment, information, or glasses, the point is that great principals assume responsibility for resources so teachers don't have to.

FINDING THE PRINCIPALS WE NEED

Though they most often affect student outcomes indirectly, good principals are typically the individuals most essential to creating schools that leverage the strengths of staff members and students. Unfortunately, many school districts fail to fully understand that such a complex and pivotal role calls for finding people with the right talents upon which to build.

Carrying out that search as a generation of principals retires means identifying individuals with talents similar to those of the district's best principals and then providing opportunities for those people to build on that foundation. The training for these prospective leaders must be individualized and geared toward helping them recognize the potential of their talents as the foundation of strengths. And they should be given administrative duties and assignments with real responsibility for outcomes. If a district's succession program is working, the school leaders emerging from it should be capable of performing at the same level as the best in the district.

In 1984, John Goodlad maintained that most principal selection and training programs are more "casual" than management training programs found in the private sector. That remains true today.[60] Principal training programs typically accept most applicants automatically and offer standard training regimens for all participants. Trainees are rarely required to demonstrate what they will do when faced with real challenges. And most leadership training programs are evaluated on the perceived quality and variety of the training provided rather than participant *outcomes*.

Many of these programs contribute little to the district's ability to identify and develop future leaders. Worse, they may actually do harm by giving the impression that anyone can become a principal by completing a series of training components. Moreover, making such training the gateway to principal positions often prevents districts from establishing a more careful set of criteria for leadership succession.

In planning leadership succession for principals, district leaders should keep four keys in mind:

1. *Assistant principals should meet the same criteria used to identify outstanding principals.* Principals may occasionally be hired from outside the organization, but in most school districts, the majority are appointed from the ranks of existing assistant principals. Typically, however, assistant principals are a shallow talent pool from which to select principals for this reason: Most assistant principals were chosen by a principal to fill a specific need, not for their potential to become a principal down the road.

   To correct this situation, district leaders must take a broader view. Appointing an assistant principal should be seen as an opportunity to create "bench strength," a pool from which to select future principals. It should require a vote of confidence from both the principal ("This candidate is a good fit to meet the needs in my school") and the district ("This candidate has the talent to be like our best principals").

2. *District leaders should actively recruit individuals who display leadership talent.* Too many principal training programs rely on a self-selected pool made up of walk-ons and volunteers. Effective succession planning programs leave nothing to chance when it comes to finding talented leaders. They require district and school administrators to function as talent scouts, identifying and referring individuals with evidence of leadership promise. The range may still vary, so it's important to gauge the "fit"

of each individual prior to admission to the program rather than assume that everyone has the same potential to be a principal.

3. *Districts should seek proven, research-based selection methods.* Selection processes that have proven predictive of success obviously require more time and money than those that are less rigorous. But if those who emerge from the program are more likely to be successful as principals, the potential return on investment — through positive outcomes like improved teacher turnover — is considerable.

Unfortunately, the methods currently used in many school districts to select principals and other administrators are largely unreliable. They typically consist of one or two interviews that are, most frequently, unstructured with no research basis for the questions asked or the hoped-for applicant responses. Because such interviews tend to wander in different directions, direct comparison between interviews becomes impossible. What's more, interviewers tend to listen for their own answers to the questions — and those responses aren't always predictive of success.

That's not good enough. The presence of principals who can effectively leverage teacher talent is simply too important.

There remains one critical area to consider in the development of schools rooted in talent and dedicated to strengths development. Once a school has secured a "critical mass" of teacher talent and principal talent, how should they be calibrated so all that talent is fully engaged and working to maximize student success? That's the question we'll tackle next.

CHAPTER NINE

ENGAGED SCHOOLS: SETTING THE STAGE FOR GREATNESS

"In the end, management doesn't change culture. Management invites the workforce itself to change the culture."
— Lou Gerstner, former chairman and CEO of IBM

A few months after he signed on to help me assemble this book, my writing partner, Steve, was sitting with his fiancée, an elementary school art teacher, at a coffee shop outside Washington, D.C. They happened to overhear part of a conversation between two teachers at the next table. So, they introduced themselves.

They learned that Megan and Jamie, longtime friends who are teachers in different D.C. suburbs, regularly get together to share what's happening in their lives. They often talk about their work, partly because both are passionate about teaching as a profession, but also because they appreciate the opportunity to relate to someone who fully understands their successes and frustrations.

That day, they had been talking about how things were going in Jamie's new school. She said she was much happier there and said that her relationship with the principal was the biggest difference. Her new principal took the time to know each teacher personally, and she trusted him to be concerned with her development as an educator. Megan, on the other hand, described her principal as the source of much of her discontent with her own school. The principal seemed to continually chase the latest education cure-all, Megan said, all the while treating the teachers condescendingly.

Jamie noted that, even though she liked her new principal, she still had misgivings about the way she was treated as a professional. At a recent staff meeting, administrators had told the faculty to keep the "hobby teaching" to a minimum, meaning they should avoid using projects or illustrations that were not part of the prescribed standards tested by the state. Jamie complained that this felt like a lack of respect for teachers' opinions and judgment, amounting to being told, "Who you are is getting in the way of your job performance."

During the course of the conversation, both teachers complained about the lack of respect they were shown by parents who questioned them when their children received a poor grade or were disciplined. For these teachers who felt they had sacrificed much by going into a tough, low-paying field out of a love for students and education, having their judgment questioned was particularly tough to take. Pinched between a lack of autonomy and parental mistrust, they felt boxed in. They still loved teaching, but their enthusiasm was constantly dampened by the little injustices and sense of career inertia they grappled with every day.

Megan's and Jamie's frustration underscores the idea that a disproportionate amount of concern over what happens in schools is focused on the "what" of education — the standards and curriculum. The workplace conditions that help teachers and other staff members keep students engaged and learning are typically neglected. Megan and Jamie each teach in schools that are relatively well off in terms of funding and the socioeconomic status of the kids they serve — schools where you might expect workplace dynamics to be comparatively healthy. But despite their passion for teaching, both expressed considerable disillusionment about their careers and the level of fulfillment afforded by their schools. The way teachers feel about their work environment is critical. It influences whether they will stay in education and how engaged they are in their jobs — and, in turn, how effectively they promote student achievement.

This brings us to the fifth faulty assumption: *Differences in workplace culture are largely irrelevant to schools, because a teacher's working environment doesn't make much difference in the classroom.* The evidence clearly demonstrates that this assumption is wrong, costs school districts huge amounts of money, and hurts teachers and students.

TEACHER TURNOVER

Let's start with the dollar costs of neglecting the workplace climate in schools. The problem begins with the turnover statistics for beginning teachers. An alarming 40% to 50% of new teachers hired in a given year will leave the teaching profession within five years. Figure 10 shows the cumulative estimated attrition of beginning teachers in their first through fifth years, based on an analysis of three Department of Education datasets by University of Pennsylvania researcher Richard Ingersoll.[1]

FIGURE 10

Cumulative Percentage of Beginning Teachers Leaving Teaching by Year

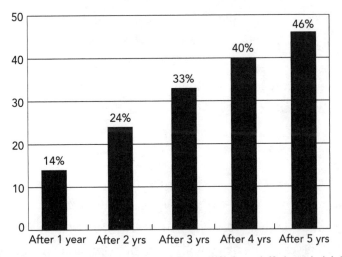

Source: National Commission on Teaching and America's Future. (2003, January). *No dream denied: A pledge to America's children.*

According to conventional wisdom, rising enrollment figures and the graying of the teacher workforce are driving the nation's current teacher shortage. But the single biggest cause lies elsewhere. In 2003, Ingersoll took a close look at the problem and debunked the idea that there aren't enough aspiring educators in the pipeline to offset the upcoming retirement of baby-boom teachers. Using the U.S. Department of Education's Schools and Staffing Survey and Teacher Follow-Up Survey, Ingersoll found that each year, more teacher vacancies resulted from teacher turnover than from retirement or student population growth.

Turnover statistics include "movers," teachers who voluntarily move from one school or district to another and "leavers," teachers who actually leave the profession. Movers and leavers constitute similar percentages of the overall turnover rate. Both create headaches for districts faced with quickly filling these vacancies. The nationwide turnover rate for teachers has been fairly consistent in recent years, ranging from a low of 13.2% in the 1991-1992 school year to a high of 15.7% in 2000-2001. By comparison, the estimated national turnover rate across all types of jobs over the previous decade was 11.9%.[2]

Data from the 1999-2000 and the 2000-2001 school years (Figure 11) demonstrate the magnitude of the teacher turnover problem and why it costs districts so much to deal with it. At the beginning of the 1999-2000 school year, 534,861 teachers entered their schools for the first time. But by the beginning of the following school year, 539,778 teachers had moved from one school to another or left teaching altogether. That means that nearly one-third of the entire nation's 3,451,316 teachers either changed schools or left teaching altogether, and more left than entered the previous year. That instability robs school after school of experience and momentum, creating a "revolving door," as Ingersoll describes it, of vacancies and new teachers.[3] All of this often happens with students needing stability the most.

FIGURE 11

Teacher Transition for the 1999 and 2000 School Years

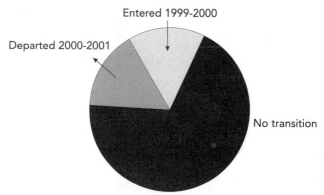

Source: Ingersoll, R. M. (2003, September). *Is there really a teacher shortage?* University of Washington, Center for the Study of Teaching and Policy.

The costs to school districts of high turnover include the resources needed to recruit, select, train, and evaluate new teachers — not to mention the lost productivity of the departing teachers. The total expense is alarming, although in most districts, it's hard to fully gauge because most of the actual costs of replacing a teacher who leaves are built into existing budgets.

There have been some attempts to fully estimate those costs in a realistic manner, but the results vary considerably. The Texas Center for Educational Research reviewed a number of estimation models and studied three representative Texas school districts. They concluded that the districts spent 20% of a departing teacher's annual salary to replace him or her, amounting to a conservative estimate of $329 million statewide each year.[4] In a 2004 study of teacher retention, the Alliance for Excellent Education estimated that the costs associated with teacher attrition are about $12,500 per teacher,[5] and concluded that the cost in the 2000 school year could have been nearly $2.1 billion across the nation.[6] The Charlotte Advocates for Education, an organization supporting the Charlotte-Mecklenburg Schools, puts the cost of replacing a single teacher in their district at $11,500.[7]

Using very conservative numbers, let's calculate the turnover cost for a single school district. If the district has 1,000 teachers and an average annual turnover rate of 15%, we could expect 150 teachers to resign in any given year. Using an estimated national average salary for first-year teachers of $30,496 for the 2003-2004 school year[8] and 20% of the teacher's salary as the cost to the district (the lowest estimate listed above), the cost to replace a single teacher would be $6,099.20. Multiplying that by 150 teachers to be replaced results in a total approaching $1 million in a single year for a single school district.

- 1,000 teachers x 15% turnover = 150 departing teachers

- $30,496 x 20% = $6,099.20 to replace one first-year teacher

- $6,099.20 x 150 = **$914,880** total annual expense

But budget expenditures aren't the biggest cost. Teacher turnover also diminishes the quality of instruction available to students. The resources devoted to hiring new teachers each year could be far better spent keeping talented teachers engaged and growing continually more productive over the course of their careers. Annual turnover rates of 10% or more make it fairly likely that some students will have first-year teachers several times, repeatedly learning from teachers who are themselves finding their way in the classroom. Turnover is especially high among math, science, and special education teachers. Among public schools, it is most rampant in urban schools and high-poverty areas.[9] Is it a coincidence that the most talked-about problems plaguing public schools — unfavorable international comparisons and the seemingly intractable achievement gap — involve areas heavily affected by teacher turnover?

Turning Turnover Around

Discouraging workplace conditions have created a huge blind spot for many districts that are desperately looking for ways to slow the revolving door. In the long run, solving the turnover problem will require forging the political will to set a higher standard for teacher salaries nationwide. That will have to happen, but it's a frustratingly slow process. Still, it doesn't mean that individual districts faced with budget limitations should just shrug their shoulders and accept high turnover as a fact of life.

Many school leaders aren't aware of the levers available to them when it comes to keeping teachers fully engaged in their jobs. Consider these findings as examples:

- Statewide surveys of 34,000 teachers in North Carolina and 15,200 teachers in South Carolina conducted by the Southeast Center for Teaching Quality in 2004 revealed a strong connection between working conditions and teacher retention. The most important factors? A collegial atmosphere, instructional leadership by the principal, empowerment among high school teachers, and professional development opportunities among elementary school teachers.[10]

- In the Charlotte-Mecklenburg schools, most teachers left after less than three years in the district. In 2004, the Charlotte Advocates for Education conducted a retention study focusing on principals as the key to lowering the district's high turnover rate. The group identified 20 principals from high-need schools with two important characteristics: They had relatively high teacher-retention rates and strong student achievement records. In focus groups and then a written survey, the 20 principals identified seven strategies for improving retention. The list is strikingly similar to the factors that emerged from the large-scale teacher surveys: 1) allocating time for teachers to work together, 2) meeting facility and resource needs, 3) setting overarching goals and a vision for the school, 4) empowering teachers, 5) providing opportunities for professional development, 6) supporting new teachers, and 7) assisting groups of teachers in using achievement data to improve student learning.[11]

The effects of high teacher turnover ripple through a school, increasing the workloads and stress levels of those teachers who remain and eventually stunting student achievement. All school districts need to fully appreciate the psychological impact their working conditions have on teachers. And just as importantly, they should understand the effect that teachers' feelings about their workplaces have on their students.

IF WE CAN'T HAVE GREAT PLACES FOR TEACHERS TO WORK . . .

Until recently, the quality of the workplace received little attention from principals and superintendents. Schools tend to look a lot alike from the outside, so there has been little pressure on administrators to improve — or even assess — their effectiveness as workplaces. Even when differences in workplace climate are recognized, pinpointing their causes and effects is difficult because the most important issues typically spring from the quality of relationships — particularly those between teachers and between teachers and administrators. As longtime educator Roland Barth maintained in his 1990 book *Improving Schools From Within*, "The relationships among adults in schools are the basis, the precondition, the *sine qua non* that allow, energize, and sustain all other attempts at school improvement. Unless adults talk with one another, observe one another, and help one another, very little will change."[12]

Because so much policy is set at the district level, we tend to think about the schools within a district as a uniform bloc, each only marginally different from those nearby. In reality, even schools a few blocks apart can be like night and day in terms of the conditions that foster engagement among teachers and other staff members.

With the publication of *A Place Called School* in 1984, John Goodlad challenged the assumption that America's schools are all pretty much the same for teachers and students. Goodlad and his team conducted a massive survey of more than 1,300 teachers, nearly 13,000 students, and more than 8,000 parents, along with 1,000 observations of classrooms in 38 high schools.

Based on this large database, Goodlad concluded that schools vary considerably on the basis of the relationships between students and teachers, teachers and principals, and school staff and parents, as well as the freedom granted to teachers and principals to do their work. Goodlad found that in schools where the relationships were seen by teachers, students, and parents as constructive, the overall perceptions of the schools held by those same groups were also rated more highly. When one measure went up, so did the other.[13]

Moreover, students, parents, and teachers who perceived harmony between their groups were more likely to express satisfaction with the school overall. In the schools scoring lower on overall satisfaction, 57% of the principals interviewed cited "staff relations" as a problem, compared to only 20% of the principals in schools with higher satisfaction.

In reviewing the satisfaction ratings given to schools by teachers, students, and parents, Goodlad made a sobering observation about school improvement. Singling out the "less satisfying schools," he cast doubt on their ability to take significant steps toward improving student achievement, saying:

> They are not healthy organisms. They simply are not good candidates for tackling the difficult tasks of curricular and pedagogical reform. The first step is for them to become more effective in their conduct of present business and in the process to become more satisfying places for those associated with them. They need data about their present condition and considerable support and encouragement in the needed process of renewal.[14]

In his 2003 study, Ingersoll similarly found large differences among individual schools with regard to the quality of relationships within them. He concluded that "Significant numbers of secondary schools have high levels of conflict between staff and students, have high levels of conflict among teachers, and have a high level of conflict between teachers and principals. . . ."[15] Examining the administrative structures of various schools, Ingersoll suggested that those involving teachers in important decision-making processes tend to experience less student, teacher, and principal conflict and lower teacher turnover. "In other words," he wrote, "decentralized schools appear to have fewer problems with student misbehavior, more collegiality and cooperation among teachers and administrators, and a more committed staff."[16]

Engaged workplaces, like engaged classrooms, maintain a critical balance between control and flexibility. In its "No Dream Denied" report, the National Commission on Teaching and America's Future made it clear that the highly directive leadership "designed for the factory-era schools of the 19th century" is inappropriate for the task of managing teachers today. Instead, the commission expressed the need for shared decision making between teachers and principals and professional learning communities that endow groups of highly motivated teachers with the knowledge and skills to improve student achievement in whichever way works best for them.[17]

The pressure to perform well on state accountability tests pushes principals and superintendents to exercise greater control over what takes place in the classroom. No Child Left Behind has prodded many schools even further toward the control side of the scale; many now enforce a prescribed uniform curriculum. But without some measure of autonomy, resentment and resistance are likely to grow among teachers.[18] Nothing kills the growth of a true learning community faster. "We read proposals every day suggesting ways to attract, train, retain, and retrain the best and the brightest to work with our children in school," writes Barth in *Improving Schools From Within*. "Yet, on the very next page, we read more and more demands that such individuals comply with the exacting requirements of externally controlled predetermined, routinized, carefully monitored jobs."[19]

School leaders should consider the downward spiral created by similar efforts in the private sector. Many organizations turn to micromanagement in an attempt to control unproductive or disengaged employees, with disastrous results. Jim Collins writes in *Good to Great,* "Most companies build their bureaucratic rules to manage the small percentage of wrong people on the bus, which in turn drives away the right people on the bus, which then increases the percentage of wrong people on the bus, which increases the need for more bureaucracy to compensate for incompetence and lack of discipline, which then further drives the right people away, and so forth."[20]

Regardless of the type of work we do, our workplaces have a strong bearing on our happiness as human beings. We typically spend about a third of our waking lives at work. Positive Psychology studies continue to investigate the correlation between work satisfaction and life satisfaction.[21] For many of us, much of our self-concept is tied up in our jobs. This is particularly true of talented teachers, most of whom see their work as a personal calling. A workplace that recognizes and reflects that self-concept will earn their full engagement.

As high teacher turnover rates suggest, schools can no longer afford to ignore the psychological climate in which their teachers work. The best teachers always have the most opportunities to leave workplaces that fail to give them a degree of autonomy and make them feel like part of a community of professionals.[22]

That brings us to the bottom line: If we can't have great places for teachers to work, we won't have great places for students to learn. Student achievement relies too heavily on the full deployment of teacher talent. We need to ensure that every teacher in this country works in an environment that promotes his or her own engagement in order to fully tap students' potential.

THREE PERSPECTIVES: CULTURE, CLIMATE, AND EMPLOYEE ENGAGEMENT

Improving working conditions requires examining schools from an unfamiliar perspective: from the inside out. Building on Goodlad's work, educators like Roland Barth, Terry Deal, and Kent Peterson have made the case that too many reform efforts focus on driving improvement from the outside through mandates and policies, and too few look at changing schools from within.[23] As Curt Coffman and Gabriel Gonzalez-Molina concluded from Gallup's studies with private-sector companies, great organizations "look inward in order to move forward."[24]

The terms "climate" and "culture" have been commonly used to describe the unique attributes of a school. "Climate" found its way into school studies from its use by industrial psychologists and has served as an umbrella term to describe teachers' perceptions of their overall work environment. In particular, climate has come to refer to the quality of relationships within the school and how those relationships affect staff members' experience.[25] In the previous chapter, we described how principals promote a healthy climate by:

- communicating a clear mission and vision
- fostering collaboration among teachers
- encouraging teachers' involvement in decision making
- setting high expectations for teachers and students
- developing a sense of teamwork and trust
- stimulating thinking and reflection on teaching

"Culture," as applied to schools, takes a broader view of the organization and people. It commonly refers to the traditions and expectations in an organization or workgroup — the shared ways of doing things inside a school that have evolved over time. A school's culture influences "the way people act, how they dress, what they talk about or avoid talking about, whether they seek out colleagues for help or don't, and how teachers feel about their work and their students," write Deal and Peterson.[26] Culture is revealed anytime someone says, "That's just the way we've always done it around here."

Great managers in any industry use culture and climate to generate high levels of employee engagement.[27] That engagement, in turn, helps sustain a culture of positivity and productivity. The simplest definition of employee engagement is employees' level of involvement with and enthusiasm for their work and its outcomes. Employees make day-to-day decisions about what they will and will not do — and the attitude with which the activities they *will* do are done — that ultimately drive outcomes. When engaged, employees are emotionally committed to their work and are intrinsically motivated to strive for excellence. That motivation can be infectious because it raises the ambient level of energy and expectation for all employees. Just as negativity can breed more negativity, active engagement can breed even higher engagement.

GALLUP'S WORKPLACE RESEARCH

Qualitative and quantitative workplace studies spanning more than three decades have taught Gallup researchers much about the causes and effects of employee engagement. This research has unwaveringly followed the principle of studying success — the characteristics of productive workgroups and leaders — as opposed to what *doesn't* work in organizations.[28]

Perhaps the most significant result of all this research has been a better understanding of the critical role the workgroup-level manager plays in influencing employees' psychological involvement with their work. In the case of a school, that person is typically the principal or department head, depending on the school's size. A second — and related — consistency has been the finding that when it comes to improving workplace conditions, focusing on the workgroup level yields the best results. Local cultural and climatic conditions account for most of the significant differences found in all manner of long, detailed, organization-wide satisfaction surveys.[29] The good news is that local workgroup conditions aren't that difficult to assess and change — and doing so affects an employee's satisfaction, loyalty, and pride, not to mention his or her intent to remain with the organization.[30]

In the late 1990s, a comprehensive analysis of the most productive workgroups Gallup had studied over the years identified a standard set of commonly found characteristics. These were narrowed down to 12 items most indicative of engagement at the workgroup level — and most predictive of success. Here they are:

1. I know what is expected of me at work.

2. I have the materials and equipment I need to do my work right.

3. At work, I have the opportunity to do what I do best every day.

4. In the last seven days, I have received recognition or praise for doing good work.

5. My supervisor, or someone at work, seems to care about me as a person.

6. There is someone at work who encourages my development.

7. At work, my opinions seem to count.

8. The mission or purpose of my company makes me feel my job is important.

9. My associates or fellow employees are committed to doing quality work.

10. I have a best friend at work.

11. In the last six months, someone at work has talked to me about my progress.

12. This last year, I have had opportunities at work to learn and grow.

A hierarchical model of workplace needs is presented in Figure 12. The 12 items are grouped into four levels, the most basic of which must be addressed first.

- **Level 1: Basic needs.** The most fundamental requirements of all employees are an understanding of what is expected of them and the materials and equipment they need to do their jobs.

- **Level 2: Management support.** The next level addresses management issues — in the case of schools, mostly teacher-administrator relationships. These include ensuring that teachers are given opportunities to do what they do best, that they receive frequent recognition, that they feel cared about at work, and that their professional development is encouraged.

- **Level 3: Teamwork.** The third level addresses the relationships among employees and between employees and the organization itself. In education, it measures commitment to the mission of the school, trust and friendships among fellow teachers, teachers' sense that they have a voice in the important decisions affecting the school, and confidence in colleagues doing quality work.

- **Level 4: Growth**. The highest level of the engagement pyramid contains items addressing personal growth. Does the employee feel that the organization is contributing to his development? Is it in fact committed to helping him feel fulfilled?

FIGURE 12

Gallup Q¹² Engagement Hierarchy

The 12 items are intended to gauge the overall culture and climate of the workplace; only one refers directly to a "supervisor," and even this question is tempered with "or someone at work." As the quote from Lou Gerstner at the beginning of this chapter suggests, *everyone* in the organization — from executives to part-time staffers — is responsible for establishing and maintaining a healthy, constructive culture.

Nevertheless, another key insight from Gallup's engagement work across industries is this: People don't leave bad companies; they leave bad *managers*. The principal is the one who must take the lead in establishing an environment that values behaviors supportive of these conditions.[31] Working in collaboration with staff members, he or she is in the best position to introduce changes that promote staff engagement. Once those changes are initiated, all staff members share in the responsibility for sustaining and building on them.

EMPLOYEE ENGAGEMENT AND OUTCOMES

In 2006, Gallup researchers completed the latest in a series of meta-analyses examining a massive amount of employee engagement data. A meta-analysis allows researchers to combine data from a number of smaller studies to identify relationships that apply consistently across different contexts.

The 2006 meta-analysis included a total of 166 proprietary surveys with 125 separate organizations, including 20 from outside the United States. Responses from a total of 681,799 employees in 23,910 workgroups were included. The 125 organizations included a diverse range of enterprises; in fact, six were school districts, representing 10,496 of the employees included in the study. The analysis aggregated employee responses at the workgroup level and correlated them to outcome measures such as customer loyalty, productivity (student achievement for schools), profitability, turnover, and safety.[32]

The analysis revealed a strong relationship between a workgroup's aggregated responses to the 12 items and its performance on several important outcomes. Workgroups with engagement scores in the top 50% of their organizations performed significantly better than those with scores in the lower 50%. Those workgroups whose engagement scores were the highest demonstrated, on average, 56% greater success on customer loyalty measures, 44% lower turnover rates, 38% higher productivity outcomes, and 27% higher profitability.[33]

Focusing on the school studies alone demonstrated more specifically that employee engagement is related to student achievement. The school data came from districts in Texas, which enabled Gallup researchers to compare performance levels on the Texas Assessment of Academic Skills (TAAS) tests among schools with different average employee engagement scores. The study found a significant positive relationship between employee engagement and student performance by individual school. An analysis of two large districts found that in those schools in the top 15% with regard to average teacher engagement scores, 8.7% more students passed all of the tests than in schools in the bottom 15%. Comparing two 500-student elementary schools, this means that about 44 more students passed all the TAAS tests in the school with high engagement scores than in the school with low engagement scores.

Exactly what do these data tell us? We should be careful not to automatically infer a direct line of causality from teacher engagement to student achievement; other factors may be supporting high levels of both. But even if that's the case, those factors start at the individual school level, because the variation in schools' average employee engagement levels tends to be just as high between different schools *within* a district as it is between schools in *different* districts.

That brings us back to the principal. Principals are critical to the success of schools in many ways. But laying the groundwork for teacher engagement is the single area in which the principal can most effectively contribute to success in the classroom.

WHAT CAN THE PRINCIPAL DO TO MAINTAIN A HEALTHY WORKPLACE?

Like all great managers, outstanding principals successfully cultivate the 12 fundamental conditions in the employee engagement pyramid. In doing so, they foster positive relationships throughout the school and keep talented teachers highly involved and upbeat.

Level 1: Basic Needs

The two basic needs at the base of the pyramid are: a clear understanding of expectations and access to needed materials and equipment. Fulfilling these needs gives the organization a baseline level of credibility with employees. If these needs are not met, employees tend to be frustrated and resentful, focusing on their own survival as opposed to the success of the organization or its customers.[34]

1. *"I know what is expected of me at work."*

   "What do I have to do to be seen as successful?" For employees who are unclear on the answer to that question, it's virtually impossible to remain fully engaged because they have no clear objective in which to invest their full attention. Clear expectations give employees a platform from which to apply their talents.

   But principals must resist the temptation to go overboard with expectations. As we've noted, great principals help teachers find their own way to student achievement outcomes. They operate similarly to Collins' "good-to-great" companies, which established "a consistent system with clear constraints, but they also gave people freedom and responsibility within the framework of that system. They hired self-disciplined people who didn't need to be managed, and then managed the system, not the people."[35]

   Principals and other school administrators play a critical role in helping teachers sort out often-conflicting demands and integrating them into the common vision that has been established for the school. Good administrators work to keep teachers from feeling buffeted by such demands so they can focus on achieving outcomes.

2. *"I have the materials and equipment I need to do my work right."*

Providing resources in a variety of areas is a primary responsibility of the principal. If teachers are deprived of the "stuff" they need to achieve the outcomes expected of them, they naturally feel a sense of betrayal. "We have to nurture teachers," said one participant in a Gallup focus group of principals. "I really view my role as a principal as being the resource person. Whatever it is that teachers need to do their jobs, it becomes my job to provide it for them."

Unfortunately, that's not the case in many schools. A survey of 1,467 public school teachers reported that they spent an average of $443 of their own money on supplies for students in 2000.[36] In another study with beginning middle school and high school teachers who were considering leaving teaching, lack of resources and materials was cited as one of the main problems.[37]

Keeping employees well-supplied is the very least an organization can do to show them that they're valued and that their efforts are supported. "We really have tried to provide the teachers with all the right materials so they feel like we view them as professionals," says Nancy Oberst of Omaha's Liberty Elementary.

Level 2: Management Support

Once these lower level needs are met, administrators can turn to ensuring that teachers feel supported. That means building relationships, acknowledging successes, and helping teachers and other staff members develop and make full use of their strengths. Effective administrators elicit self-confidence and productivity from teachers in much the same way that great teachers do from students: by establishing supportive partnerships.

3. *"At work, I have the opportunity to do what I do best every day."*

Great principals start setting teachers up for success during the recruiting process. They hold out for reliable indications of the necessary talents in the teachers they invite to work with students — indications that a teaching role will allow them to do what they naturally do well. This requires talking to applicants about the specific needs and demands of the role so that the principal and the new recruit agree on the fit.

After teachers are hired, effective principals act as guides in helping teachers identify and stay focused on what they do best. This assessment of "fit" occurs again and again in assignment of grade levels, subjects, students, and teams.

4. *"In the last seven days, I have received recognition or praise for doing good work."*

No one suffers from over-recognition. Great leaders never pass up the opportunity to recognize individuals who are performing at excellence. But in many schools, recognition of staff members is so rare that an outsider might assume it had to be deducted from employees' paychecks. Frequent recognition is a staple of healthy workplaces. It has incredible power to promote engagement if it: 1) is genuine and deserved, and 2) occurs regularly but also spontaneously and creatively, in order to avoid the tedious "employee of the month" syndrome.[38]

In *How Full Is Your Bucket?*, Tom Rath and Don Clifton make an important point about recognition: To be truly meaningful, it must be tailored to each individual. Some people love public recognition, while others are embarrassed by it. Some like notes or small gifts to commemorate their achievement; others want their families to know about it.[39] Principals and administrators who are in doubt about the best form of recognition for a given teacher should use the occasion to open a dialogue with the teacher and get to know her or him better.

But any form of positive recognition is better than none at all. The bottom line here is this: Mediocre performance will become the norm if excellent performance goes unrecognized. We get more of what we celebrate. We rarely get more of what we ignore.

5. *"My supervisor, or someone at work, seems to care about me as a person."*

Just as students work harder for some teachers than for others, teachers work harder for some principals. The bond is strongest when a principal or manager consistently makes it clear through words and actions that she cares about each employee as a person. As in the case of recognition, that sense of caring can mean different things to different people. Administrators must be aware of and respond to the unique needs of each teacher. Moreover, they should help teachers make connections between their own needs and those of the students and the school.[40]

This item may strike some as unrealistic. After all, how can a principal or assistant principal have time to establish caring bonds with dozens of teachers who may or may not have any interest in a relationship with her? The most successful principals understand that caring about a person doesn't have to be about close personal familiarity. It can simply imply a focus on doing what is right for the person and on helping the individual flourish. Great principals know such caring simply means knowing enough about each person to help him or her succeed.

6. *"There is someone at work who encourages my development."*

This item more directly taps into that sense of support. Encouraging development begins with a highly individualized, rather than a prescriptive, approach to growth. It means acting on what principals and administrators know about the interests and needs of each teacher, by holding up a mirror to provide feedback and then providing resources for further development. It's a constant process that needs to occur outside of formal evaluation conferences, in a setting where it is understood that the only agenda is promoting the developmental and career growth of the teacher.

Level 3: Teamwork

The teacher-administrator relationship is perhaps the most important in the school, but it is by no means the *only* important connection. A strong network of relationships among colleagues supports engagement in any type of workplace. In schools, supporting this network poses a special challenge in the creation of opportunities for teachers — who spend most of their time isolated from each other in their classrooms — to talk and share ideas.

Strong teams exist when individuals have a significant degree of ownership for shared goals and can sense that their fellow team members feel that ownership as well. Out of these perceptions come close relationships that further strengthen the team. The next four items address those feelings of ownership and trust that bind the workgroup members together.

7. *"At work, my opinions seem to count."*

Data from schools across the country indicate that most teachers have little or no involvement in important decisions that affect their jobs on a daily basis.[41] That finding was reflected in Gallup's focus groups in which teachers were least likely to agree that their opinions count. "Our job now is teaching the test," said one instructional assistant. "Here's what you teach; this is the information. If you have a chance to elaborate more on that, try to — but don't burden yourself with anything extra that you might think is relevant to the topic."

Educator Roland Barth believes that the culture in most U.S. schools suffers from a crippling lack of collegiality that trickles all the way down to students:

> The biggest problem besetting schools is the primitive quality of human relationships among children, parents, teachers, and administrators. Many schools perpetuate infantilism. School boards infantilize superintendents; superintendents, principals; principals, teachers; and teachers, children. This leads to children and adults who frequently behave like infants, complying with authority from fear or dependence, waiting until someone's back is turned to do something "naughty." To the extent that teachers and principals together can make important school decisions, they become colleagues. They become grown-ups. They become professionals.[42]

In schools where teachers and staff participate in meaningful decisions about how to do their jobs, teachers perceive principals as more communicative and supportive.[43] Empowerment results in strong connections between teachers and their schools.[44]

8. *"The mission or purpose of my company makes me feel my job is important."*

A strong sense of mission infuses work with meaning, importance, and a broader perspective that can inspire high performance. As I noted in Chapter 8, great principals understand the power of tapping teachers' natural altruism by explicitly connecting the specific mission of the school to the values of the individual staff members in clear, understandable language.

The mission of education may seem obvious, but in many schools, it tends to recede in staff members' consciousness amid all their daily trials and challenges. Often, the principal and staff members take the school's underlying mission for granted. Worse yet, many teachers feel high levels of mission at the outset of their careers, but the flame isn't fanned by regular recognition and ample opportunity to fulfill that mission. Eventually, it burns out, and those teachers become disheartened or leave the school. Important outcomes characteristic of the school must be constantly communicated and reinforced — and their achievement celebrated to the fullest — or the emotion dims.

9. *"My associates or fellow employees are committed to doing quality work."*

Confidence in their fellow staff members is important to sustaining high engagement among great teachers. Without it, teachers have to constantly justify to themselves why they're working harder than their colleagues for little added reward.

Principals influence this item by selecting teachers with high standards for themselves and their students and clearly communicating how quality is defined and measured at the school. Great principals also provide staff members with opportunities to discuss desired outcomes with each other and how best to achieve them.[45] Collegiality is the key here — the sense that "we're all in this together." "What we had in middle school was the team concept," said one teacher in our focus groups. "And that really was, for me, a great engagement tool because you're working with four or five other teachers who are teaching the same small group of students, so you can compare notes. . . . Where they can create schools within a school, I think would probably help toward [teacher] engagement."

10. *"I have a best friend at work."*

Principals and other managers tend to vary considerably in their opinions about friendships in the workplace, but the research results are very clear on this point: The presence of strong friendships represents a critical difference between more successful and less successful workgroups.[46] Friendships between staff members provide them with social capital that they can rely on when negative things happen.[47]

Ann Wilson, a veteran teacher in Ft. Worth, Texas, told me about a workplace relationship she's particularly proud of. "Leanne is a colleague here on this campus, and we use each other's strengths as partners," Ann said. "I love working with her because, I'm telling you, Leanne just makes things happen. We make great partners because I work more at keeping people working together and continuing to learn. We have seen now that without the other one, we couldn't have accomplished anywhere near what we've done on this campus. Neither of us could have done it without the other."

Friendships in the workplace increase the overall level of shared trust among team members.[48] These relationships affect how teachers see their jobs, their workplaces, and themselves. Notice that this item is further up the pyramid than those addressing positive teacher-administrator relationships and employees' feelings of ownership. When those conditions are in place, administrators can rest assured that friendships among teachers won't result in an "us versus them" mentality, instead tying the friends closer to the organization as a whole.

In schools, this "teamwork" level of the pyramid is particularly tough to address — but again, the impact of collegiality on teacher engagement can't be overstated. Consider the following story told by Diane, a veteran elementary school teacher who oversees a research program for others at her school:

A young teacher who had been teaching for seven years was about ready to quit. In the course of our conversation, she said she was really worried about her ESL students not being able to read independently, and she asked, "How can I address that?" And I said, "Well, that would be a good question for the teacher research team." So she joined the team and worked collaboratively with the ESL teacher. That's key number 1 — she found a friend. And this friend had a common interest: What can we do to help ESL students with reading? Key number 2 is the fact that this friend and she were supported by another community of friends who showed an interest in what they were doing.

At the end of the year, she came to me and she said, "I feel so grown up." I asked, "What do you mean?" She replied, "For the first time in my seven years, I feel that what I was doing was validated, that other people were interested in what I was doing and what I was doing actually helped, contributed to a problem that we all have with students." All of those factors helped energize her and renew her interest in teaching.

Level 4: Growth

At the peak of the engagement pyramid are two items that directly address how effectively the organization helps teachers develop. Keep in mind that if the lower levels of the pyramid — fulfillment of basic needs, administrative support, and a sense of belonging — are weak, the two growth conditions will neither help retain teachers nor keep them engaged in serving students. But unless these two items *are* addressed, teachers will never be as engaged with the school as they could be. As we saw in Chapter 7, passionate teachers are invariably passionate learners. Too often, schools overlook talented teachers' insatiable thirst to add new knowledge and skills to their repertoire.

11. *"In the last six months, someone at work has talked to me about my progress."*

   Employees everywhere need periodic feedback about their progress and contributions. The common once- or twice-a-year evaluation conference with experienced teachers is typically too little, too late, and too prescribed. It tends to be a stressful process for teachers and administrators alike because it occurs so rarely and the stakes are so high. It doesn't have to be this way. By scheduling regular sessions to talk about progress and successes outside of formal evaluation scenarios, great principals and administrators provide more timely input and encouragement regarding the contributions of the individual staff members.

   Staff members and principals benefit from taking ample time to discuss progress. All too frequently, teachers feel like they have few ways to demonstrate the impact of their own personal development on their effectiveness in the classroom. Great principals notice staff members succeeding and use those successes to suggest further learning opportunities.

12. *"This last year, I have had opportunities at work to learn and grow."*

   Individuals who are fully engaged in their lives yearn to learn and grow. This characteristic of human nature is universal and quite remarkable. But different people learn and grow best in different ways. Classes and seminars are one way to learn, but there are myriad other ways too. Allowing employees to choose their mode of learning adds vitality to the organization because it supplements the sum total of its knowledge and skills in unexpected ways.[49]

Just as teachers make use of different classroom strategies to achieve similar learning outcomes, they need distinct learning opportunities that correspond to their individual talents. Expensive, large-scale staff development programs that are intended to address perceived gaps in the "competency" of the staff are likely to result in cynicism and low returns on investment. "When a school or school system deliberately sets out to foster new skills by committing everyone to required workshops, little happens except that everyone feels relieved, if not virtuous, that they have gone through the motions of doing their job," notes Barth. "So, by and large, the district staff development activities we employ insult the capable and leave the incompetent untouched."[50] The key to successful investment is first finding out what staff members need and want, then devising strategies to help them go out and get it.

PRINCIPALS AND THE WORKPLACE

The first step to improving retention of talented teachers is to challenge the assumption that the conditions found in fulfilling workplaces somehow don't apply to schools. To be sure, there are conditions set outside of the school environment that dramatically influence retention — low salaries being the most obvious. But the day-to-day engagement of teachers and other staff members is equally affected by the climate and culture particular to each school.

A great principal, just like any other manager, is critical to retention because, as noted earlier, most people don't leave organizations, they leave supervisors. If the principal expresses a clear, unwavering commitment to building a positive workplace on a daily basis, the rest of the staff will follow suit.

When teachers and other staff members find their schools to be supportive, stimulating places to work, those schools will be far more likely to keep the people they work so hard to recruit, select, and train. Like any type of organization, schools can't afford to keep losing their most important asset — the right people — through a revolving door. It's time to face a fundamental reality: In the long run, schools can't be great places for students to learn if they are not great places for adults to work. The attitudes of those serving always rub off on those being served. A supportive, collaborative workplace that fully engages talented teachers and administrators — that's the only setting in which we can be truly confident that students have opportunities to reach their full potential.

CHAPTER TEN

ENGAGED COMMUNITIES: RALLYING AROUND THE SCHOOLS

"Whether a school succeeds or fails in its mission depends in no small measure on the degree of support received from the nation and from the community it serves."
— *Ernest Boyer, university professor and writer*

There's hardly a more iconic image of the tightly knit communities of America's past than the little red schoolhouse. When cities and schools were smaller, there was a greater sense that the schools belonged to the community. Teachers knew their students' families and where they lived and thought nothing of paying a visit to their homes. Parents and teachers routinely ran into each other in worship services and at the local grocery store. They were often friends and true partners in the healthy development of the community's children.

As more people moved to the cities and communities became larger, that routine contact largely disappeared, and with it a significant source of familiarity and trust. In addition, with the rise of the standards movement in recent decades, more decisions affecting schools have been taken out of the hands of community leaders. As a result, schools have come to seem more like extensions of federal or state governments than organizations designed to serve local communities and reflect local values.[1] Not surprisingly, the distance between the schools and the rest of the community has, in many cases, widened considerably.

That's troubling, because to create an engaged school, it's important to rally people *outside* the school setting. Parents and leaders in the community served by the school can have an enormous impact on the perceptions of those within it. To the extent that those people are actively engaged in supporting and establishing positive partnerships with the school, the community's "education culture" flourishes. Whether those partnerships are initiated within the school through the efforts of teachers and principals or outside the school by community groups or individual parents, they are essential to keeping those inside *and* outside the school engaged in improving the future of the community and its children.

EDUCATION CULTURE

Recent research on leadership in education reveals that the broader education culture in which students are immersed outside of school is a critical element of their success *within* the school. The norms and beliefs regarding education that are manifest in a community — and in individual families — help determine how relevant young people feel education is to their lives.

This culture varies widely among communities and among families in the same community, regardless of their economic or social circumstances. The messages it sends include expectations regarding work ethic, the value of academic achievement, the importance of devoting resources and support to schoolwork, and the connection between education and work.[2] The way a community or family approaches each of these issues makes a big impression on students and teachers.

Strong educational cultures can be found in all types of communities and in families of all ethnic groups and income levels. The significance a community attaches to learning helps explain certain students' motivation, work ethic, and persistence. The educational culture of a family or a school neighborhood may be a more direct predictor of school success than socioeconomic status.[3]

Yet too often, school leaders underestimate the potential for schools to foster strong education cultures by establishing positive dialogues with anyone invested in the success of students. Just as the workplace culture within a school can be geared to promote constructive relationships, so can the broader culture among the school and those it serves. The education cultures within families can be strengthened, but schools can't influence them unless they realize this and take the initiative to help.

How? There are many approaches to increasing parents' and community members' level of engagement with the public schools. But they all require overcoming some difficult barriers and improving the quality of interactions at two important connecting points:

- the teacher/parent juncture, which is too often characterized by mistrust and lack of collaboration

- the juncture between school leaders — principals, superintendents, and other administrators — and social, political, and business leaders interested in promoting a successful future for the community

At both points, the two sides have a strong mutual interest. Even so, their interactions are frequently mired in apathy or defensiveness. By failing to recognize that through these two junctures they can broaden their base of support and participation, schools too often miss out on potent sources of positive energy. They overlook important means for further engaging students, teachers, and principals — not to mention the community upon which public schools depend.

Let's start by considering how the most fundamental connection, that between teachers and parents, can be developed to improve the education culture to which students are exposed.

TEACHERS AND PARENTS

In 2005, the PDK/Gallup Poll asked Americans the following question: *In your opinion, who is most important in determining how well or how poorly students perform in school — the students themselves, the students' teachers, or the students' parents?* Forty-three percent chose the students' parents; 33% chose their teachers; and 20% chose the students themselves.[4]

In a 2002 survey by the Educational Testing Service, a majority of educators (58%) cited "lack of parental involvement" as a cause of problems in public schools. Many parents themselves agreed; nearly 4 in 10 (39%) parents rated low parent involvement as a cause of problems.[5] In a 1999 study, more than 8 in 10 (82%) parents agreed with the statement: "Too many parents expect the school to do their job for them."[6]

Schools blessed with a community in which families tend to have strong education cultures have a distinct advantage in terms of keeping students engaged. Parents' support and involvement indicates to their children that the family puts a high priority on ensuring their success at school. That, in turn, boosts children's confidence and keeps them from forming broad negative conclusions — like "I'm not cut out to be a good student" — in the face of temporary frustration. Families with strong education cultures help kids see that their education is an ongoing process of self-discovery and that as long as they continue to apply themselves, they can't help but reap the benefits of it.

Congress recognized the importance of a close working relationship between schools and parents in framing the Goals 2000 education reform act passed in 1994. That law established the expectation that "By the year 2000, every school will promote partnerships that will increase parental involvement and participation in promoting the social, emotional, and academic growth of children."[7] A number of state efforts to do so were established and supported.

But more than a decade later, many public schools still view parental contact as a necessary evil rather than a key to academic growth and part of the lifeblood of the school. It has proven very difficult to shake the sixth prevailing assumption that *though greater involvement in America's schools is needed, schools can do little to improve parents' commitment to their children's education.* That's simply not true. In fact, unless schools *do* take the initiative to establish positive relationships, even those parents who are eager to be actively involved can threaten, rather than support, engagement in the school.

Improving the Connection

Teachers seem to view positive partnerships with parents as rare. A 1999 Public Agenda survey of 1,000 teachers and 1,220 parents tapped into basic attitudes toward public involvement in schools. Fully two-thirds of teachers said that parents of students in their school did a "fair" or "poor" job of being involved with their children's education.[8] Teachers often express irritation about lack of parental participation even in formal parent-teacher conferences.

Homework is another area of frequent disconnect between parents and teachers. In the 1999 Public Agenda study, most teachers (57%) said they preferred that parents check to be sure homework was correct and completed. But nearly 8 in 10 (78%) believed that parents paid little attention to the accuracy of homework or even whether or not it was done. For their part, parents were most likely to say that they were making an effort to ensure their child did his or her homework, but that it was an uphill struggle. Half of parents reported one or more serious and emotional conflicts with their children during the past year over homework. Moreover, some parents expressed doubt that all of the homework required was important to learning, feeling some of it was "busy work."[9]

In some instances, parents may not fully realize the importance of supporting their children's schooling at home. Some may be more concerned that their children develop independence and the ability to handle challenges on their own. In other cases, cultural norms may discourage parents from "interfering" with the work of schools and authority figures like teachers.[10] The resulting lack of involvement can be misinterpreted by teachers as a lack of caring.

Sometimes, teachers' negative perceptions further discourage parental participation, creating a vicious cycle. Parent-teacher conferences often focus on the open gradebook for a review of the student's progress. If the grades are less than stellar, the implied question becomes, "Why aren't you a better parent?" One father described his interaction with his son's teachers to researchers this way: "They expect me to go to school so they can tell me my kid is stupid or crazy. They've been telling me that for three years, so why should I go and hear it again? They don't do anything. They just tell me my kid is bad."[11] When these kinds of encounters discourage parents from getting involved, teachers may grow even more critical — and the cycle continues.

On the other hand, nearly every teacher can tell a horror story about parents who are overly controlling (some call them "helicopter parents" because they seem to constantly hover over their children's teachers).[12] As an East Coast principal in a Gallup focus group said, "You want parents in the school, but you need teachers to view them as advocates, not as pains in the neck. At the same time, you need to help parents realize that teachers are their partners. Teacher and parent have to be mutually supportive."

When parent-teacher interactions start with defensiveness on both sides, neither is open to the other's point of view. If schools can pre-empt those negative first steps, they can avert the vicious cycle and even replace it with a positive cycle in which parental involvement leads to positive relationships, which in turn leads to further involvement.

START ON A POSITIVE NOTE

Lisa, another colleague of mine who lives in Omaha, told me about a parent-teacher conference that she says will stick with her forever:

"Miss Vancleave was a brand new teacher, fresh out of college. So we thought, hmmm, is this going to work? But I decided I should give her the benefit of the doubt.

"So the dreaded first parent-teacher conference got scheduled, and I was very nervous about it because I just don't like to hear all the negative stuff that you kind of associate with parent-teacher conferences. We sat down and I said, 'So how is he doing?' She's like, 'First of all, I've just got to tell you Jack is one of my favorite students.' She said, 'Here are some of the things that I asked him to pull out of his work. These are some of his favorite pieces that he's worked on this quarter. These are the things that he is most proud of and he wanted to share with you.' And I was like, 'This is great!'

"At the end of the conference, she said, 'I've got one other thing that I need you to do for me.' And she handed me this sheet of paper with a star on it. She said, 'Before he goes to bed tonight, I want you to list out at each tip of the star the things that you are so happy with about him right now and place it on his pillow.' She was trying to get at things like his spelling, his math, and just all the good highlight points of that conference.

"I just thought it was very cool for Jack to have a teacher like that. I was so ready to think, 'Oh, this brand new teacher — we're going to have to be the ones that give her the experience that she's going to need for other children down the road.' But she really, to me, had it. It's her makeup, it's just who she is."

All too frequently, parents' contacts with teachers occur as a result of a problem. To many parents, any communication from a teacher means bad news. Savvy teachers also start parent-teacher conferences by listening intently to parents, asking for their insights about the student and how best to work with him or her. What does the parent think that the student does best? What are the student's accomplishments? What are her interests? What's the best way to give her recognition? How does she respond to being corrected? Who are her best friends? These teachers understand that knowing more about students' strengths pays off in the classroom — but also that the information-sharing approach invites collaboration.

Making the initial contact with a parent a positive one goes a long way toward building a trusting relationship. The parent will approach future calls from the teacher more optimistically, and the teacher is acknowledged on a more personal level. In fact, a Gallup study found "a positive beneficial contact with a parent" as one of five factors most closely related to overall parental satisfaction.[13]

Reaching Out to Preschool and Kindergarten Parents

There are many examples of programs that involve parents early in their children's schooling, strengthening the family's education culture and establishing positive parent-school interaction from the start. Early Head Start provides programs in parenting and specific developmental activities for low-income parents of infants and toddlers to use with their children at home. In 2001, an independent study including 3,000 families compared two-year-olds whose parents had been enrolled in the program for at least a year to randomly assigned toddlers whose parents had not received the training. The Early Head Start toddlers demonstrated higher scores on a standardized developmental assessment and displayed more cooperative behavior, and their parents created more stimulating environments at home.[14]

Project EASE (Early Access to Success in Education) helps parents in Minnesota nurture verbal language and literacy skills in kindergarten students. The program provides training, materials, and specific activities for parents to carry out with their children at home. A 2000 study of its effects found that kindergarteners whose parents participated made significantly greater gains than did a randomly selected group. What's more, by the end of the program, those kindergarteners who displayed poor language abilities but received structured help from their parents were performing as well as those who began with strong language abilities but didn't receive help.[15] Programs like these give parents a positive orientation toward their children's education very early on, increasing the chances that they will be productively engaged throughout their children's school years.

Reaching Out to Elementary and Middle School Parents

Constructive teacher-parent partnerships may have the greatest long-term impact in the elementary and middle school years. Consider, for example, a 2001 study that focused on teacher outreach to parents in 71 Title I elementary schools in high-poverty communities. That outreach included: a) asking for in-person meetings, b) making telephone calls to parents, and c) providing materials for parents to use in helping their children at home. Results showed that when teachers and schools made sustained efforts to involve the parents of low-achieving *third grade* students, those students showed 50% greater growth in reading and 40% greater growth in mathematics on standardized tests two years later in *fifth grade* than did students whose schools reported low parental outreach levels for the third grade.[16]

As part of a 2004 study, 129 high-poverty elementary schools adopted a specific set of strategies for involving parents. Those schools posted significantly higher gains on state tests than did matched schools with no such strategies — higher also than the average gain for the state.[17] The researchers suggested that efforts by teachers and the schools to involve parents created higher levels of trust and respect. They went on to recommend the following efforts by schools:

- Make expectations clear, communicate students' progress to parents, and provide examples of what parents can do to help.

- Develop opportunities for parents and teachers to talk about the role parents can play in helping students.

- Create parent education programs.

- Build relationships with parents through a continuous conversation about teachers' and parents' roles in student learning.

In effect, the program emphasized positive steps in providing learning opportunities for parents and creating an ongoing dialogue between parents and teachers.

The list could go on. The common element among programs like these is that they successfully manage teachers' and parents' perceptions of the role parents play in their children's schooling. In order to reach parents, schools first openly acknowledge that their help is needed, that the school alone can't handle the task of educating their children. Effective programs then establish an ongoing dialogue about children's talents and strengths, help parents develop the confidence to be involved in cultivating those talents and strengths, and provide specific suggestions and training for parents.

Parental Involvement in High Schools

What about parents' involvement at the high school level? Speaking of the limited role of the environment in shaping kids' behavior, Matt Ridley says in *Nature via Nurture*, "Parenting is a revelation to most people. Having assumed you would now be the chief coach and sculptor of a human personality, you find yourself reduced to the role of little more than a helpless spectator cum chauffeur."[18] Around age 16, even the chauffeur role ends.

Schools can help keep parents from being relegated to the sidelines by encouraging dialogue about students' academic choices beginning in high school. After all, if schools are to get better at identifying and leveraging students' talents, parents' insights are essential. What's more, helping a child think about his greatest talents can help his parents anchor their relationship with him through a time of potential emotional turmoil.

TALK *WITH* ME, NOT *AT* ME

The other connecting point that is important to engaged schools is the one between school leaders and the community. Most administrators believe that they are doing a good job of communicating to parents and other community members. But according to a 2003 MetLife survey (Figure 13), teachers and parents aren't as convinced.

While 89% of principals and 72% of teachers strongly felt that their school "is welcoming to parents," fewer parents (61%) agreed. Ninety-one percent of principals said their schools have "a lot" of "open communication," but only 58% of teachers and 58% of parents agreed. Sixty-nine percent of principals strongly felt their school "is connected with the neighborhood or community," but just 58% of teachers and 49% of parents felt the same way.[19]

FIGURE 13

Principals', Teachers', and Parents' School Descriptions

Percentage responding "a lot"

	Principals n=800 %	Teachers n=1,017 %	Parents n=1,107 %
Shows concern for students	97	83	66
Is welcoming to parents	89	72	61
Has open communication	91	58	58
Is connected with the community	69	58	49

Source: MetLife. (2003). *The MetLife survey of the American teacher: An examination of school leadership.* Based on a Harris Interactive poll.

Obviously, it's more difficult for principals to criticize their own schools than for parents to do so. But the size of the gaps, particularly with regard to "open communication," is striking. When it comes to perceptions of openness and connectedness, it's the parents' point of view that's important. If schools are to garner the support of their communities, they can't be viewed by the people they serve as isolated or inhospitable.

Some school leaders may need to reconsider how they think about community partnerships. When asked to describe public engagement in the 2001 Public Agenda study, most of the 686 superintendents surveyed discussed one-way communication activities designed to garner public support and improve the image of schools. Moreover, almost three in four superintendents (73%) said their own school leaders typically communicate to rally support for policies and programs rather than listening to concerns or needs.[20]

These descriptions echo teachers' views of their own voice in school matters. In response to the same Public Agenda survey, 70% of teachers said they personally felt left out of discussions and decisions in their school districts. Only about half (49%) said they felt school leaders listen to teachers' views and take them into account.[21] Teachers can be a school's best community ambassadors through their ongoing dialogue with parents — or they can be the school's biggest detractors. Keeping teachers informed and ensuring that their input is sought not only helps keep teachers engaged at work, it also makes them more likely to get parents involved in school issues. After all, if teachers feel shut out of active involvement with their own schools, what chance do parents have?

Administrators tend to view their outreach role as a traditional "PR" function, largely consisting of outbound "marketing." But in the age of information, customers and constituents of all kinds — from consumers opting to receive customized alerts from amazon.com to citizens e-mailing their opinions to local congressional representatives — increasingly expect to be active participants in a dialogue rather than passive recipients of mass-market communications. Savvy marketers know that dialogue has become critical to customer engagement; school leaders should recognize the same with regard to engaging parents and community leaders.

255

COMMUNITY FEEDBACK

It's a tricky proposition to convince most people that the schools in their communities would benefit from their involvement, especially if they seem to be doing fine. As Figure 14 shows, of those members of the general public who rated their schools as "excellent" or "good" in a 2001 Public Agenda survey, three-fourths (76%) said they were comfortable leaving school policy decisions to educators (although we should note that even so, 52% of this group also indicated a desire for more community involvement in the schools). Among those who felt their schools were "fair" or "poor," 48% were comfortable leaving those decisions to educators, while the number who perceived a need for more public involvement grew to 74%.[22]

FIGURE 14

Comparison of Public Schools Rating and Involvement — General Public

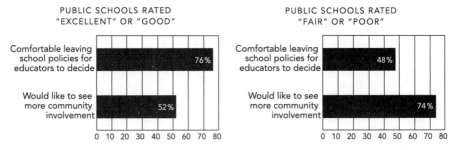

Source: Farkas, S., Foley, P., & Duffet, A. (2001). *Just waiting to be asked? A fresh look at attitudes on public engagement.* Public Agenda.

Some educators may be tempted to agree with those who feel schools are best left alone. But there are dangers in failing to actively involve parents and the broader community in the life of the school. In the case of parents, it sends a message that they play only a minor role in their children's education and that the school can handle the responsibility on its own. That perception can in turn be harmful to engagement among those *within* the school. Ernest Boyer pointed out in his 1983 book *High School: A Report on Secondary Education in America*, "The indifference of parents can be almost as destructive as criticism; it undermines staff morale, erodes standards, and slows students' progress."[23]

In addition to a scarcity of positive feedback from administrators, teachers often say that they feel a lack of respect from the public at large, and parents in particular. That can be enough to dishearten even the most committed individuals. Though most teachers derive intense satisfaction from seeing students grow, talented teachers also need — and deserve — to hear about the positive impact they've made. The active involvement of community members underscores to teachers and principals that those outside the school recognize the critical nature of their work.

In the 2001 Public Agenda study, superintendents and board members agreed that they typically hear only from community members who have complaints.[24] Among the most common complaints are demands for the removal of books or other materials. The debate over teaching evolution versus creationism is a good example — these challenges come from sharply different value positions and are fueled by distrust of schools as institutions. While these complaints typically come from a small minority of constituents, they consume tremendous amounts of time and energy. Absent hearing from parents and community members with a broader perspective and experience, teachers, principals, and district administrators begin to see this vocal minority as representing *all* parents. When only those who are unhappy with the school district get involved, the typical result is a blame game rather than a new collaboration to address a shared problem.

Parents in particular need more positive avenues by which to feel they have a voice in how their kids are taught. As David Mathews, president of the Kettering Foundation, has pointed out, such initiatives as charter schools, vouchers, and home-schooling represent efforts by segments of the public to take control of their children's education.[25] Would opportunities to become more closely involved in their local public schools and develop positive relationships with teachers make parents less likely to pursue these alternatives? It might. Certainly, alternatives like adopting a siege mentality, as the railroads did, or simply assuming that new competitors don't present a serious threat, as IBM did, will not ensure the viability of public schools in the future.

Community involvement provides an opportunity to not only tell the schools' story to a wider audience, but also to learn from the schools' customers in the community. The American public consistently makes it clear in polls that it supports public education rather than finding another approach for schools, but Americans want to see public schools improved.[26] School leaders must invite parents and the public into schools to build a broad-based commitment to education in their communities. Only by letting more of the public into our schools and making them active participants will community members — with or without children in the schools — see the public schools as their own.

THE SCHOOL AS THE HUB OF AN ENGAGED COMMUNITY

Earlier, I referred to Liberty Elementary School in Omaha as an example of a school established with a powerfully compelling mission, one of inclusiveness and positive change. The school is located in the heart of the city's growing Hispanic community; it serves a working-class, largely non-English-speaking population. Clearly, Liberty's principal, Nancy

Oberst, and her staff faced a daunting challenge in attempting to engage parents and the community in the life of the school.

So instead, they decided to engage the school in the life of the community. In the summer of 2002, Oberst and a team of educators canvassed the neighborhood, going door to door to let residents know the new school would be a positive, highly inclusive place — that they would be welcome there as active partners in their children's education. "We wanted everyone to know that it was going to be a school that was owned by the neighborhood and all the people," Oberst recalls.

Once she and her staff had begun to sell parents on the school, Oberst turned to businesses and other community organizations. The school was to be housed in an old bus warehouse for two years while a new building was constructed. Oberst considered this an opportunity to form strong partnerships with the community resources near the school. Students went to the nearby YMCA for gym classes, to the children's museum across the street for art, and took frequent trips to the children's theater and the local fire station.

Oberst tirelessly lobbies on behalf of Liberty's students, applying for grants and seeking donations from Omaha companies and organizations to provide basic necessities like clothes and medicine — and even food and rent in some cases for indigent families. The school serves as a de facto social services center, connecting families with social agencies like shelters and mental health providers. Healthcare clinics are held at Liberty once a week, GED classes take place daily in the mornings and afternoons, and ESL classes occur there regularly. In addition, the school recycles clothes and furniture for area residents, and parents are invited to come into the breakfast room every morning and eat with their kids.

"We want people to come in and talk to us and help us, you know, understand their situation. And we have people who can help people navigate through social situations and settings," Oberst says. "We have felt that our community was one that did not have the benefit of some of the social systems in place that other communities have. Nor do our families have the flexibility that people who are professionals have in their workplace which allows you to be more a part of your children's school."

The connections and positivity have generated an atmosphere that promotes the development of Liberty's students and the area as a whole. A *Medium Magazine* article called it "an anchor of hope and a catalyst for change" in its community.[27] That spirit makes parents and other community members want to be involved. "It's a feeling," Oberst says. "You walk in the building, and you catch the feeling. People are laughing, and children run up and hug people all the time. We talk to them; we laugh with them. We don't always speak the same language, but we're friendly and they feel welcome."

The "community schools" concept goes back at least to the 1930s, when industrialist Charles Stewart Mott, concerned about the welfare of his adopted community in Flint, Michigan, established a foundation that organized school-based recreational activities. Since then, the foundation has grown into a nationwide community education program.[28] Viewing the local school in a neighborhood as the hub on a wheel, the approach then adds spokes in the form of youth service groups, health and social agencies, public and private community service groups, and businesses. The goal is to use the school as a rallying point to: 1) expand community connections for young people, and 2) provide needed services for neighborhood residents through a variety of formal and informal partnerships.[29]

Rather than being one of many separate entities in the neighborhood, a community school builds bridges to other community sectors by inviting the public into the school at every opportunity. It provides services before, during, and after normal school hours for students as well as parents and non-parents. A school and community center in one, it partners with one or more local agencies to run activities that make full use of the school's facility to involve and enrich the community. No cookie-cutter program will work for such a school. Instead, the principal and teachers, parents, community agencies, and other interested community members develop the program for a community school cooperatively, based on local needs.[30]

The central goal of a community school is the same as any other: to provide students with a high-quality education. The principal's core responsibility, as in any school, is to provide a program and environment that promotes student achievement. But the means for arriving at those ends tend to be more diverse than in less well-connected schools. Activities for students in these schools may not cease at the end of the school day. After-school and evening programs combine educational, recreational, and mentoring activities. These less-structured activities give students a chance to more freely investigate their talents.[31]

Companion services for others in the school's neighborhood might include early-childhood, literacy, and job-skills training programs, as well as health services that otherwise might be scattered across the community. In exchange for arranging such services, which draw more community members into positive engagement with the school, administrators can say to assorted social and governmental agencies and the citizens of the neighborhood, "Forget about bricks and mortar; use the schools."[32]

Two large studies demonstrate the success of community school programs. The University of California, Irvine conducted an evaluation of the California After School Learning and Safe Neighborhoods

Partnerships Program in 2000 and 2001. A variety of activities is provided under this umbrella effort, but all programs must provide educational support, such as homework assistance and/or tutoring and enrichment programs in a number of areas.[33] The evaluation found that students participating in the program scored higher on standardized tests in reading and math, and their school attendance improved. Their grade-point averages also improved.[34]

The American Youth Policy Forum summarized 13 studies of "out-of-school time" programs. The programs varied widely but included combinations of academic help, cultural enrichment activities, drug and alcohol initiatives, life-skills training, mentoring, parent support activities, and recreation programs before and after normal school hours. In 11 of 13 evaluations with academic results, most of the programs found that participants improved on academic measures, earned higher scores on state tests, and were more likely to graduate than students who did not participate.[35]

Kenneth Leithwood and his colleagues describe the importance of the wider community in providing learning environments for students everywhere. Speaking of the broad group of organizations typically involved in community schools, they said, "In the best of circumstances, these networks, people and agencies form strong communities based on familiarity, interdependence, and commitment to a common purpose; they may add to the capital provided by healthy family cultures or compensate for unhealthy cultures."[36]

A commitment to community schools also offers returns to teachers and principals. By extending and complementing their work, community schools create a broader sense of belonging, of working together toward a common end. Without the engagement of the community, teachers and principals all too often feel as if they single-handedly fight a desperate battle to help students. Many teachers describe the resulting frustration as a factor in the profession's high turnover rate. Schools that invite the neighborhood in develop a very different role for teachers and other educators in the community.

The logistical difficulties associated with establishing and sustaining community schools are real, which explains why many communities that need such a resource don't have one. Principals can't assume the additional responsibilities, and in most instances, a full-time coordinator, hired through community sources, coordinates the additional community school programs. Ironing out tricky issues like facility usage and ownership of programs requires a fervent belief in the enormous potential of community schools to cultivate engagement both inside and outside the school walls.

But in the end, promoting community engagement with the school may help the country make the most of its education system. Not only does it give students more opportunities for applied learning, it gives more community members exposure to student talent. Such connections generate opportunities that wouldn't otherwise exist. In describing the result of globalization to Thomas Friedman, Bill Gates said, "We're going to tap into the energy and talent of five times as many people [worldwide] as we did before."[37] If that's true, American communities desperately need the capacity to reach into the schools and help discover and promote talent in more students than ever before.

IMPROVING EDUCATION FROM THE GROUND UP

Though school-community connections typically originate within the schools, they don't always. There are many people outside the schools who are interested in forging such partnerships. David Mathews defines the public as "a diverse body of people who have joined together to try to promote the well-being of all" and notes that "Without a public, public schools can't exist."[38]

Some efforts to foster grass-roots community involvement with the schools have begun by rallying anyone with an impulse to support them: educators, community leaders, political leaders, taxpayers, parents, and citizens with no school-aged children. This approach starts with a positive assumption: People want to be involved in improving their schools if given the opportunity and a concrete reason to do so.[39]

The power of PEN

For a good example of this strategy, consider the efforts of the Public Education Network (PEN). In PEN initiatives, local action in a community moves through what are known as local education foundations or funds. Created as non-profit support organizations for public schools, these groups initially made grants to schools by soliciting community donations and organizing fundraisers. Other foundations filled a need in providing services to school districts, such as the arrangement of staff development activities.

Dedicated to supporting public schools, but independent of the school district itself, these foundations serve as a connection between a community's business and civic leadership and its school districts. They support bond election campaigns for school construction and levy elections to raise more money for public schools. They work to generate support for education proposals of which many community members would otherwise have never been aware.[40]

The concept developed by PEN calls for working with three broad groups in the community. The largest group of residents in any given school district today has no school-aged children. This group includes not just childless people, but those with grown children and those

264

whose children haven't yet reached school age. Demographically, this group will continue to grow, and the vast majority of its members have little or no relationship with the schools.[41]

A second broad category consists of key stakeholder groups, including parent organizations, unions, chambers of commerce, business associations, and civic organizations. And the third group is made up of policymakers at the state, local, and school district levels. PEN's approach is to bring these groups together as partners who are involved in critical issues.[42]

The program calls for moving people from self-interest to common interests — that is, moving everyone involved toward Mathews' criterion: a public that is supportive of the public good. The local education foundation calls groups together to identify and confront problems, thereby establishing relationships where none existed before. Individuals and groups are more likely to work together and assume responsibility for an outcome because of these contacts.

Information is power. So collecting data about specific areas that influence the quality of education in a community is essential. As a supporter of the school district and also as a representative of the community, the local education foundation can elicit trust from both sides in collecting and analyzing data. The resulting analysis is accepted as an objective presentation of the issue that helps rally everyone around a specific plan for improvement.[43]

Once collected, the data are disseminated as widely as possible. Individuals trained by the local education foundation to facilitate groups lead discussions on the issue with all interested groups in the community. This process of constituency building among stakeholders requires considerable time and effort, but the result is that a critical mass of the public understands the issue and agrees on a plan of action. The highly structured nature of the process leads to more ideas from the grass-roots level, stronger advocacy for meaningful change, and a greater commitment by all kinds of community leaders to stay involved in improving the schools.

Schools as "Community Learning Centers"

When it comes to demonstrating how community-school ties can co-alesce to benefit everyone involved, the Community Learning Centers in Lincoln, Nebraska, are among the best examples I've encountered. I learned about them from Barbara Bartle, Executive Director of the Foundation for Lincoln Public Schools (NE), who shared with me the following history:

> In 1995, the Foundation for Lincoln Public Schools board formed a strategic plan, and the board was shocked to learn that 75% of the citizens in Lincoln had no children in the public schools. This realization caused us to question how we could get the public to stay involved and interested in the schools when they didn't have children in them. We published the results of a community survey with action steps to inform and involve that provided some understanding of the community's priorities and challenges.
>
> From there, we decided to focus on some of the highest need schools where there weren't a lot of volunteers. At a Rotary kickoff meeting, a person from the housing industry in the audience was talking with one of the elementary principals and learned about the high student mobility in her school. From this came the idea that if renters could be moved to homeowners, people would stay and build the neighborhood around the school, and student achievement would increase.

So we started bringing together people in the housing business to meet with the principal. We soon learned that you can't talk about housing without Health and Human Services or workforce development representatives. Pretty soon, our table was looking like the community and talking about strengthening families with the child in the center. At the same time, I was going to grant meetings about after-school programming, and it became clear that we had to bring all of these people together.

From four pilots, begun with a study grant from the Lincoln Community Foundation, we had 19 community learning centers in 2005. Around each of those schools, there is a school neighborhood advisory committee that identifies the needs, suggests programs, and makes an annual plan. In each school, there is a broker, a staff person who works with the agencies that are already in the community to bring the programs into the school.

One of the programs [promoted by the advisory committees] involves starting at the school and working block by block to find out the greatest need for that block — whether it's eliminating a crack house or finding flowerpots. The concept is that if one block makes improvements, then the next block is more likely to do something. It involves getting people back to caring for the safety and well-being of the children in a local neighborhood.

The block projects also get people to know one another, start to trust one another, and start seeing the school as a friendly place. A lot of people didn't have good experiences in school themselves. So coming to school for a positive reason and having a good experience can change parents' attitudes, increase participation, and build support for students.

Another program found that out of 400 students in one of the schools, 160 had been identified as needing counseling or having inappropriate behavior, but only 14 were qualifying for counseling through Medicaid. Family Services and Title I collaborated and put their counselor in a space provided by the school instead of in a branch office, reducing transportation difficulties for community members and serving many more children than they were in their normal offices.

Obviously, this arrangement offers untold opportunities for students, both through the services provided for students and the spirit of active involvement instilled in school and community members. "Public engagement is all about building relationships and trust," Bartle concluded. "Then, by creating partnerships and collaboration, we can accomplish so much more for students."

COMMUNITY INVOLVEMENT AND THE GRADE GAP

Unfortunately, such a high level of public involvement in the schools has become relatively rare. Most schools are still a mystery to too many members of their local communities. When asked to grade their *local public schools*, people without children in their local schools give lower average ratings than do parents with school-aged children. In 2005, 45% of the public *without* school-aged children gave the local schools an "A" or "B," but a significantly higher 57% of those *with* children in K-12 schools gave the local schools an "A" or "B." Regardless of how Americans overall have rated the public schools over the last 25 years, those who have exposure to those schools have been more likely to rate them highly than those who do not.

We see a different — but related — gap between respondents' ratings of the nation's public school system as a whole and their ratings of the public schools in their area (Figure 15). The grades given to the system as a whole are always considerably lower than the grades people assign to the schools in their community — an effect we see among those with school-aged kids and those without.[44]

FIGURE 15

Grading the Public Schools, 1974-2005
Phi Delta Kappa/Gallup Polls

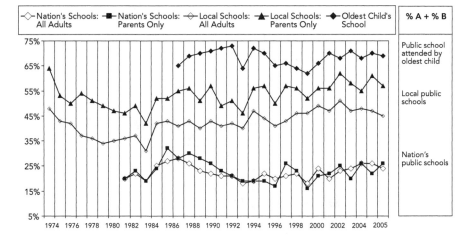

What grade, A, B, C, D, or Fail, would you give the public schools in **your community**?
...the public schools in **the nation**?
...the public school **attended by your oldest child**?

What's the point here? There are different ways to interpret the gap. Certainly, a sense of loyalty may be an influence, particularly given that we see the "better in my backyard" effect in Americans' ratings of other services, such as healthcare facilities, as well. Nonetheless, it seems encouraging that the more likely it is that the respondent has firsthand knowledge of the schools he or she is rating, the more likely he or she is to have a positive perception of them.

Those who have no firsthand knowledge are most likely to base their perceptions of the public schools on media reports, which tend to dwell on negatives like low test scores and school violence. In 2002, the PDK/Gallup Poll asked Americans: *What are the sources of information you use to judge the quality of schools in your community — that is, where do you get your information about the schools?* Newspapers were the dominant source of information about the quality of schools for 43% of those surveyed, followed by other people (35%), children or students (17%), and television (16%). Communications from the schools themselves tied with unspecified media for last place at 6%.[45]

FIGURE 16

Information on the Quality of Schools — 2002 Phi Delta Kappa/Gallup Poll

What are the sources of information you use to judge the quality of schools in your community — that is, where do you get your information about the schools?

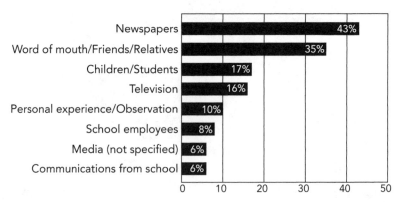

Source: Rose, L. C., & Gallup, A. M. (2002, September). The 34th Annual Phi Delta Kappa/Gallup Poll of the public's attitudes toward the public schools. *Phi Delta Kappan, 84*(1), 41-57.

In 1984, John Goodlad asserted, "Our schools will get better and have continuing good health only to the degree that a significant proportion of our people, not just parents, care about them."[46] Ninety-seven percent of superintendents, 95% of board members, and 94% of teachers indicated in a 2001 poll that providing opportunities to see schools from the inside was the best way to generate that kind of support.[47]

Just as teachers can tap the talents of a student only by actively engaging her, schools can tap the talents of the community surrounding them only by working to engage it in the education process so vital to its future. All of this is hard work to be sure, and it must be done in addition to the core responsibility of helping students learn day to day.

But broader efforts in school districts of all types will likely reap rewards. Many teachers have the sense that they are constantly swimming upstream in the face of a lack of understanding among parents and community leaders regarding all of the expectations piled on them. They would be relieved by a process through which stakeholders from across the community honestly discuss and jointly plan ways to be sure those expectations are realistic and that talented teachers have the support they need to fulfill them.

One more point: Engaging more community members in more positive relationships with the schools may help break up the education reform logjam that has made it harder for the schools to evolve with changing social conditions. The more community leaders and school leaders share information about what actually works in the classroom, the more the national debate between the "insider" and "outsider" perspectives on education reform becomes moot. District by district, school by school, more people are likely to be on the same page, working to build schools in which teachers and students are more fully engaged.

CONCLUSION

"It is not the strongest of the species that survives, nor the most intelligent, but the one most responsive to change."
— *Charles Darwin*

Despite his company's status as the leader in consumer electronics retailing in 2002, Brad Anderson, CEO of Best Buy, worried about the competition. Anderson was most concerned not about the number-two electronics retailer, Circuit City, but about competition from totally different sources: Wal-Mart and Dell Computer. Wal-Mart's pervasiveness and Dell's mastery of online retailing made these two companies serious threats to Best Buy's future success.

How could Best Buy better position itself to meet these challenges? One answer was to focus on further improving one of the chain's strengths: the consumer electronics knowledge of its employees and their helpful-yet-unobtrusive manner of providing advice.

Best Buy also conducted an extensive study of its customers, which led the retailer to implement a radical shift in store operations. Identifying five types of highly profitable customers, the analysis suggested that one or more of these groups could be associated with an existing store's location. Then a strategy emerged: Each store would be given greater flexibility and autonomy regarding product display and inventory. So some stores might focus more heavily on home theater components, while others might stock more brightly colored iPods. In theory, this more nuanced understanding of each store's customers would boost sales and increase the odds that every location would be able to meet the needs of the customers it serves.

The strategy marked a significant departure from the fairly centralized process of decision making on products and store layout. Within Best Buy, the initial reaction was mixed, as the chain's existing strategies seemed to be working well. Nevertheless, many stores were converted to the new approach beginning in 2003. Throughout the rollout process in test stores, dissent was encouraged rather than suppressed so that issues could be worked out. Skepticism remained, but sales and profit gains by first quarter 2005 showed the strategy was working, and current plans call for conversion of all Best Buy stores by 2008.[1]

What does Best Buy's new marketing approach have to do with public schools? It's a good example of the kind of forward thinking that might have allowed the railroad companies to navigate sweeping social and technological changes and could have saved IBM a considerable amount of pain in the 1980s. Unlike the railroads and IBM, Best Buy demonstrated an understanding of the need to constantly assess the goals, strategies, and strengths of an organization in order to respond to changing conditions. The retailer illustrates the idea that simply assuming an approach that has been successful in the past will continue to be so can blind an organization (or industry) to opportunities to build a more sustainable future.

A FINAL ASSUMPTION

In Chapter 10, I noted that Americans give strikingly higher ratings to their local schools than they give to the nation's public schools as a whole. Certainly, there's an element of loyalty in those responses. There's also the likelihood that most Americans have little direct knowledge of their local schools and assume that no news is good news. Parents may simply hold the assumption that *if their son or daughter receives good grades, seems happy with school, has friends, and feels safe, the school must be doing a good job.*

And yet, we become alarmed when we hear that American kids are testing below those in Japan and Singapore, that business leaders are fretting about our country's future competitiveness, and that we are only tapping the true potential of a fraction of our students. Many people have the impression that America's schools haven't kept pace with new realities, but they may find it difficult to criticize the schools in their area because those schools seem to be doing all the things that people are used to seeing schools do.

The current strategy for improving America's public schools both feeds on and reinforces that impression: We don't need to think differently about schools' priorities or structure, we just need to enforce expectations better than we have in the past. That might be an effective strategy if we were competing against our own past performance. Unfortunately, that's no longer the case.

THE COMING STORM

The continued use of assumptions that are outdated or only partially correct will increasingly interfere with American students' ability to maintain world-class performance as the definition of "world-class" changes. Describing America's high schools as "obsolete," Bill Gates charges that, "Even when they're working exactly as designed, [they] cannot teach our kids what they need to know today."[2] As of yet, there's not enough pressure to break though the logjam in education reform, partly because conditions have changed so rapidly that it's hard to be clear on what's at stake. As Thomas Friedman points out in *The World Is Flat*, "We are blithely sailing along, heading straight for the storm, with both politicians and parents insisting that no dramatic changes or sacrifices are required now. After all, look how calm and sunny it is outside, they tell us. . . . Don't be fooled by the calm. That's always the time to change course — not when you're just about to get hit by the typhoon."[3]

Neither the public nor political leaders seem fully aware that, as in Best Buy's case, the real test for America's schools increasingly comes from outside the traditional comparison group. Instead of a school in the same school district or in a neighboring community or the state's average test scores, the new competitive benchmarks for America's public schools are in China, India, and other countries whose rising educational standards are fueled by their skyrocketing economic development. On the basis of the latest international benchmark tests, we're now in the middle of the pack among the industrialized nations — and slipping.

In a 2005 *Education Week* commentary, educator Mary Catherine Swanson argued that the "silent majority" of "average" American students has been neglected in recent years. "It's time to re-energize the discussion on how to serve those 'average' students," Swanson wrote. "Today, we're consigning millions of students to low expectations, ignoring their true potential, and denying them the education they need to get ahead. Schools are not making the achievement gains they could. And we're contributing to greater economic and racial polarization in our country, while failing to address national workforce and economic realities."[4]

Swanson is right. In the long run, it won't be the chronically estranged students or the slowest learners who are our biggest problem. It will be the much larger group that is simply going through the motions — those millions of students who feel no excitement about their own development and whose vital talents are left untapped.

I'm convinced that the ongoing failure to develop schools that better cultivate the talents and enthusiasm of students and teachers will eventually result in the declaration of an education crisis in this country. And you can be sure that the resulting sense of urgency will only intensify support for alternatives to public education. As Kettering Foundation President David Mathews suggests, "We have to face the fact that we might not have a public school system in the 21st century." While public schools may not go away altogether, they may become "to our educational system what Medicaid is to our healthcare system."[5] The result is a stark picture in which parents abandon public schools in droves, with the poor trapped in those that remain.

Let's consider once again the errors of the railroads and IBM, and this time compare them more directly to current trends in education reform.

- To ward off mounting criticism as they increasingly failed to meet passengers' expectations, the railroads adopted a siege mentality, but it couldn't protect them from change. Similarly, educators ignored the calls for testing that came in the 1980s, saying that education was too complicated to measure. But governors and state legislatures created standards and accountability testing in spite of educators' criticisms — and the federal government made it a national mandate in No Child Left Behind. As a result, both sides have become entrenched in their opposing positions, reducing their likelihood to share ideas and develop creative alternatives.

- The railroads and IBM clung to narrow views of their missions, missing opportunities to stay ahead of their respective competitors. America's public schools will fall into the same trap if they behave as if their mission is simply to maintain the schools of the past. In the working world, progress is inescapable. It should be a similarly inescapable element of students' experiences in school. Public schools will remain relevant only as long as leaders continually revise their mission with an eye toward the future.

- The near-monopoly status of public schools won't protect them from the alternative systems that will emerge if Americans begin to fear that a national education crisis has reached the schools in their own neighborhoods. It may seem inconceivable that America's public schools could become so obsolete that they are beyond repair. But the railroad barons once monopolized transportation, and IBM's market share once seemed unassailable. Both suffered from complacency, and both were crippled by more forward-looking competitors.

CHALLENGING THE ASSUMPTIONS

There are no silver bullets when it comes to revitalizing America's class-rooms. But we can take specific steps to challenge the old assumptions, adopt new perspectives, and construct engaged schools where students, teachers, principals, and communities develop to their full potential.

Starting With Strengths

Most fundamentally, it's time to recognize that the development of strengths, not the remedial approach so often taken in our society, leads to excellence. The differences between individuals should be acknowledged and celebrated, rather than downplayed in favor of standardization, or even viewed as detrimental. The schools should construct the means to allow students to run with their talents, rather than create institutional hurdles to talent development. An important part of every young person's education should be the identification and development of his or her greatest talents, guided by an individualized approach.

Every student needs to learn the basics. But ultimately, fulfillment for most students comes from the opportunity to develop their natural inclinations in ways that lead to personal and professional success. A focus on weakness fixing and remediation leads to an emphasis on getting all students to average, not to excellence in an area of great potential. The one-size-fits-all approach still dominant in our schools today actually fits very few, and it results in a great deal of needless disillusionment. A strengths-development approach will demonstrate just the opposite: Individual students possess unique talents and differing learning needs. And they are energized when those differences are attended to by their teachers.

Recognizing That Schools Are People-Driven

School leaders and communities must recognize that the abilities of teachers, principals, and other school personnel are paramount to the success of students. No longer can we give lip service to the importance of talented educators while behaving as if they are interchangeable parts in a machine. Teacher talent clearly affects student outcomes more than any curricular change or prescribed instructional technique.

School leaders should start with the realization that their schools will be no better than the people who work with students.

This means that finding the right people must become the highest priority in every school and school district. Principals have no job more critical than selecting the teachers and other staff members who will help students learn. Selecting principals who are both good managers and inspiring leaders is, in turn, one of the most important functions at the district level. It's worth saying one more time: The success of every other effort depends on the identification, cultivation, and deployment of teacher talent and principal talent.

Building Engaged School Cultures

Each school's environment influences how the students and teachers within it perform. Underestimating the need to actively construct a positive culture can make any organization stagnant — but especially a school. The fact that some leaders understand this better than others produces wide variations in the working conditions between schools, and even within some schools.

The good news is that every school's environment can be improved if principals, teachers, and other staff members work together with the express purpose of doing so. Supportive environments can slow the revolving door of teacher turnover and increase teachers' loyalty and enthusiasm. Within those environments, teachers and other staff members feel that their basic needs are provided for, that they're supported, that they belong, and that they have opportunities to grow. Only at that point are teachers and support staff capable of making students feel the same way.

Involving Those Outside the School

School leaders must recognize that the active support of parents and the surrounding community can extend and amplify the learning that takes place during normal school hours. Great schools engage parents in relationships that help parents develop a more thorough understanding of their child and of the role they play in his or her learning. One of the key benefits of such outreach is stronger, more trusting partnerships between parents and teachers.

Moreover, schools can't make the necessary changes alone. School leaders must take the first step and reach out to their communities. Then, communities must rally around initiatives intended to keep students keenly interested in unlocking their own potential. One of the largest obstacles to creating engaged schools is the complacency of parents and the public to changes in America's schools. As the cartoon character Pogo said, "We have met the enemy, and he is us."

Improving Measurement

Encouraging decision makers to think differently about accountability testing is an extremely difficult challenge, because the current system is encased in state and federal law. But our measurement strategies must quickly become more flexible and sophisticated to accommodate the goal of cultivating development in students' areas of strongest interest and talent and to provide more useful instructional information. America can't match the pace of global competition by continuing to set student achievement goals that amount to the lowest common denominator.

The current accountability testing approach appears far more suitable for the past than the future. By these measures, too many "good" schools are deemed superior not through their own efforts, but because of the stronger family educational cultures and socioeconomic advantages of the students in them. Measurement of students' relative growth provides a much better yardstick of a school's capacity to keep its staff and students fully engaged in the learning process.

CHANGING COURSE

Inertia among those most closely associated with our public schools is the biggest obstacle to their development. To many parents and community members, the idea that we need to substantively change the way we think about schooling can be distressing because it forces us to recognize that the means by which we ourselves were educated are no longer entirely adequate.[6] Failing to break with the comfortable past results in school leaders attempting to drive into the future by looking in the rear-view mirror.

As institutions, school districts appear just as likely to support business as usual. School board members, superintendents, and principals live in a political world. Without a public mandate, changes tend to be limited to areas considered the province of professionals — most notably, curriculum and instruction. The resulting pressure to provide rigor and structure forces teachers to teach like they themselves were taught, perpetuating an education model from the past. Teachers now work so hard on a day-to-day basis to conform with standards that they rarely have time to step back and question what's being done. The end result of all this inertia is, in futurist Alvin Toffler's terms, "a second-rate, factory style organization pumping out obsolete information in obsolete ways."[7]

Shaking the system out of its rut won't be easy, but there's reason to think it's increasingly attainable. Business leaders and globalization experts have sounded a clear alarm that we can no longer afford to let the obstacles to education reform keep us from taking bold new steps.

As stakeholders in the educational system, they can lay the groundwork in forcing local, state, and national political figures to re-examine how schools might better prepare their students. But ultimately, only when parents and the public are convinced of the need for change will it occur on a large scale. In order to spark the public's imagination, school and community leaders must paint bold and innovative visions of fully engaged schools.

Those visions should incorporate the dreams we all have for our children: That beyond learning the basics, they will discover and explore their talents as naturally unique individuals. That their teachers will have the ability to see the best in them, and serve as guides in bringing it out. That their schools will provide them with positively charged environments alive with exploration and optimism. That they will be challenged and learn that hard work pays off.

Admittedly, it may be impossible to find a school in which every single student is fully engaged and developing his or her unique potential. But schools can get far closer to that ideal than they are today. And we can certainly have schools in which more teachers and principals are engaged in their work. America's public schools kindled hopes of economic and social advancement that fueled the American dream for nearly 200 years. They must continue to be sources of hope by overcoming the lethargy that now plagues them.

Futurist John Schaar said, "The future is not some place we are going to, but one we are creating. The paths are not to be found, but made, and the activity of making them, changes both the maker and the destination." I am confident that building engaged schools will change America's students, teachers, principals, and communities in meaningful and positive ways. It's time to create the future.

LEARN MORE

To learn more about building an engaged school:

- Call Gallup's Education Division at 402-951-2003.

- Contact us by e-mail at engagedschools@gallup.com

- Visit our Web site at http://education.gallup.com

- Subscribe to the *Gallup Educator*, the Education Division's online journal, at http://education.gallup.com/educator/

ACKNOWLEDGEMENTS

As a teacher, I understand all too well that no book is "by" its author alone. In many ways, writers stand on the shoulders of their teachers, mentors, and fellow scholars to describe what they see. And they rely on dedicated partners to help turn their ideas into printed reality.

The teacher and mentor who contributed most to this book is Donald O. Clifton, Ph.D. (1924-2003). Ever the learner, Don spent his life researching successful people in all walks of life, but he had a special passion for teachers. His enduring legacy is his tireless mission to help people find the right "fit" for their talents, in order to develop the very best in them. Don created the first engaged school in Gallup's own Child Development Center.

I am greatly indebted to Steve Crabtree, my writing partner on this book, for his assistance, counsel, and involvement in crafting these pages. Steve is an extraordinarily gifted writer who helped me bring the concepts of the engaged school to life. He also spent countless hours studying the education field so that he could bring myriad insights and suggestions for improvement to this book. Steve's total commitment to this project has made *Building Engaged Schools* possible. I deeply value his partnership and his belief in making our schools better.

The people with whom I have the privilege of working every day provided constant support and encouragement throughout the writing of this book. A big thank you goes to Judy Bailey, Irene Burklund, Dee Drozd, Gary Evans, Ella Turrentine Hall, Denise Hinkley, Kelly Peaks Horner, Rosanne Liesveld, Jo Ann Miller, JerLene Mosley, and Mark Pogue. Their commitment to the students of America is truly inspiring. A special thanks goes to Connie Rath for her belief in Gallup's work in education and her personal support of me. Sherry Ehrlich, a mentor and friend, remains one of the best teachers I've ever known.

A special mention goes to our gifted editor Paul Petters for his keen insights into strengths theory and deep understanding of Gallup's research. Paul deserves tremendous credit for ensuring this work stays true to Gallup's research base and to the unique language of strengths. The ever-meticulous Mark Stiemann took great pains to ensure that the manuscript was logically consistent and that all the facts checked out; I thank him for his considerable efforts throughout the process. Thanks also to our copyeditor Kelly Henry for lending her sharp and discerning eye to the text, and to graphic designer Sarah Schenck for ensuring that the finished product has a polished and distinctive look.

Geoff Brewer, our editorial director, earned a great deal of gratitude for his support and guidance. Geoff always knew when to ask for more and when to acknowledge the struggle that comes with putting ideas on paper.

To Larry Emond and Jim Clifton go my appreciation for their support and commitment to Gallup's involvement with education and to writing a book about the people who make schools great learning places for students. To Piotrek Juszkiewicz, my many thanks for his publishing expertise as well as his diligent work in getting this book produced.

My deepest appreciation goes to the thousands of teachers and principals in America's schools as well as the managers and leaders in numerous fields Gallup has had the pleasure to study over the years. Gallup's research was made possible by your cooperation.

Lastly, my heartfelt thanks go to Nancy, my most critical editor and biggest supporter. My wife and best friend, Nancy, improved the ideas and kept my spirits up throughout the project. Without her, this book would likely be a wish rather than a reality.

— Gary Gordon

NOTES

Introduction

[1] National Commission on Excellence in Education. (1983, April). *A nation at risk: The imperative for educational reform*. Retrieved March 6, 2006, from http://www.ed.gov/pubs/NatAtRisk/risk.html

[2] Ibid.

[3] Friedman, T. L. (2005). *The world is flat: A brief history of the twenty-first century*. New York: Farrar, Straus and Giroux.

[4] National Center for Education Statistics. *Trends in international mathematics and science study (TIMSS) 2003*. Retrieved March 6, 2006, from http://nces.ed.gov/timss/TIMSS03Tables.asp?figure=1&Quest=1 (4th grade) and http://nces.ed.gov/timss/TIMSS03Tables.asp?figure=5&Quest=1 (8th grade)

[5] Lerner, R. (2004, December 6). *The release of the Program for International Student Assessment (PISA)*. Retrieved March 6, 2006, from http://nces.ed.gov/whatsnew/commissioner/remarks2004/12_6_2004.asp

[6] Ibid.

[7] Sum, A. M., Kirsch, I. S., & Taggart, R. (2002). *The twin challenges of mediocrity and inequality: Literacy in the U.S. from an international perspective.* Retrieved March 6, 2006, from the Educational Testing Service Web site: http://www.ets.org/Media/Research/pdf/PICTWIN.pdf

[8] Organisation for Economic Co-operation and Development. (2004, September 14). *Education at a glance 2004.* Retrieved March 8, 2006, from http://www.oecd.org/dataoecd/34/55/33714494.pdf

[9] Lyons, L. (2005, June 7). Reforms fail to raise confidence in education. *Gallup Poll Tuesday Briefing.* Retrieved March 17, 2006, from http://poll.gallup.com/content/default.aspx?ci=16657

[10] Hart, P. D., & Winston, D. (2005). *Ready for the real world? Americans speak on high school reform.* Retrieved March 17, 2006, from the Educational Testing Service Web site: http://www.ets.org/Media/Education_Topics/pdf/2005highschoolreform.pdf and http://www.ets.org/Media/Education_Topics/pdf/2005surveypresentation.pdf

[11] Gardner, H. (2000). *The disciplined mind: Beyond facts and standardized tests, the K-12 education that every child deserves.* New York: Penguin.

[12] Fairfax County Public Schools (2005, August 11). *Fairfax County public schools to open on Tuesday, September 6.* Retrieved March 17, 2006, from http://www.fcps.k12.va.us/suptapps/newsreleases/newsrelease.cfm?newsid=50

Ulysses S. Grant High School. (n.d.). *School profile.* Retrieved March 14, 2006, from http://www.granths.org/profile.jsp?rn=3956

[13] Gardner, H. (1993). *Multiple intelligences: The theory in practice.* New York: Basic Books.

[14] Ibid.

Chapter 1 — Old Assumptions, New Perspectives

[1] Stover, J. F. (1997). *American railroads.* (2nd ed.). Chicago: University of Chicago Press.

[2] Ibid.

[3] Thompson, G. L. (1993). *The passenger train in the motor age: California's rail and bus industries, 1910-1941.* Columbus: Ohio State University Press.

[4] Carroll, P. (1993). *Big blues: The unmaking of IBM.* New York: Crown Publishers.

See also Chposky, J., & Leonsis, T. (1988). *Blue magic: The people, power and politics behind the IBM personal computer.* New York: Facts on File.

[5] Ibid.

[6] Ibid.

[7] Hutzler, C., & Linebaugh, K. (2004, December 8). For Lenovo, a bold gambit. *The Wall Street Journal,* p. B2.

Lohr, S., & Sorkin, A.R. (2004, December 9). A tale of two nations. *Kansas City Star,* p. B1.

[8] Chposky, J. & Leonsis, T. (1988). *Blue magic: The people, power and politics behind the IBM personal computer.* New York: Facts on File.

[9] Brandwein, P. F. (1981). *Memorandum: On renewing schooling and education.* New York: Harcourt Brace Jovanovich.

Chapter 2 — The Reform Standoff

[1] Rugg, H., & Shumaker, A. (1928). *The child-centered school.* New York: World Book.

[2] National Commission on Excellence in Education. (1983, April). *A nation at risk: The imperative for educational reform.* Retrieved March 6, 2006, from http://www.ed.gov/pubs/NatAtRisk/risk.html

[3] Boyer, E. L. (1983). *High school: A report on secondary education in America.* New York: Harper & Row.

[4] Goodlad, J. I. (1984). *A place called school: Prospects for the future.* New York: McGraw-Hill.

[5] Thomson, S. D. (1983). *College admissions: new requirements by state universities.* Reston, VA: National Association of Secondary School Principals.

[6] Weiss, S. (2000, January-February). Standards. *The Progress of Education Reform 1999-2001, 1*(5), 4. Retrieved March 15, 2006, from Education Commission of the States Web site: http://www.ecs.org/html/educationIssues/ProgressofReform.asp

[7] National Conference of State Legislatures. (2005, February). *Task force on No Child Left Behind: Final report.* Retrieved March 28, 2006, from http://www.ncsl.org/programs/educ/nclb_report.htm

[8] Ingersoll, R. M. (2002, June). The teacher shortage: A case of wrong diagnosis and wrong prescription. *NASSP Bulletin, 86*(631), 16-31.

[9] Washington, B. T. (1901). *Up from slavery: an autobiography.* New York: Doubleday, Page and Company.

[10] Temes, P. S. (2002). *Against school reform (and in praise of great teaching): Getting beyond endless testing, regimentation, and reform in our schools.* Chicago: Ivan R. Dee.

[11] Phelps, G. (2004). Looking for the perfect process? *Gallup Management Journal.* Retrieved March 28, 2006, from http://gmj.gallup.com/content/default.aspx?ci=13522

[12] Wheatley, M. (1997, Summer). Goodbye, command and control, *Leader to Leader, 5,* 21-28.

[13] Willis, S. (2002, April). Customization and the common good: A conversation with Larry Cuban. *Educational Leadership. 59*(7), 6-11.

[14] National Conference of State Legislatures. (2005, February). *Task force on No Child Left Behind: Final report.* Retrieved March 28, 2006, from http://www.ncsl.org/programs/educ/nclb_report.htm. See tables that picture the differences in these groups of students and schools. See p. 54 for a list of sanctions under NCLB.

[15] Ghezzi, P. (2005, May 8). Student testing craze will pass, experts say. *Atlanta Journal-Constitution*, p. A1.

[16] Goodlad, J. I. (1984). *A place called school: Prospects for the future.* New York: McGraw-Hill.

[17] Bender, W. (2005, July 24). *Differentiated instruction: Teaching smarter, not harder.* Paper presented at the Teacher's Workshop Speaker's Bureau, Virginia Beach, VA.

[18] Thompson, S. (2001, January). The authentic standards movement and its evil twin [Electronic version]. *Phi Delta Kappan, 82*(5), 358-362.

[19] Mathews, J. (2004, February 17). Seeking alternatives to standardized testing. *The Washington Post.* Retrieved March 15, 2006, from http://www.washingtonpost. com/ac2/wp-dyn/A47699-2004Feb17?language=printer

[20] See Sanders, W. L., & Horn, S. P. (1994). The Tennessee value-added assessment system (TVAAS): Mixed-model methodology in educational assessment. *Journal of Personnel Evaluation in Education, 8*(1), 299-311.

Sanders, W. L., & Rivers, J. C. (1996). *Cumulative and residual effects of teachers on future student academic achievement.* Knoxville: University of Tennessee Value-Added Research and Assessment Center.

Wright, S. P., Horn, S. P., & Sanders, W. L. (1997, April). Teacher and classroom context effects on student achievement: Implications for teacher evaluation. *Journal of Personnel Evaluation in Education, 11*(1), 57-67.

Sanders, W. L., & Horn, S. P. (1998, September). Research findings from the Tennessee value-added assessment system (TVAAS) database: Implications for education and research. *Journal of Personnel Evaluation in Education, 12*(3), 247-256.

[21] U.S. Department of Education. (2005, November 18). *Secretary Spellings announces growth model pilot, addresses chief state school officers' annual policy forum in Richmond.* Retrieved March 15, 2006, from http://www.ed.gov/news/pressreleases/2005/11/11182005.html

[22] Wood, G. H. (1992). *Schools that work: America's most innovative public education programs.* New York: E. P. Dutton.

[23] Gardner, H. (1999). *The disciplined mind: Beyond facts and standardized tests, the K-12 education that every child deserves.* New York: Penguin.

[24] Palmer, P. J. (1997). *The courage to teach: Exploring the inner landscape of a teacher's life.* San Francisco: Jossey-Bass.

[25] Gates, B. (2005, February 26). Prepared remarks presented at 2005 National Education Summit on High Schools. Retrieved July 7, 2005, from http://www.nga.org/cda/files/es05gates.pdf

[26] Ibid.

Chapter 3 — A Common Hurdle: The Weakness Trap

[1] Reavis, G. H. (1999). *The Animal School.* Peterborough, NH: Crystal Springs Books. With grateful appreciation to Phi Delta Kappa, the professional education association, for its assistance in the use of the animal story within this book.

[2] Buckingham, M., & Clifton, D. O. (2001). *Now, discover your strengths.* New York: Free Press.

[3] Ibid.

[4] Gallup Poll, based on telephone interviews with 1,016 national adults, aged 18 and older, conducted February 19-21, 2001. For results based on the total sample of national adults, one can say with 95% confidence that the maximum margin of sampling error is ±3 percentage points.

[5] Seligman, M. E. P. (2002). *Authentic happiness: Using the new positive psychology to realize your potential for lasting fulfillment.* New York: Free Press.

[6] Hall, T. (1998, April 28). Seeking a focus on joy in field of psychology. *New York Times,* p. F7.

[7] Tomlinson, C. A. (1999). *The differentiated classroom: Responding to the needs of all learners.* Alexandria, VA: Association for Supervision and Curriculum Development.

[8] Austin, D. (2005). *The effects of a strengths development intervention program upon the self-perceptions of students' academic abilities.* Unpublished doctoral dissertation, Azusa Pacific University, Azusa, CA.

[9] Clifton, D. O., & Harter, J. K. (2003). Investing in strengths. In K. S. Cameron, J. E. Dutton, & R. E. Quinn (Eds.), *Positive organizational scholarship: Foundations of a new discipline* (pp. 111-121). San Francisco: Berrett-Koehler.

[10] Hallowell, E. M. (2002). *The childhood roots of adult happiness: Five steps to help kids create and sustain lifelong joy.* New York: Ballantine Books.

[11] Ridley, M. (2003). *Nature via nurture: Genes, experience, & what makes us human.* New York: HarperCollins.

[12] Ibid.

[13] Buckingham, M., & Coffman, C. (1999). *First, break all the rules: What the world's greatest managers do differently.* New York: Simon & Schuster.

[14] Thompson, M., & Barker, T. (2004). *The pressured child: Helping your child find success in school and life.* New York: Ballantine Books.

[15] Barab, S. A., & Plucker, J. A. (2002). Smart people or smart contexts? Cognition, ability, and talent development in an age of situated approaches to knowing and learning. *Educational Psychologist, 37*(3), 165-182.

[16] Buckingham, M., & Coffman, C. (1999). *First, break all the rules: What the world's greatest managers do differently.* New York: Simon & Schuster.

[17] Ingersoll, R. M. (2003). *Who controls teachers' work? Power and accountability in America's schools.* Cambridge, MA: Harvard University Press.

[18] Clifton, D. O., & Nelson, P. (1992). *Soar with your strengths.* New York: Delacorte Press.

Chapter 4 — A Common Goal: Engagement in the Classroom

[1] Elam, S. M., & Rose, L. C. (1995, September). The 27th annual Phi Delta Kappa/Gallup Poll of the public's attitudes toward the public schools. *Phi Delta Kappan* 77(1), 41-56.

Rose, L. C., & Gallup, A. M. (2004, September). The 36th annual Phi Delta Kappa/Gallup Poll of the public's attitudes toward the public schools. *Phi Delta Kappan,* 86(1), 41-56.

[2] Hersch, P. (1998). A *tribe apart: A journey into the heart of American adolescence.* New York: Ballantine Books.

[3] Bruner, J. (1960). *The process of education: A landmark in educational theory.* New York: Random House.

[4] Csikszentmihalyi, M. (1990). *Flow: The psychology of optimal experience.* New York: Harper & Row.

[5] Wrzesniewski, A. E. (1999). *Jobs, careers, and callings: Work orientation and job transitions.* Unpublished doctoral dissertation, University of Michigan, Ann Arbor.

[6] Florida, R. (2005). *The flight of the creative class: The new global competition for talent.* New York: HarperCollins.

[7] Superville, D. (2005, July 14). Nine-year-olds said better in math, reading. *Blackamericaweb.com News.* Retrieved March 17, 2006, from http://www.tjms.com/site.aspx/bawnews/tests715

[8] Friedman, T. L. (2005). *The world is flat: A brief history of the twenty-first century.* New York: Farrar, Straus, and Giroux.

[9] Goodlad, J. I. (1984). *A place called school: Prospects for the future.* New York: McGraw-Hill.

[10] Tyre, P. (2006, January 30). The trouble with boys. *Newsweek, 147,* 44-52.

[11] Winters Keegan, R. (2006, February 13). Looking for a lab-coat idol. *Time, 167*(7), 26-27.

[12] Schlechty, P. C. (2001). *Shaking up the schoolhouse: How to support and sustain educational innovation.* San Francisco: Jossey-Bass.

[13] Gallup Youth Survey, based on Web surveys with a randomly selected national sample of 600 teenagers, aged 13 to 17, in the Gallup Poll Panel of households. All surveys were completed between July 6 and September 4, 2005. For results based on this sample, one can say with 95% confidence that the maximum error attributable to sampling and other random effects is ±4 percentage points.

[14] Ibid.

[15] Crabtree, S. (2005, September 27). Youth poll: What makes the best classes different? *Gallup Poll Tuesday Briefing.* Retrieved March 17, 2006, from http://poll.gallup.com/content/default.aspx?ci=18808

[16] Tomlinson, C. A. (1999). *The differentiated classroom: Responding to the needs of all learners.* Alexandria, VA: Association for Supervision and Curriculum Development.

[17] Levine, M. (2002). *A mind at a time.* New York: Simon & Schuster.

[18] Crabtree, S. (2004, January 27). Students sound off on fixing U.S. education. *Gallup Poll Tuesday Briefing.* Retrieved March 20, 2006, from http://poll.gallup.com/content/default.aspx?ci=10420

[19] DuFour, R., DuFour, R., Eaker, R., & Karhanek, G. (2004). *Whatever it takes: How professional learning communities respond when kids don't learn.* Bloomington, IN: National Educational Service.

[20] Gardner, H. (2000). *The disciplined mind: Beyond facts and standardized tests, the K-12 education that every child deserves.* New York: Penguin.

Chapter 5 — Engaged Students: In Pursuit of Strengths

[1] Levine, M. (2002). *A mind at a time.* New York: Simon & Schuster.

[2] Jensen, E. (1998, November). How Julie's brain learns. *Educational Leadership, 56*(3), 41-45.

[3] D'Arcangelo, M. (1998, November). The brains behind the brain. *Educational Leadership, 56*(3), 20-25.

4   Ridley, M. (2003). *Nature via nurture: Genes, experience, & what makes us human.* New York: HarperCollins.

5   Ibid.

6   Ibid.

7   Buckingham, M., & Clifton, D. O. (2001). *Now, discover your strengths.* New York: Free Press.

8   Ibid.

9   Ibid.

10   Clifton, D. O., & Nelson, P. (1992). *Soar with your strengths.* New York: Delacorte Press.

11   Buckingham, M., & Coffman, C. (1999). *First, break all the rules: What the world's greatest managers do differently.* New York: Simon & Schuster.

12   Ibid.

13   Gallup Workplace Poll. (2002, July). Internal research document, The Gallup Organization.

14   Clifton, D. O., & Harter, J. K. (2003). Investing in strengths. In K. S. Cameron, J. E. Dutton, & R. E. Quinn (Eds.), *Positive organizational scholarship: Foundations of a new discipline* (pp. 111-121). San Francisco: Berrett-Koehler.

15   Gallup Poll, based on nationally representative samples of about 1,000 employed adults aged 18 and older. Interviews were conducted by telephone April 1-30, 2004. For results based on samples of this size, one can say with 95% confidence that the maximum error attributable to sampling and other random effects is ±3 percentage points.

16   Black, B. (2001, December 15). The road to recovery. *Gallup Management Journal.* Retrieved March 28, 2006, from http://gmj.gallup.com/content/default.aspx?ci=772

17   Connelly, J. (2002, March 15). All together now. *Gallup Management Journal.* Retrieved March 28, 2006, from http://gmj.gallup.com/content/default.aspx?ci=763

[18] Collins, J. (2001). *Good to great: Why some companies make the leap …
and others don't*. New York: HarperCollins.

[19] Bloom, B. S., & Sosniak, L. A. (1981, November). Talent development vs.
schooling. *Educational Leadership, 39*(2), 86-94.

[20] Toor, R. (2001). *Admissions confidential: An insider's account of the
elite college selection process*. New York: St. Martin's Press.

[21] Gallup Poll, based on telephone interviews with a randomly selected
national sample of 1,000 adults in the Gallup Poll Panel of households,
aged 18 and older, conducted March 1-22, 2005. For results based on
this sample, one can say with 95% confidence that the maximum error
attributable to sampling and other random effects is ±3 percentage
points.

[22] Levine, M. (2002). *A mind at a time*. New York: Simon & Schuster.

[23] As Alan Greenspan has noted, "The heyday when a high school or
college education would serve a graduate for a lifetime is gone. Today's
recipients of diplomas expect to have many jobs and to use a wide
range of skills over their working lives. Their parents and grandparents
looked to a more stable future — even if in reality it often turned out
otherwise."— Greenspan, Alan. (1999, February 16). Economy and
change: Investing in an educated future. Remarks presented at the
81st Annual Meeting of the American Council of Education. Retrieved
March 21, 2006, from http://www.federalreserve.gov/boardDocs/
speeches/1999/19990216.htm

[24] Friedman, T. L. (2005, April 29). 'What, me worry?' *New York Times*, p.
A25.

[25] Williamson, J. (2002). *Assessing student strengths: Academic
performance and persistence of first-time college students at a private,
church-affiliated college*. Unpublished doctoral dissertation, Mount
Vernon Nazarene University, Mount Vernon, OH.

[26] Ibid.

[27] Cantwell, L. D. (2005). *A comparative analysis of strengths-based
versus traditional teaching methods in a freshman public speaking
course: impact on student learning and academic engagement*.
Unpublished doctoral dissertation, Azusa Pacific University, Azusa, CA.

28 Clifton, D. O., & Anderson, E. (2002). *StrengthsQuest*. Washington, DC: Gallup Press.

29 Harter, J. K. (1999, September). Youth perceiver and student outcomes: A four-year longitudinal study. *Gallup Educator, 4*(5).

30 Austin, D. (2005). *The effects of a strengths development intervention program upon the self-perceptions of students' academic abilities.* Unpublished doctoral dissertation, Azusa Pacific University, Azusa, CA.

31 Mika, S. (2005). Start small, but dream big. *Gallup Educator.* Retrieved March 21, 2006, from http://education.gallup.com/content/default. aspx?ci=22510

32 Meier, D. (2002). *In schools we trust: Creating communities of learning in an era of testing and standardization.* Boston: Beacon Press.

Chapter 6 — Engaged Teachers, Part 1: Heroes of the Classroom

1 United States Department of Education. (n.d.). *What does "highly qualified" mean for teachers?* Retrieved March 22, 2006, from http:// www.ed.gov/teachers/nclbguide/toolkit_pg6.html#provision

2 Palmer, P. J. (1998). *The courage to teach: Exploring the inner landscape of a teacher's life.* San Francisco: Jossey-Bass.

3 Buckingham, M., & Coffman, C. (1999). *First, break all the rules: What the world's greatest managers do differently.* New York: Simon & Schuster.

4 Ibid.

5 Buckingham, M., & Clifton, D. O. (2001). *Now, discover your strengths.* New York: Free Press.

6 Palmer, P. J. (1998). *The courage to teach: Exploring the inner landscape of a teacher's life.* San Francisco: Jossey-Bass.

7 Buckingham, M., & Coffman, C. (1999). *First, break all the rules: What the world's greatest managers do differently.* New York: Simon & Schuster.

[8] Ibid.

[9] Collins, J. (2001). *Good to great: Why some companies make the leap ... and others don't.* New York: HarperCollins.

[10] Coffman, C., & Gonzalez-Molina, G. (2002). *Follow this path: How the world's greatest organizations drive growth by unleashing human potential.* New York: Warner Books.

[11] Buckingham, M., & Clifton, D. O. (2001). *Now, discover your strengths.* New York: Free Press.

[12] Clifton, D. O., & Nelson, P. (1992). *Soar with your strengths.* New York: Delacorte Press.

[13] Buckingham, M., & Coffman, C. (1999). *First, break all the rules: What the world's greatest managers do differently.* New York: Simon & Schuster.

[14] Stephenson, F. (2001). *Extraordinary teachers: The essence of excellent teaching.* Kansas City, MO: Andrews McMeel.

[15] Cuban, L. (1988). *The managerial imperative and the practice of leadership in schools.* Albany, NY: State University of New York Press.

[16] Temes, P. S. (2002). *Against school reform (and in praise of great teaching): Getting beyond endless testing, regimentation, and reform in our schools.* Chicago: Ivan R. Dee.

[17] Gallup Youth Survey, conducted via an online research panel with 517 respondents, aged 13 to 17, between August 1 and August 29, 2003. For results based on the total sample, one can say with 95% confidence that the maximum margin of sampling error is ±5 percentage points.

[18] Gallup Youth Survey, conducted via an online research panel with 785 respondents, aged 13 to 17, between January 22 and March 9, 2004. For results based on the total sample, one can say with 95% confidence that the maximum margin of sampling error is ±4 percentage points.

[19] Phi Delta Kappa/Gallup Poll, based on telephone interviews with 4,189 national adults, aged 18 and older, conducted May 1-30, 1999. For results based on the total sample of national adults, one can say with 95% confidence that the maximum margin of sampling error is ±2 percentage points.

[20] Phelps Deily, M. E. (2002, July 10). Teaching quality viewed as crucial. *Education Week.* Retrieved March 17, 2006, from http://72.14.203.104/search?q=cache:qqfd-JGl4lsJ:secure.edweek.org/ew/newstory.cfm%3Fslug%3D42PEN.h21+education+week+phelps+deily+july+10&hl=en&gl=us&ct=clnk&cd=3

[21] Hart, P. D., & Teeter, R. M. (2002). *A national priority: Americans speak on teacher quality.* Retrieved March 22, 2006, from the Educational Testing Service Web site: http://ftp.ets.org/pub/corp/survey2002.pdf

[22] Ibid.

[23] Gallup Poll, based on telephone interviews with 1,017 national adults, aged 18 and older, conducted August 9-11, 2004. For results based on the total sample of national adults, one can say with 95% confidence that the maximum margin of sampling error is ±3 percentage points.

[24] Goldhaber, D. (2002, Spring). The mystery of good teaching. *Education Next.* Retrieved March 22, 2006, from http://www.educationnext.org/20021/50.html

[25] Ibid.

[26] Hill, D. (2000, May). He's got your number. *Teacher Magazine, 11*(8), 42-47.

Sanders, W. L., & Rivers, J. C. (1996). *Cumulative and residual effects of teachers on future student academic achievement.* Knoxville: University of Tennessee Value-Added Research and Assessment Center.

Sanders, W. L., & Horn, S. P. (1998, September). Research findings from the Tennessee Value-Added Assessment System (TVAAS) database: Implications for educational evaluation and research. *Journal of Personnel Evaluation in Education,* 12(3), 247-256.

[27] Sanders, W. L., & Rivers, J. C. (1996). *Cumulative and residual effects of teachers on future student academic achievement.* Knoxville: University of Tennessee Value-Added Research and Assessment Center.

[28] Mendro, R. L. (1998, September). Student achievement and school and teacher accountability. *Journal of Personnel Evaluation in Education, 12*(3), 257-267.

[29] Sanders, W. L., Wright, S. P., & Horn, S. P. (1997, April). Teacher and classroom context effects on student achievement: Implications for teacher evaluation. *Journal of Personnel Evaluation in Education, 11*(1), 57-67.

[30] Ibid. See also Sanders, W. L., & Rivers, J. C. (1996). *Cumulative and residual effects of teachers on future student academic achievement.* Knoxville: University of Tennessee Value-Added Research and Assessment Center.

[31] Sanders, W. L., & Rivers, J. C. (1996). *Cumulative and residual effects of teachers on future student academic achievement.* Knoxville: University of Tennessee Value-Added Research and Assessment Center.

[32] Hill, D. (2000, May). He's got your number. *Teacher Magazine, 11*(8), 42-47.

[33] Darling-Hammond, L., & Youngs, P. (2002). Defining highly qualified teachers: What does scientifically-based research actually tell us? *Educational Researcher, 31*(9), 13-25.

Chapter 7 — Engaged Teachers, Part 2: What Do They Do Differently?

[1] Clifton, D. O., & Nelson, P. (1992). *Soar with your strengths.* New York: Delacorte Press.

[2] Ibid.

[3] Noblit, G. W., Rogers, D. L., & McCadden, B. M. (1995, May). In the meantime: The possibilities of caring. *Phi Delta Kappan, 76*(9), 680-685.

[4] Rogers, C. R. (1957). The necessary and sufficient conditions of therapeutic personality change. *Journal of Consulting Psychology, 21*(2), 95-103.

[5] Ibid.

[6] Moulthrop, D., Calegari, N. C., & Eggers, D. (2005). *Teachers have it easy: The big sacrifices and small salaries of America's teachers.* New York: New Press.

[7] Wrzesniewski, A. (1999). *Jobs, careers, and callings: Work orientation and job transitions.* Unpublished doctoral dissertation, University of Michigan, Ann Arbor.

[8] Farkas, S., Johnson, J., & Foleno, T. (2000). *A sense of calling: Who teaches and why.* Retrieved March 24, 2006, from the Public Agenda Web site: http://www.publicagenda.org/research/research_reports_details.cfm?list=28

[9] Ibid.

[10] Ibid.

[11] Liesveld, R., & Miller, J. A. (2005). *Teach with your strengths: How great teachers inspire their students.* New York: Gallup Press.

[12] Andrews, P. & Hatch, G. (2002). Initial motivations of serving teachers of secondary mathematics. *Evaluation and Research in Education, 16*(4), 185-201.

[13] Richardson, P., & Watt, H. M. G. (2002, December). A survey investigation of influences and choices in attracting graduates into teaching. Paper presented at the 2002 annual AARE Conference, Brisbane, Australia.

[14] Goodlad, J. I. (1984). *A place called school: Prospects for the future.* New York: McGraw-Hill.

[15] Bosworth, K. (1995, May). Caring for others and being cared for: Students talk caring in school. *Phi Delta Kappan, 76*(9), 686-693.

[16] Boyer, E. L. (1983). *High school: A report on secondary education in America.* New York: Harper & Row.

[17] Aspy, D. N., & Roebuck, F. N. (1977). *Kids don't learn from people they don't like.* Amherst, MA: Human Resource Development Press.

[18] Ibid.

[19] Ferreira, M. M., & Bosworth, K. (2001, Spring). Defining caring teachers: Adolescents' Perspectives. *Journal of Classroom Interaction, 36*(1), 24-30.

[20] Wentzel, K. R. (1997). Student motivation in middle school: The role of perceived pedagogical caring. *Journal of Educational Psychology, 89*(3), 411-419.

[21] Ibid. See also Noblit, G. W., Rogers, D. L., & McCadden, B. M. (1995, May). In the meantime: The possibilities of caring. *Phi Delta Kappan, 76*(9), 680-685.

[22] Bosworth, K. (1995, May). Caring for others and being cared for: Students talk caring in school. *Phi Delta Kappan, 76*(9), 686-693.

[23] Noblit, G. W., Rogers, D. L., & McCadden, B. M. (1995, May). In the meantime: The possibilities of caring. *Phi Delta Kappan, 76*(9), 680-685.

[24] Bosworth, K. (1995, May). Caring for others and being cared for: Students talk caring in school. *Phi Delta Kappan, 76*(9), 686-693.

[25] Noblit, G. W., Rogers, D. L., & McCadden, B. M. (1995, May). In the meantime: The possibilities of caring. *Phi Delta Kappan, 76*(9), 680-685.

[26] Bosworth, K. (1995, May). Caring for others and being cared for: Students talk caring in school. *Phi Delta Kappan, 76*(9), 686-693.

[27] Nieto, S. M. (2003, May). What keeps teachers going? *Educational Leadership, 60*(8), 14-18.

[28] Stephenson, F. (2003). *Extraordinary teachers: The essence of excellent teaching.* Kansas City, MO: Andrews McMeel.

[29] Croom, D. B. (2004, February 29). Are there any questions? *Teachers College Record.* Retrieved March 24, 2006, from http://www.tcrecord.org/AuthorDisplay.asp?aid=18391

[30] Banner, J. M., Jr., & Cannon, H. C. (1997). *The elements of teaching.* New Haven, CT: Yale University Press.

[31] Liesveld, R., & Miller, J.A. (2005). *Teach with your strengths: How great teachers inspire their students.* New York: Gallup Press.

[32] Banner, J. M., Jr., & Cannon, H. C. (1997). *The elements of teaching.* New Haven: Yale University Press.

[33] Stephenson, F. (2003). *Extraordinary teachers: The essence of excellent teaching.* Kansas City, MO: Andrews McMeel.

[34] Schlechty, P. C. (2001). *Shaking up the schoolhouse: How to support and sustain educational innovation.* San Francisco: Jossey-Bass.

[35] Bosworth, K. (1995). Caring for others and being cared for. *Phi Delta Kappan.* 76, 686-693.

[36] Rogers, S., & Renard, L. (1999, September). Relationship-driven teaching. *Educational Leadership 57*(1), 34-37.

[37] National Association of Manufacturers. (2005). *The looming workforce crisis.* Washington, D.C.: Author. Retrieved March 24, 2006, from http://www.nam.org/s_nam/bin.asp?CID=201825&DID=235064&DOC=FILE.PDF

Chapter 8 — Engaged Principals: Helping the Heroes

[1] Cuban, L. (1988). *The managerial imperative and the practice of leadership in schools.* Albany, NY: State University of New York Press.

[2] Murphy, J., & Hallinger, P. (1992, September). The principalship in an era of transformation. *Journal of Educational Administration, 30*(3), 77-88.

[3] Cuban, L. (1988). *The managerial imperative and the practice of leadership in schools.* Albany, NY: State University of New York Press.

[4] Leithwood, K. (1994). Leadership for school restructuring. *Educational Administration Quarterly, 30*(4), 498-518.

[5] Leithwood, K., Seashore Louis, K., Anderson, S., & Wahlstrom, K. (2004). *How leadership influences student learning.* Retrieved from the Wallace Foundation Web site: http://www.wallacefoundation.org/NR/rdonlyres/E3BCCFA5-A88B-45D3-8E27-B973732283C9/0/ReviewofResearchLearningFromLeadership.pdf

[6] Cuban, L. (1988). *The managerial imperative and the practice of leadership in schools.* Albany, NY: State University of New York Press.

[7] Buckingham, M., & Coffman, C. (1999). *First, break all the rules: What the world's greatest managers do differently.* New York: Simon & Schuster.

[8] Leithwood, K., Seashore Louis, K., Anderson, S., & Wahlstrom, K. (2004). *How leadership influences student learning.* Retrieved from the Wallace Foundation Web site: http://www.wallacefoundation. org/NR/rdonlyres/E3BCCFA5-A88B-45D3-8E27-B973732283C9/0/ ReviewofResearchLearningFromLeadership.pdf

[9] Davis, S., Darling-Hammond, L., LaPointe, M., & Meyerson, D. (2005). *School leadership study: Developing successful principals.* Retrieved March 24, 2006, from the Stanford Educational Leadership Institute Web site: http://seli.stanford.edu/research/documents/SELI_sls_ research_review.pdf

Waters, T., & Grubb, S. (2004). *Leading schools: Distinguishing the essential from the important.* Retrieved March 24, 2006, from the Mid-Continent Research for Education and Learning Web site: http:// www.mcrel.org/PDF/LeadershipOrganizationDevelopment/4005IR_ LeadingSchools.pdf

Goodlad, J. I. (1984). *A place called school: Prospects for the future.* New York: McGraw-Hill.

[10] National Principal Study. Based on telephone interviews with 1,000 national adults, aged 18 and older, conducted August-September 2001. For results based on the total sample of national adults, one can say with 95% confidence that the maximum margin of sampling error is ±3 percentage points.

[11] Farkas, S., Johnson, J., & Duffett, A. (2003). *Rolling up their sleeves.* Retrieved March 24, 2006, from the Public Agenda Web site: http://www. publicagenda.org/specials/rollingup/rollingup.htm

[12] Leithwood, K., Seashore Louis, K., Anderson, S., & Wahlstrom, K. (2004). *How leadership influences student learning.* Retrieved from the Wallace Foundation Web site: http://www.wallacefoundation. org/NR/rdonlyres/E3BCCFA5-A88B-45D3-8E27-B973732283C9/0/ ReviewofResearchLearningFromLeadership.pdf

See also Davis, S., Darling-Hammond, L., LaPointe, M., & Meyerson, D. (2005). *School leadership study: Developing successful principals.* Retrieved March 24, 2006, from the Stanford Educational Leadership Institute Web site: http://seli.stanford.edu/research/documents/SELI_ sls_research_review.pdf

[13] Ibid.

[14] Mendro, R. L. (1998, September). Student achievement and school and teacher accountability. *Journal of Personnel Evaluation in Education, 12*(3), 257-267.

[15] Leithwood, K., Seashore Louis, K., Anderson, S., & Wahlstrom, K. (2004). *How leadership influences student learning.* Retrieved from the Wallace Foundation Web site: http://www.wallacefoundation. org/NR/rdonlyres/E3BCCFA5-A88B-45D3-8E27-B973732283C9/0/ ReviewofResearchLearningFromLeadership.pdf

[16] Murphy, J., & Hallinger, P. (1992, September). The principalship in an era of transformation. *Journal of Educational Administration, 30*(3), 77-88.

[17] Leithwood, K. (1994). Leadership for school restructuring. *Educational Administration Quarterly, 30*(4), 498-518.

[18] Zheng, H. Y. (1996, April). *School contexts, principal characteristics, and instructional leadership effectiveness: a statistical analysis.* Paper presented at the annual meeting of the American Educational Research Association, New York, NY.

[19] Leithwood, K. (1994). Leadership for school restructuring. *Educational Administration Quarterly, 30*(4), 498-518.

Hallinger, P., & Murphy, J. (1985, November). Assessing the instructional management behavior of principals. *Elementary School Journal, 86*(2), 217-247

Murphy, J., & Hallinger, P. (1992, September). The principalship in an era of transformation. *Journal of Educational Administration, 30*(3), 77-88.

[20] Leithwood, K., Seashore Louis, K., Anderson, S., & Wahlstrom, K. (2004). *How leadership influences student learning.* Retrieved from the Wallace Foundation Web site: http://www.wallacefoundation. org/NR/rdonlyres/E3BCCFA5-A88B-45D3-8E27-B973732283C9/0/ ReviewofResearchLearningFromLeadership.pdf

[21] Hallinger, P., Bickman, L., & Davis, K. (1996). School context, principal leadership, and student reading achievement. *The Elementary School Journal, 96*(5), 527-549.

[22] Murphy, J., & Hallinger, P. (1992, September). The principalship in an era of transformation. *Journal of Educational Administration, 30*(3), 77-88.

Leithwood, K. (1994). Leadership for school restructuring. *Educational Administration Quarterly, 30*(4), 498-518.

[23] Ingersoll, R. M. (2003). *Who controls teachers' work? Power and accountability in America's schools.* Cambridge, MA: Harvard University Press.

[24] Leithwood, K., Seashore Louis, K., Anderson, S., & Wahlstrom, K. (2004). *How leadership influences student learning.* Retrieved from the Wallace Foundation Web site: http://www.wallacefoundation. org/NR/rdonlyres/E3BCCFA5-A88B-45D3-8E27-B973732283C9/0/ ReviewofResearchLearningFromLeadership.pdf

[25] Bossert, S., Dwyer, D., Rowan, B., & Lee, G. (1982). The instructional management role of the principal. *Educational Administration Quarterly, 18*(3), 34-64.

[26] Leithwood, K., Seashore Louis, K., Anderson, S., & Wahlstrom, K. (2004). *How leadership influences student learning.* Retrieved from the Wallace Foundation Web site: http://www.wallacefoundation. org/NR/rdonlyres/E3BCCFA5-A88B-45D3-8E27-B973732283C9/0/ ReviewofResearchLearningFromLeadership.pdf

[27] Ibid.

[28] Buckingham, M., & Coffman, C. (1999). *First, break all the rules: What the world's greatest managers do differently.* New York: Simon & Schuster.

[29] Mendro, R. L. (1998, September). Student achievement and school and teacher accountability. *Journal of Personnel Evaluation in Education, 12*(3), 257-267.

[30] Farkas, S., Johnson, J., & Duffett, A. (2003). *Rolling up their sleeves.* Retrieved March 24, 2006, from the Public Agenda Web site: http://www.publicagenda.org/specials/rollingup/rollingup.htm

[31] Collins, J. (2001). *Good to great: Why some companies make the leap ... and others don't.* New York: HarperCollins.

[32] Deal, T. E., & Peterson, K. D. (1999). *Shaping school culture: The heart of leadership.* San Francisco: Jossey-Bass.

[33] Leithwood, K. (1994). Leadership for school restructuring. *Educational Administration Quarterly, 30*(4), 498-518.

[34] Results for Liberty Elementary School retrieved April 10, 2006, from http://www.schoolmatters.com/app/location/q/stid=28/llid=118/stllid=287/locid=995615/catid=-1/secid=-1/compid=-1/site=pes

[35] Andrews, R. L., & Soder, R. (1987, March). Principal leadership and student achievement. *Educational Leadership, 44*(6), 9-11.

[36] Hallinger, P., Bickman, L., & Davis, K. (1996). School context, principal leadership, and student reading achievement. *The Elementary School Journal, 96*(5), 527-549.

[37] Sebring, P. B., & Bryk, A. S. (2000). School leadership and the bottom line in Chicago. *Phi Delta Kappan, 81*(6), 440-443.

[38] Clifton, D. O., & Nelson, P. (1992). *Soar with your strengths.* New York: Delacorte Press.

[39] Sebring, P. B., & Bryk, A. S. (2000). School leadership and the bottom line in Chicago. *Phi Delta Kappan, 81*(6), 440-443.

[40] Schlechty, P. C. (2001). *Shaking up the schoolhouse: How to support and sustain educational innovation.* San Francisco: Jossey-Bass.

[41] Hallinger, P., Bickman, L., & Davis, K. (1996). School context, principal leadership, and student reading achievement. *The Elementary School Journal, 96*(5), 527-549.

[42] Sebring, P. B., & Bryk, A. S. (2000). School leadership and the bottom line in Chicago. *Phi Delta Kappan, 81*(6), 440-443.

[43] Clifton, D. O., & Nelson, P. (1992). *Soar with your strengths*. New York: Delacorte Press.

[44] Sebring, P. B., & Bryk, A. S. (2000). School leadership and the bottom line in Chicago. *Phi Delta Kappan, 81*(6), 440-443.

[45] Aspy, D. N., & Roebuck, F. N. (1977). *Kids don't learn from people they don't like*. Amherst, MA: Human Resource Development Press.

[46] Tomlinson, C. A. (1999). *The differentiated classroom: Responding to the needs of all learners*. Alexandria, VA: Association for Supervision and Curriculum Development.

[47] Leithwood, K., Seashore Louis, K., Anderson, S., & Wahlstrom, K. (2004). *How leadership influences student learning*. Retrieved from the Wallace Foundation Web site: http://www.wallacefoundation. org/NR/rdonlyres/E3BCCFA5-A88B-45D3-8E27-B973732283C9/0/ ReviewofResearchLearningFromLeadership.pdf

[48] Sebring, P. B., & Bryk, A. S. (2000). School leadership and the bottom line in Chicago. *Phi Delta Kappan, 81*(6), 440-443.

[49] Coffman, C., & Gonzalez-Molina, G. (2002). *Follow this path: How the world's greatest organizations drive growth by unleashing human potential*. New York: Warner Books.

[50] Blase, J., & Blase, J. (1999). Principals' instructional leadership and teacher development: Teachers' perspectives. *Educational Administration Quarterly, 35*(3), 349-378.

[51] Farkas, S., Johnson, J., & Duffett, A. (2003). *Stand by me: What teachers really think about unions, merit pay, and other professional matters*. Retrieved March 24, 2006, from the Public Agenda Web site: http://publicagenda.org/research/research_reports_details.cfm?list=10

[52] Buckingham, M., & Coffman, C. (1999). *First, break all the rules: What the world's greatest managers do differently*. New York: Simon & Schuster.

[53] DuFour, R., DuFour, R., Eaker, R., & Karhanek, G. (2004). *Whatever it takes: How professional learning communities respond when kids don't learn*. Bloomington, IN: National Educational Service.

[54] Leithwood, K., Seashore Louis, K., Anderson, S., & Wahlstrom, K. (2004). *How leadership influences student learning.* Retrieved from the Wallace Foundation Web site: http://www.wallacefoundation. org/NR/rdonlyres/E3BCCFA5-A88B-45D3-8E27-B973732283C9/0/ ReviewofResearchLearningFromLeadership.pdf

[55] DeMoss, K. (2002). Leadership styles and high-stakes testing: Principals make a difference. *Education and Urban Society, 35*(1), 111-132.

[56] Ingersoll, R. M. (2003). *Who controls teachers' work? Power and accountability in America's schools.* Cambridge, MA: Harvard University Press.

[57] Heck, R. H., & Marcoulides, G. A. (1993, May). Principal leadership behaviors and school achievement. *NASSP Bulletin, 77*(553), 20-28.

[58] Sebring, P. B., & Bryk, A. S. (2000). School leadership and the bottom line in Chicago. *Phi Delta Kappan, 81*(6), 440-443.

[59] Andrews, R. L., & Soder, R. (1987, March). Principal leadership and student achievement. *Educational Leadership, 44*(6), 9-11.

[60] Goodlad, J. I. (1984). *A place called school: Prospects for the future.* New York: McGraw-Hill.

Chapter 9 — Engaged Schools: Setting the Stage for Greatness

[1] National Commission on Teaching and America's Future. (2003, January). *No dream denied: A pledge to America's children.* Retrieved March 24, 2006, from http://www.nctaf.org/search/search_results. php?c=4&sc=16

[2] Ibid. See also, Ingersoll, R. M. (2003, September). *Is there really a teacher shortage?* Retrieved March 24, 2006, from University of Washington, Center for the Study of Teaching and Policy Web site: www.ctpweb.org

[3] Ibid.

[4] Texas Center for Educational Research. (2000, November). *The cost of teacher turnover.* Retrieved March 24, 2006, from the Texas State Board for Educator Certification Web site: http://www.sbec.state.tx.us/ SBECOnline/txbess/turnoverrpt.pdf

[5] Alliance for Excellent Education. (2004). *Tapping the potential: Retaining and developing high-quality new teachers.* Retrieved March 24, 2006, from http://www.all4ed.org/publications/TappingThePotential/ TappingThePotential.pdf

[6] Alliance for Excellent Education. (2005, August). *Teacher attrition: A costly loss to the nation and to the states.* Retrieved March 24, 2006, from http://www.all4ed.org/publications/TeacherAttrition.pdf

[7] Charlotte Advocates for Education. (2004, February). *Role of principal leadership in increasing teacher retention: Creating a supportive environment.* Retrieved March 24, 2006, from http://www. advocatesfored.org/publications/Principal%20Final%20Report.pdf

[8] American Federation of Teachers. (2003). *Actual average beginning teacher salaries 2002-03, estimated 2004.* New York: Author. Retrieved March 24, 2006, from http://www.aft.org/salary/2003/ download/2003Table2.pdf

[9] National Commission on Teaching and America's Future. (2003, January). *No dream denied: A pledge to America's children.* Retrieved March 24, 2006, from http://www.nctaf.org/search/search_results. php?c=4&sc=16

[10] Southeast Center for Teaching Quality. (n.d.). *Teacher working conditions are student learning conditions: A report to Governor Mike Easley on the 2004 North Carolina Teacher Working Conditions Survey.* Retrieved on March 24, 2006, from http://www.teachingquality. org/pdfs/TWC_FullReport.pdf

Southeast Center for Teaching Quality. (n.d.). *Listening to the experts: A report on the 2004 South Carolina Teacher Working Conditions Survey.* Retrieved March 24, 2006, from http://www.teachingquality. org/pdfs/TWC_SCFinalReport.pdf

[11] Charlotte Advocates for Education. (2004, February). *Role of principal leadership in increasing teacher retention: Creating a supportive environment.* Retrieved March 24, 2006, from http://www.advocatesfored.org/publications/Principal%20Final%20Report.pdf

[12] Barth, R. S. (1990). *Improving schools from within: Teachers, parents, and principals can make the difference.* San Francisco: Jossey-Bass.

[13] Goodlad, J. I. (1984). *A place called school: Prospects for the future.* New York: McGraw-Hill.

[14] Ibid.

[15] Ingersoll, R. M. (2003). *Who controls teachers' work? Power and accountability in America's schools.* Cambridge, MA: Harvard University Press.

[16] Ibid.

[17] National Commission on Teaching and America's Future. (2003, January). *No dream denied: A pledge to America's children.* Retrieved March 24, 2006, from http://www.nctaf.org/search/search_results.php?c=4&sc=16

[18] Ingersoll, R. M. (2003). *Who controls teachers' work? Power and accountability in America's schools.* Cambridge, MA: Harvard University Press.

[19] Barth, R.S. (1990). *Improving schools from within: Teachers, parents, and principals can make the difference.* San Francisco: Jossey-Bass.

[20] Collins, J. (2001). *Good to great: Why some companies make the leap … and others don't.* New York: HarperCollins.

[21] Harter, J. K., Schmidt, F. L., & Keyes, C. L. M. (2002). Well-being in the workplace: A review of the Gallup studies. In C. L. M. Keys & J. Haidt (Eds.), *Flourishing: Positive Psychology and the life well-lived* (pp. 205-224). Washington, D.C.: American Psychological Association.

[22] Temes, P. S. (2002). *Against school reform (and in praise of great teaching): Getting beyond endless testing, regimentation, and reform in our schools.* Chicago: Ivan R. Dee.

[23] Deal, T. E., & Peterson, K. D. (1999). *Shaping school culture: The heart of leadership.* San Francisco: Jossey-Bass.

[24] Coffman, C., & Gonzalez-Molina, G. (2002). *Follow this path: How the world's greatest organizations drive growth by unleashing human potential.* New York: Warner Books.

[25] Hoy, W. (1990). Organizational climate and culture: A conceptual analysis of the school workplace. *Journal of Educational and Psychological Consultation, 1*(2), 149-168.

[26] Deal, T. E., & Peterson, K. D. (1999). *Shaping school culture: The heart of leadership.* San Francisco: Jossey-Bass.

[27] Harter, J. K., Schmidt, F. L., & Hayes, T. L. (2002). Business-unit-level relationship between employee satisfaction, employee engagement, and business outcomes: A meta-analysis. *Journal of Applied Psychology, 87*(2), 268-279.

[28] Harter, J. K., Schmidt, F. L., & Keyes, C. L. M. (2002). Well-being in the workplace: A review of the Gallup studies. In C. L. M. Keys & J. Haidt (Eds.), *Flourishing: Positive Psychology and the life well-lived* (pp. 205-224). Washington, D.C.: American Psychological Association.

[29] Harter, J. K., Schmidt, F. L., & Hayes, T. L. (2002). Business-unit-level relationship between employee satisfaction, employee engagement, and business outcomes: A meta-analysis. *Journal of Applied Psychology, 87*(2), 268-279.

[30] Harter, J. K., Schmidt, F. L., & Killham, E. A. (2003, July). *Employee engagement, satisfaction, and business-unit-level outcomes: a meta-analysis.* Omaha, NE: The Gallup Organization.

[31] Harter, J. K., Schmidt, F. L., & Keyes, C. L. M. (2002). Well-being in the workplace: A review of the Gallup studies. In C. L. M. Keys & J. Haidt (Eds.), *Flourishing: Positive Psychology and the life well-lived* (pp. 205-224). Washington, D.C.: American Psychological Association.

[32] Harter, J. K., Schmidt, F. L., Killham, E. A., & Asplund, J. W. (2006, March). Q^{12} *meta-analysis.* Omaha, NE: The Gallup Organization.

[33] Ibid.

[34] Harter, J. K., Schmidt, F. L., & Keyes, C. L. M. (2002). Well-being in the workplace: A review of the Gallup studies. In C. L. M. Keys & J. Haidt (Eds.), *Flourishing: Positive Psychology and the life well-lived* (pp. 205-224). Washington, D.C.: American Psychological Association.

[35] Collins, J. (2001). *Good to great: Why some companies make the leap ... and others don't.* New York: HarperCollins.

[36] National Education Association. (2003, November). *Status of the American public school teacher 2000-2001: Highlights.* Retrieved March 27, 2006, from http://www.nea.org/edstats/images/statushighlights.pdf

[37] Public Education Network. (2003, Fall). *The voice of the new teacher.* Retrieved March 24, 2006, from http://www.publiceducation.org/pdf/Publications/Teacher_Quality/Voice_of_the_New_Teacher.pdf

[38] Harter, J. K., Schmidt, F. L., & Killham, E. A. (2003, July). *Employee engagement, satisfaction, and business-unit-level outcomes: a meta-analysis.* Omaha, NE: The Gallup Organization.

[39] Rath, T., & Clifton, D. O. (2004). *How full is your bucket? Positive strategies for work and life.* New York: Gallup Press.

[40] Harter, J. K., Schmidt, F. L., & Killham, E. A. (2003, July). *Employee engagement, satisfaction, and business-unit-level outcomes: a meta-analysis.* Omaha, NE: The Gallup Organization.

[41] Ingersoll, R. M. (2003). *Who controls teachers' work? Power and accountability in America's schools.* Cambridge, MA: Harvard University Press.

[42] Barth, R. S. (1990). *Improving schools from within: Teachers, parents, and principals can make the difference.* San Francisco: Jossey-Bass.

[43] Ingersoll, R. M. (2003). *Who controls teachers' work? Power and accountability in America's schools.* Cambridge, MA: Harvard University Press.

[44] Southeast Center for Teaching Quality. (n.d.). *Teacher working conditions are student learning conditions: A report to Governor Mike Easley on the 2004 North Carolina Teacher Working Conditions Survey.* Retrieved on March 24, 2006, from http://www.teachingquality.org/pdfs/TWC_FullReport.pdf

[45] Harter, J. K., Schmidt, F. L., & Hayes, T. L. (2002). Business-unit-level relationship between employee satisfaction, employee engagement, and business outcomes: A meta-analysis. *Journal of Applied Psychology, 87*(2), 268-279.

[46] Harter, J. K., Schmidt, F. L., & Killham, E. A. (2003, July). *Employee engagement, satisfaction, and business-unit-level outcomes: a meta-analysis.* Omaha, NE: The Gallup Organization.

[47] Harter, J. K., Schmidt, F. L., & Keyes, C. L. M. (2002). Well-being in the workplace: A review of the Gallup studies. In C. L. M. Keys & J. Haidt (Eds.), *Flourishing: Positive Psychology and the life well-lived* (pp. 205-224). Washington, D.C.: American Psychological Association.

[48] Coffman, C., & Gonzalez-Molina, G. (2002). *Follow this path: How the world's greatest organizations drive growth by unleashing human potential.* New York: Warner Books.

[49] Ibid.

[50] Barth, R. S. (1990). *Improving schools from within: Teachers, parents, and principals can make the difference.* San Francisco: Jossey-Bass.

Chapter 10 — Engaged Communities: Rallying Around the Schools

[1] Schlechty, P. C. (2001). *Shaking up the schoolhouse: How to support and sustain educational innovation.* San Francisco: Jossey-Bass.

[2] Leithwood, K., Seashore Louis, K., Anderson, S., & Wahlstrom, K. (2004). *How leadership influences student learning.* Retrieved from the Wallace Foundation Web site: http://www.wallacefoundation. org/NR/rdonlyres/E3BCCFA5-A88B-45D3-8E27-B973732283C9/0/ ReviewofResearchLearningFromLeadership.pdf

[3] Ibid.

[4] Phi Delta Kappa/Gallup Poll, based on telephone interviews with a random sample of 1,000 U.S. adults, aged 18 and older, conducted from June 9-26, 2005. For results based on this sample, one can say with 95% confidence that the maximum error attributable to sampling and other random effects is ±3 percentage points.

5　Hart, P. D., & Teeter, R. M. (2002). *A national priority: Americans speak on teacher quality.* Retrieved March 22, 2006, from the Educational Testing Service Web site: http://ftp.ets.org/pub/corp/survey2002.pdf

6　Farkas, S., Johnson, J., & Duffett, A. (1999). *Playing their parts: Parents and teachers talk about parental involvement in public schools.* New York: Public Agenda.

7　Goals 2000: Educate America Act. H.R. 1804. (1994). Retrieved March 27, 2006, from http://www.ed.gov/legislation/GOALS2000/TheAct/sec102.html

8　Farkas, S., Johnson, J., & Duffett, A. (1999). *Playing their parts: Parents and teachers talk about parental involvement in public schools.* New York: Public Agenda.

9　Ibid.

10　Finders, M., & Lewis, C. (1994, May). Why some parents don't come to school. *Educational Leadership, 51*(8), 50-54.

11　Ibid.

12　Gibbs, N., (2005, February 21). Parents behaving badly. *Time, 165*(8), 40-49.

13　Gallup Internal Study. (1995, July). Presented at USC Superintendents' Conference, Los Angeles, CA.

14　U.S. Department of Health & Human Services. (2001, January). Building their futures: How early Head Start programs are enhancing the lives of infants and toddlers in low-income families. Summary Report. Retrieved March 27, 2006, from the Administration for Children & Families Web site: http://www.acf.hhs.gov/programs/opre/ehs/ehs_resrch/reports/building_summary/building_exesum.pdf

15　Jordan, G. E., Snow, C. E., & Porche, M. V. (2000, October-December). Project EASE: The effect of a family literacy project on kindergarten students' early literacy skills. *Reading Research Quarterly, 35*(4), 524-546.

[16] U.S. Department of Education. (2001). *The longitudinal evaluation of school change and performance (LESCP) in Title I schools.* Retrieved March 27, 2006, from http://www.ed.gov/offices/OUS/PES/esed/lescp_vol1.pdf

[17] Redding, S., Langdon, J., Meyer, J., & Sheley, P. (2004, November). *The effects of comprehensive parent engagement on student learning outcomes.* Retrieved March 27, 2006, from Harvard Graduate School of Education Web site: http://www.gse.harvard.edu/hfrp/content/projects/fine/resources/research/redding.pdf

[18] Ridley, M. (2003). *Nature via nurture: Genes, experience, & what makes us human.* New York: HarperCollins.

[19] MetLife. (2003). *The MetLife survey of the American teacher: An examination of school leadership.* Retrieved March 27, 2006, from http://www.metlife.com/WPSAssets/20781259951075837470V1F2003%20Survey.pdf

[20] Farkas, S., Foley, P., & Duffet, A. (2001). *Just waiting to be asked? A fresh look at attitudes on public engagement.* Retrieved March 27, 2006, from the Public Agenda Web site: http://www.publicagenda.org/pubengage/pdfs/just_waiting_to_be_asked.pdf

[21] Ibid.

[22] Ibid.

[23] Boyer, E. L. (1983). *High school: A report on secondary education in America.* New York: Harper & Row.

[24] Farkas, S., Foley, P., & Duffet, A. (2001). *Just waiting to be asked? A fresh look at attitudes on public engagement.* Retrieved March 27, 2006, from the Public Agenda Web site: http://www.publicagenda.org/pubengage/pdfs/just_waiting_to_be_asked.pdf

[25] Mathews, D. (1999, June). Whose schools? Reconnecting the public and the public schools. *American School Board Journal,* 22-24.

[26] Rose, L. C., & Gallup, A. M. (2005, September). The 37th Annual Phi Delta Kappa/Gallup Poll of the public's attitudes toward the public schools [Electronic version]. *Phi Delta Kappan, 87*(1), 41-57. Retrieved March 27, 2006, from http://www.pdkintl.org/kappan/k0509pol.pdf

[27] Biga, L. A. (2003, May). Lady Liberty. *Medium Magazine.*

[28] Charles Stewart Mott Foundation. (n.d.). *Man of vision led with his heart.* Retrieved March 27, 2006, from www.mott.org/about/founder.asp.

[29] Coalition for Community Schools. (n.d.). *Community schools: Partnerships for excellence.* Retrieved March 27, 2006, from http://www.communityschools.org/CCSDocuments/partnerships.html

[30] Ibid.

[31] Ibid.

[32] Blank, M. J., Jehl, J., & Neary, M. (2005, Summer). Engaging the community: Strategies that work. *Threshold*, 7-9. Retrieved March 27, 2006, from the Cable in the Classroom Web site: http://www.ciconline.com/NR/rdonlyres/

Coalition for Community Schools. (n.d.). *Community schools: Partnerships for excellence.* Retrieved March 27, 2006, from http://www.communityschools.org/CCSDocuments/partnerships.html

Blank, M. J., Melaville, A., Shah, B. P. (2003, May). *Making the difference: Research and practice in community schools.* Washington, D.C.: Coalition for Community Schools.

[33] California Department of Education. (2002, February 1). *Substantial gains made in reading and math for students in after school programs.* Retrieved March 28, 2006, from http://www.cde.ca.gov/nr/ne/yr02/yr02rel08.asp

[34] University of California, Irvine. (2002). *Evaluation of California's After School Learning and Safe Neighborhoods Partnerships Program: 1999-2001.* Retrieved March 28, 2006, from the California Department of Education Web site: http://www.cde.ca.gov/ls/ba/as/execsummary.asp

[35] American Youth Policy Forum. (2003). *Finding fortune in thirteen out-of-school time programs.* Retrieved March 28, 2006, from http://www.aypf.org/publications/Compendium2003.pdf

[36] Leithwood, K., Seashore Louis, K., Anderson, S., & Wahlstrom, K. (2004). *How leadership influences student learning.* Retrieved from the Wallace Foundation Web site: http://www.wallacefoundation.org/NR/rdonlyres/E3BCCFA5-A88B-45D3-8E27-B973732283C9/0/ReviewofResearchLearningFromLeadership.pdf

[37] Friedman, T. L. (2005). *The world is flat: A brief history of the twenty-first century.* New York: Farrar, Straus and Giroux.

[38] Mathews, D. (1999, June). *Whose schools? Reconnecting the public and the public schools. American School Board Journal,* 22-24.

[39] Public Education Network. (2004). *Taking responsibility: Using public engagement to reform our public schools.* Retrieved March 28, 2006, from http://www.publiceducation.org/pubs_publicengagement. asp

[40] Ibid.

[41] Mathews, D. (1999, June). Whose schools? Reconnecting the public and the public schools. *American School Board Journal,* 22-24.

[42] Public Education Network. (2004). *Taking responsibility: Using public engagement to reform our public schools.* Retrieved March 28, 2006, from http://www.publiceducation.org/pubs_publicengagement. asp

[43] Ibid.

[44] Rose, L. C., & Gallup, A. M. (2005). Combined analysis of annual PDK/Gallup Poll of the Public's Attitudes Toward the Public Schools. Washington, DC: The Gallup Organization.

[45] Phil Delta Kappa/Gallup poll, based on telephone interviews with a randomly selected national sample of 1,000 adults, aged 18 and older, conducted June 5-26, 2002. For results based on this sample, one can say with 95% confidence that the maximum error attributable to sampling and other random effects is ±3%.

[46] Goodlad, J. I. (1984). *A place called school: Prospects for the future.* New York: McGraw-Hill.

[47] Farkas, S., Foley, P., & Duffet, A. (2001). Just waiting to be asked? *A fresh look at attitudes on public engagement.* Retrieved March 27, 2006, from the Public Agenda Web site: http://www.publicagenda.org/ pubengage/pdfs/just_waiting_to_be_asked.pdf

Conclusion

[1] Chakravarthy, B. (2005, July/August). If it ain't broke, fix it. *Business Life*. London: Cedar Communications, 22.

Form 10-Q for Best Buy Co Inc. (2005, October 6). Retrieved March 24, 2006, from http://biz.yahoo.com/e/051006/bby10-q.html

[2] Gates, B. (2005, February 26). Prepared remarks presented at 2005 National Education Summit on High Schools. Retrieved July 7, 2005, from http://www.nga.org/cda/files/es05gates.pdf

[3] Friedman, T. L. (2005). *The world is flat: A brief history of the twenty-first century*. New York: Farrar, Straus and Giroux.

[4] Swanson, M. C. (2005, November 2). It's time to focus on the forgotten middle. *Education Week, 25*(10), 31, 33.

[5] Mathews, D. (1999, June). Whose schools? Reconnecting the public and the public schools. *American School Board Journal*, 22-24.

[6] Deal, Terrence E. & Kent D. Peterson. (1999). *Shaping school culture: The heart of leadership*. San Francisco: Jossey-Bass.

[7] Daly, J. (2000, September 26). Interview with Alvin Toffler. Business 2.0. Retrieved March 28, 2006, from http://www.ghandchi.com/iranscope/Anthology/Alvin_Toffler00.htm

ABOUT THE AUTHOR

Gary Gordon, Ed.D., is Vice President and Practice Leader of The Gallup Organization's Education Division. Before joining Gallup in 1994, Dr. Gordon's career spanned more than 20 years in public education as a teacher, assistant principal, high school principal, personnel director, and assistant superintendent. Dr. Gordon currently consults with school districts and businesses on human resources, leadership, and workplace management. He has been published in the *State Education Standard* and *Phi Delta Kappan*.

Dr. Gordon's writing partner, Steve Crabtree, has developed and produced publications for The Gallup Organization since joining the company in 1993. Crabtree currently develops articles and analyses from the Gallup World Poll, and is a contributing writer for the *Gallup Management Journal*.